THE RISE OF URBAN AMERICA

CHICAGO:
A MORE INTIMATE VIEW OF URBAN POLITICS

Charles Edward Merriam

ARNO PRESS
&
The New York Times

NEW YORK • 1970

Reprint Edition 1970 by Arno Press Inc.

Reprinted from a copy in The State Historical Society of Wisconsin Library

LC# 71-112579
ISBN 0-405-02467-3

THE RISE OF URBAN AMERICA
ISBN for complete set 0-405-02430-4

Manufactured in the United States of America

CHICAGO

BY

CHARLES EDWARD MERRIAM

THE AMERICAN PARTY SYSTEM

AMERICAN POLITICAL IDEAS

FOUR AMERICAN PARTY LEADERS

CHICAGO

A MORE INTIMATE VIEW OF URBAN POLITICS

BY

CHARLES EDWARD MERRIAM

PROFESSOR OF POLITICAL SCIENCE IN THE UNIVERSITY OF CHICAGO

NEW YORK

THE MACMILLAN COMPANY

1929

Set up and printed.
Published June, 1929.

SET UP BY BROWN BROTHERS LINOTYPERS
PRINTED IN THE UNITED STATES OF AMERICA
BY THE CORNWALL PRESS

INTRODUCTION

THE observations contained in the following chapters are based upon some twenty-eight years of residence in Chicago. During this time the writer has been continuously in the department of political science of the University of Chicago, was for six years an alderman of the city, and for many years both a participant and an observer in many political scenes. I have set down these observations in the hope of making clearer some of the important aspects of the political life of a great metropolitan community.

Opinions differ as to whether the city is the hope of democracy or its despair, but unless there is a swift and radical change in modern social trends, the future of democracy rests with the cities. As goes the city, so goes the nation. In another generation in all probability the political standards, habits, practices, ideals, of cities will be those of America.

This is not a book of remedies but a study of the situation as it is. On some other occasion, perhaps, I shall set down what seems to me to be the way out, as specifically and concretely as possible. A necessary preliminary to a study of ways out is an examination of the situation as it is, and this I have tried to present in a more intimate view of urban politics.

CONTENTS

CHICAGO

CHICAGO

A MORE INTIMATE VIEW OF URBAN POLITICS

CHAPTER I

HOW CHICAGO CAME TO BE

A CITY of 4,000,000 with a history of less than a hundred years is seldom found in the annals of municipalities. When Chicago was a cluster of cabins emerging from sand and swamp around a frontier fort, New York was a city of 400,000; London an old metropolis of more than 2,000,000; Paris numbered over a million; Berlin included some 300,000; while Rome was even then celebrating its three-thousandth odd birthday. Within less than a century it was necessary to build and rebuild the physical structure of the city, establish and develop its industrial position, reconcile a maze of conflicting racial elements, contrive measures for communication, health, safety, comfort and culture, weave the web of governmental understandings, ideals and achievements without which a city cannot be.

How this was brought about is the subject for a masterpiece not yet written, containing, however, the richest of material for the historian, the novelist and the poet. Nor will such a task be attempted here. Only for the purposes of a more intimate view of urban politics, there are sketched the broad features of this great drama of urban life, losing to be sure much of the color and motion of the picture in so hasty a backward view.

CHICAGO

It is proposed to look in turn at the economic background of Chicago, at the structural side of the city, at the racial composition of the community, and at the political struggles of the municipality. In life these are all intimately related and are indeed inseparable parts of the same great unity, but for the purposes of this analysis they may be separated for a time, to be reunited again in the view of the city as a whole.

The economic history of Chicago must be interpreted in terms of the development of the Northwest and Middle West, as well as the larger economic development of America. Now the financial capital of a territory including some 50,000,000 people, greater than many nations of the world, Chicago rose to this position with the growth of the great area whose center it has come to be, resting upon one of the most productive agricultural areas in the world. Corn, wheat, cattle, foodstuffs have flowed into the city in prodigious quantities, finding their central clearing house and market.

The downward thrust of Lake Michigan fixed the lower end of the Lake as a turning point for traffic and gave Chicago a commanding position in a wide domain. Water traffic on the Great Lakes came to the aid of the city in 1833, the very year of its first charter. The Canal, opened in 1848, brought goods and men from the South. The railways found Chicago only a little later a convenient terminal point until more than a score of lines converged upon the city. The alternatives of water and rail transportation aided Chicago and contributed to its strategic advantages as a center of trade. The early rivals, St. Louis and Cincinnati, fell behind in the race for industrial supremacy when the railway lines became more important than the waterways and when the great Northwest unfolded its possibilities.

Under these conditions the industrial advance of the city

was very rapid, and Chicago grew more swiftly than the promoters of the community had dared to dream.[1] The city focused the prosperity of an enormously rich central agricultural market, and rose with the growth of this agricultural region.[2]

From 1890 on, Chicago entered a livelier phase of manufacturing development which began to take the place of the relatively declining grain, cattle and lumber market—a characteristic development of many American cities and not peculiar to Chicago. Now came great iron and steel manufactures to Chicago and the Region. Coal and iron met in a titanic union at Gary and elsewhere. Printing and publishing, clothing industries, electrical manufactures, car construction and repair, developed on a vast scale. The number of employees in five such industries more than doubled in thirty years. Chicago became a great exporter of manufactures as well as of foodstuffs. The huge agricultural clearing house remained, but giant manufactures were added and Chicago became not only the "wheat stacker and pork packer" of the world, but one of its principal manufacturing centers as well.[3] A great central market and a great central manufacturing

[1] *See* J. Paul Goode, *The Geographic Background of Chicago*; F. M. Fryxel, *The Physiography of the Region of Chicago.*

[2] A brief sketch of the development of Chicago in the earlier period is given in Riley, *The Development of Chicago and Vicinity as a Manufacturing Center Prior to 1880.*

[3] INDEX NUMBERS OF POPULATION, AGRICULTURE, AND MANUFACTURING IN THE CHICAGO REGION, 1890-1920

Year	*Index Numbers*		
	Population	*Agriculture*	*Manufacturing*
1890	100.0	100.0	100.0
1900	145.9	119.1	131.3
1910	189.3	117.5	....
1920	239.7	112.7	234.1

This table taken from Jeter, Helen R.: *Trends of Population in the Region of Chicago.*

point were thus brought together in the confines of the city or at least within the boundaries of the Chicago Region, with all the financial appurtenances that go along with marketing and manufacture on a large scale. Toward the end of the period Chicago struggled for financial independence of Eastern interests and by the development of banking and financial centers endeavored to establish itself more firmly on a local basis than heretofore. That great financial leaders such as Armours and McCormicks, Rosenwalds and Insulls, emerged, and that powerful manufacturing and credit centers were established was an inevitable part of the story. They also complicated the patterns of political behavior in the great city in many ways. Steel and railways and manufactures and banking must be read into the politics of the city along with the earlier representatives of more strictly agricultural elements as seen in the grain and cattle managers and manipulators. The Commercial Club, the Association of Commerce, the Industrial Club, the Illinois Manufacturers' Association, the Commonwealth Club, and many others became important centers of social power.

Inevitably there came also the organization of the employees in various forms. Unions were of course set up in many industries and out of these emerged after many struggles the Chicago Federation of Labor as a primary central agency. In fact, large numbers of industries were unionized in the course of time, and Chicago came to be known in many quarters as a "union town." This also is a fact regarding the history of the city that must be borne in mind in an intimate view of urban politics, for there came mighty struggles between corporations, between unions, and between employer and employee. The Haymarket massacre of 1886, the Pullman strike of 1894, the building trades struggle leading up to the "Landis award," the industrial statesmanship of the garment trades—these are all a part of the social history and political tradition of the metropolis.

Perhaps in no other great city of the world has there been presented so interesting a picture of modern industrial development, so conspicuous a transition from the agricultural to the manufacturing basis of wealth, or to a combination basis, as in the 100 years of the growth of this center both of agriculture and manufacturing, at the same time a focus of organized land transportation such as is found nowhere else in the world.

In this sense it may be said that Chicago has been and continues to be the most typically American city of the country, of the larger municipalities at any rate. No other community is more closely allied with the combined growth of rail and waterways, of agriculture and of manufacturing, than is this singularly located market place, factory, axis of air, land and waterways.

Airplane views of the structural development of Chicago would reveal three striking periods. One would show the Great Fire, its smoking ruins, the magic rebuilding of the city. Another would show the wide expansion of the city preliminary to the Columbian exposition and the rise of the White City by the Lake in 1893. A third would show the beginning of a systematic and scientific attempt to rebuild the city following the great City Plan of 1907.

In 1871 Chicago was a heap of ashes, ruined physically and financially, and only an optimistic observer, and an unreasonable one at that, would have seen here the makings of one of the world's greatest cities within a generation. But the miracle happened. The incredible catastrophe evoked a spirit of incredible energy and within a few years the marks of the devastating fire had been almost removed. The population of Chicago increased from 298,977 in 1870 to 503,185 in 1880, and its wealth and position proportionately. Out of the ashes came a great city, greater in numbers and wealth and far greater in spirit and temper.

The four hundredth anniversary of the discovery of America marked another phase in the life of Chicago. The original impulse to this development was perhaps the familiar booster spirit of the frontier, but this was transformed in the course of the year-long preparations for the event into something finer and more significant in building a city spirit. First the city was enlarged by the annexations of 1889 from an area of less than 44 to 170 square miles, chiefly on the south side of the City, and rose from 500,000 population in 1880 to 1,700,000 in 1900. When the plans for the exposition began to absorb the interest and activity of the city's leaders and of its people, they found unexpectedly artistic expression in the creation of the White City by the Lake. There can be no doubt that the imagination of the city was captured by the exposition, not merely by its lavishness of display and numbers in attendance, but by its artistic and symbolic aspects which seemed to inspire Chicago with a new spirit, in which the chief element was a broader interest in the cultural aspects of municipal life and the emergence of a new type of civic pride. The establishment of the University of Chicago near the old Fair site was the outward expression of this spirit, but not the only one.[1]

The spirit of 1893 blossomed in the City Plan of 1907. This was the creation of the Commercial Club and of Daniel Burnham, but it was also in a broader and truer sense the expression of the new life of the people of Chicago, recognizing now a new phase of urban existence—a phase in which municipal art and beauty would find a place, as well as economic utility. Technically these factors of beauty and utility,

[1] T. J. Riley, *The Higher Life of Chicago.*

of function and of form, were combined in the Plan, for it was discovered that they were not incompatible in the actual execution of a municipal design. The idea of conscious city building spread abroad, and became a part of the city's understanding of its future lines of advance. The city was henceforth to be built consciously and not merely to grow at random, without plan or purpose.

The widening of Michigan avenue and the beginning of the Lake Front development were the great symbols of this revolution. Yet they are important not merely in themselves, but also for the fact that they represent a great epoch in the building of the city, a profound transition in civic conception of urban growth and progress. Stained with graft and corruption as some of the early stages of this development were, they nevertheless mark the beginnings of a revolutionary change in the city's attitude toward itself. Elaborate parks and boulevards were the outward expression of an inner transformation in the spirit of Chicago from that of drift to that of mastery, from haphazard growth to directed plan, from real estate booming to city building in the broadest sense of the term. Zoning followed the Plan, as Housing began to follow Zoning, in the city's attempt to organize its life.

These three stages, then, the destruction by the Fire and the Rebuilding, the expansion of the city and the creation of the World's Fair, and the era of the City Plan, are important phases in the life and development of the city, essential to an understanding of its general esprit and of its political attitudes and dispositions.

Meanwhile, however, the unity of the city was seriously threatened by forces tending toward disintegration. The reluctance of the State to grant to Chicago adequate power to deal with its kaleidoscopic local situations had the effect of creating many Chicagoes instead of one. Thus as the City grew it came to include the overwhelming preponderance of the population and the wealth of Cook County; and there were two rival governments including almost the same voters;—the complicated government of Cook County on the one hand and the government of Chicago on the other, the same voters but under a different organization. The pollution of the water supply of Chicago led to the formation of the Sanitary District, an organization for sewage disposal and other purposes. This District is in the main, as far as wealth and numbers go, Chicago, but technically it is a different municipality and it must be governed as an independent unit. As the Park Boards were organized they were given a peculiar status of independence from the City. The South Park Board must be chosen by the judges of the Circuit Court of Cook County, while the Lincoln Park and the West Park Boards were to be appointed at Springfield by the Governor of the State.

To add to these elements of disintegration, there came somewhat later the movement of emigration from Chicago to the suburbs. In the early years the City pursued and kept pace with these migrations by the energetic process of annexations, the most notable of which was that of 1889, when the area of the City was extended four-fold; but in later years the City was left far behind. With the better development of suburban transportation, with the general use of the motor, and in a period of economic prosperity, population tended to press out more rapidly than ever before, and the City was unable to include all of its members in the corporate circle. In 1910 the population of Chicago was 2,185,283 and that of the metropolitan region 3,047,324; in 1920 the population of Chicago was 2,701,705, and that of the region was 3,858,818. And these tendencies were accentuated by the movements of the next decade. It is estimated that the population of Chicago in 1930 will be 3,280,000, and the region 4,900,000. This Chicago found a considerable section of its citizens—approximately one-third—outside its municipal walls, and these in many cases among its strongest from the economic and professional point of view. The bearing of this situation upon the municipal life and growth of the community is of course evident.

Chicago has struggled then for the last generation with the problem of physical integration, endeavoring to hold together the sections of the community that seem fairly to belong within the municipal corporation. This division has imposed unusually heavy burdens upon the political community of Chicago and has made far more difficult the problem of governmental organization and standards. Emigration from Chicago has been a more difficult problem than immigration into Chicago. For not only was there territorial disintegration, but also the problem of racial integration and reorganization, and these taken together made the political life of the city a very complex and difficult one. The whole process of government in Chicago must be read in the light of these movements, so vital to the life of the city.

Regional disintegration, it is true, has not been a problem peculiar to Chicago, but in fact common to all the other great cities of the world; but regional and racial disintegration taken together have been an unusual problem *outside of America.* Here many examples may be found, *notably in New York and Chicago.*

The social composition of Chicago illustrates other striking episodes in the growth of a modern city, ranging from French discovery to negro settlement. Roughly speaking, the French *found* Chicago, the native Americans settled it, the Germans and Irish and Scandinavians were its main strength in the mid-century and for a generation thereafter, the Italians, Poles and Russians and Bohemians were the second line of defense from the '90's on to the Great War. Since that time the colored man has capped the climax, although tradition has it that the first resident in Chicago was Baptiste Point De Saible, a colored man.

In the early years of its development the bulk of the Chicagoans came from the East, from New England, New York, Pennsylvania, Ohio, with a generous number journeying from the South, Kentucky, and Virginia, or other Southern sections, especially when river transportation was favorable to transit on north and south lines. In the later period when the West was settled, large numbers flooded in from all the surrounding middle western states, with others from the east and south, and of course the continuing tide of immigrants from across the sea. Strange as it may now seem, a "Know Nothing" or one hundred per cent American Mayor was elected as late as 1855.

For only a few years, however, did the native American element in the population remain in control. By 1860 the percentage of foreign born was important, and this continued until the '70's, when the figure began to decline somewhat.[1]

The German and Irish settlers helped to give the early color to the life of Chicago, and this indeed continues down to the present day. As early as 1846 German citizens protested against the refusal to appoint Charles Baumgarten as street commissioner. The Nord Seit is still known under its old name by the old-timers and Shanty town is still a

[1] Jeter's Table XXIV shows relative percentages of foreign-born population in Chicago Region, p. 34. Table XXVII gives the distribution of foreign born population in the Chicago Region from 1870 to 1910, p. 44, *Trends of Population in the Region of Chicago.*

name to recall. The second generation of both of these groups is deeply woven into the texture of the city, industrially, socially, and politically.

The more recent comers since the '90's, the Poles, the Bohemians, the Russians, the Italians, who followed the others, now outnumber the foreign born from the other nations. But if the second generation is included, the newcomers are weaker. These groups have been an important factor in the industrial and political development of the community, and without them it cannot be understood at all. Perhaps the most constant of all the immigrant elements has been the Scandinavian, including for this purpose both Swedish and Norwegian groups, who began to arrive in the '50's and continued with little abatement until the late War. The second generation of Scandinavians is firmly intrenched in the social life of the city, and an important cross section of its political life.

Latest of all is the colored man. With the shutting off of immigration at the outbreak of the War, the lines of migration to Chicago were shifted and the north and south movement began. This brought into the city great numbers of colored persons from Mississippi, Louisiana, Alabama, Georgia, and other Southern states. Their arrival had an important bearing upon the residential, the industrial, and the political life of the city—conditions later discussed in greater detail and in relation to the political situation as a whole.[1] Down to 1910, the colored population of Chicago was 44,103. In 1920 the figure had increased to 109,548, and it is now estimated that the negro in Chicago numbers 250,000.[2]

The tables which recount racial growth and composition

[1] See Chapter V.

[2] Earlier increases in negro population are found in the periods from 1860-1870, and 1890-1900.

may seem dull figures, but they are well worth the careful study of those who wish to catch the spirit of Chicago from its past, for in these forbidding columns of dusty statistics there is much to be learned about the tendencies of this great cosmopolitan city. No other of the world's great cities, with the exception of New York, has been obliged to deal with elements so complex and difficult as has this community. The rise and fall of these migrations and the still more important analysis of the adjustments and compromises made by these mingling groups thrown together on the western plain is the story of Chicago yet unwritten and indeed scarcely traced, for the modern social historian has not yet caught up with Chicago. But this way lies Chicago, and those who hurry over these basic facts will never know the town in which they live or which they aim to understand.

With only one exception, Chicago has been for a hundred years the world's greatest melting pot. In European cities the racial groups are more likely to fight than to fuse. In America, New York has been larger numerically and more powerful financially, but the industrial background of Chicago has been in many ways more complex and in many others more typically American in its mixture of trade and agriculture and in its intimate dependence upon rail transportation. Neither the industrial nor the political history of Chicago can be understood if these elements so vital to the life and growth of the city are neglected or underrated.

In scanty outline, then, this is the sketch of some of the more striking features of the development of Chicago, the two great eras in its industrial organization, the three periods of its physical and structural advance, the three successive waves of immigration which have given its ethnological composition. It would of course also be possible to blend these pictures and present a composite photograph of each successive era. Or the reader may do this for himself, perhaps. It is sufficient for this present purpose to have outlined these major features in the changing landscape of the city, to show in rough fashion what manner of a city we are dealing with as shown by how it came to be.

The political history of Chicago has been characterized by two outstanding struggles—both of which throw light upon its future—one the battle for home rule, and the other a battle for honesty and competency against graft and spoils. In successive waves or cycles these controversies have involved Chicago at intervals for the last two generations at least. There is no more dramatic chapter in the history of modern democracy than this account of the effort of a new community to adapt itself to the state of which it was a part, to reconcile and adjust the diverse elements within its border, and withal to maintain standards of justice, order, progress, appropriate to the dignity and power of one of the world's greatest cities.

Incorporated as a village in 1833, Chicago obtained a charter as a city in 1837, but the rapid growth of the population and the urban needs of the expanding Chicago soon made an 1837 charter entirely inappropriate. Chicago began its long, painful, still unended struggle to obtain the powers necessary for the government of a community widely different in size and needs from the rural districts and villages of the state of Illinois. With the mid-century the inadequacy of the powers of the city became painfully apparent, but the municipality was unable to obtain redress for its condition until the adoption of the new Constitution of 1870. The illuminating debates of this august body are full of the sufferings of Chicago, bound to the restrictions of village communities in a rapidly changing industrial and urban era and constantly subject to the raids of a corrupt legislature. The 99-year Act of 1865, in which the rights of Chicago over its streets were given away to the traction companies, over the vigorous protest of representative Chicagoans, was the high spot in a series of minor betrayals. The Constitution of 1870 was for that day a liberal document. It prevented special legislative raids on the one hand and on the other gave fairly broad grants of power to all cities of the state. For a while it eased the growing pains of the metropolis, but not for long.[1]

In the last decade of the nineteenth century Chicago again began its effort to obtain powers appropriate for the government of a great metropolis as distinguished from that of a village of a thousand population. After many delays the constitutional amendment of 1904 was adopted, designed to afford relief to the city and authorizing the Legislature of the state to enact a complete scheme of local government in and for the city of Chicago. This new plan was made subject to a referendum vote of the people of the City. But the Legislature proved unwilling to enact any plan of government acceptable to the voters of Chicago, and the deadlock continued to the detriment of the City's political and industrial life. With two million population, the City was still unable to grant a concession for checking hats or selling pop-corn on the new municipal pier without a special act of the Legislature, to say nothing of powers adequate to deal with the complicated questions of transportation and communication in a growing city, dependent for its life on free and rapid circulation of persons and goods.

Some relief was obtained by means of special "adoptive" acts and other laws classifying cities, but these means were too slender to deal with the problems of the great metrop-

[1] Sparling's *Municipal History and Present Organization of Chicago* (1898).

olis. The city fell into a vicious circle in which those in power were not trusted with real authority because they did not achieve, and not having power were not able to achieve, and not achieving were still more distrusted than before, and so on around. The effects upon the fortunes of a rapidly expanding community were unfortunate in the extreme; delayed and made difficult all great attainments in the municipal domain.

But now appears another obstacle in the path of Chicago. The down-state becomes fearful of the great city's growing power and determined to limit its representation in the state Legislature. At first merely indifferent and neglectful of the City, the State, seeing the rapid growth of Chicago, now assumes a hostile attitude and begins a campaign for permanent restriction of the City in the lawmaking body of the commonwealth of Illinois. The Constitution of the state contains an unusually clear and explicit provision requiring representation in accordance with population in the General Assembly, and to this Constitution members of the Legislature were solemnly sworn. But the wicked city must be curbed, even if members violate their oath and that without apparent compunctions of conscience. The Legislature refused to act and declined to make another reapportionment of membership. Since 1900 no new districts have been made. Almost thirty years have gone by and all the increase of Chicago's population since that time remains unrepresented in the Legislature of the state.

The population of Chicago in 1900 was 2,007,695; in 1930 it approaches 3,500,000. But 1,500,000 persons gain no representation. The 17 Senators of 1900 remain the 17 Senators of 1930, and the prospect of change seems remote; [1]

[1] For a careful study of the rivalry between Chicago and the State, see W. B. Philips' excellent monograph on *Chicago and the Down State* (1870-1927).

and likewise in the House. True, the Supreme Court of the State has held that the constitutional provision requiring a reapportionment every ten years is mandatory, but there is no remedy of a judicial nature for the enforcement of the provision.

In the Constitutional Convention of 1919-20 these questions of home rule and representation for Chicago were the storm centers of a controversy which raged for many a month. In the end a compromise was reached, by the terms of which the representation of the city was to be perpetually limited in one house and in return the city was to be given constitutional home rule. Accepted with many reservations upon both sides, the compromise in the ensuing popular vote was overwhelmingly repudiated by the voters of Chicago, who refused to purchase home rule at the price of permanent limitation of representation.

In the meantime the rivalry between city and state which had begun without specific cause except an ill-defined fear of Chicago domination began to develop more clearly in battles over the regulation of the Chicago Board of Trade, the control of the city's milk supply, the gasoline tax, the enforcement of the dry law, and other controversial questions. Chicago began to discuss its possible application for independent existence as a state, and the two sections of the state began to draw farther and farther apart, as the gap between social and economic conditions tended to effect a separation.

However, means of communication and transportation continued to draw city and country more and more closely together. Industrial and cultural bonds were constantly more and more intimate. And finally the down-state cities began to develop interest and activity in obtaining for themselves the same type of home rule which Chicago sought;

and to coöperate with Chicago in the effort to obtain a common autonomy in local affairs.

It is in the light of this half-century struggle for local home rule that the government of the city must be interpreted, if the inner meaning of the political attitudes of the people of Chicago is to be understood. Upon this question the city has been united as upon no other major issue of governmental life, and no other factor has done as much to weld together the various elements of the urban populace as the common consciousness of the wrongs inflicted upon them by the failure of the state to grant the city either its just representation in the state Legislature, or its reasonable claim to self-government in the local affairs of the community.

Other great cities are administered in some measure by the national governments of which they are capitals, as in the case of Paris or London or Berlin. Or they are supervised by nations with strongly developed agencies for central administrative control. Illinois provides neither central supervision of local affairs of cities, nor local home rule, and Chicago is left in a condition unparalleled among the great cities of the world;—without the freedom of the free, or the protection and tutelage of the slave.

And this is an important section of the life of the great city it is proposed to study.

The other great central struggle in the life of Chicago has been the battle for honesty and competency against graft and spoils, the effort to build up intelligent political control on the one hand and technically competent administration on the other, ready to do the will of the community when it has spoken.

At its birth in 1833 Chicago inherited the spoils system —a legacy of the Jacksonian democracy, and of course applied it to the system of the day. At first when the city was small and the duties of government simple little harm seemed to result. But as Chicago grew and as its affairs became more and more complex and the number of public servants larger and larger, the urban spoils system began to extort a vicious toll from the citizens. Political loafers, blacklegs, gamblers, purveyors of gambling and prostitution, crooked contractors, all the camp followers of the spoils system, appeared in Chicago, and began to stalk their prey. They did not succeed in organizing any institution of the centralized and permanent type of Tammany, developing simultaneously in New York, although local machines and local scandals were to be found a plenty. It is a curious fact that Chicago has never had an effective boss of the New York or Philadelphia type, with a well-organized machine capable of holding out against public opinion for any length of time. But a series of petty feudal chieftains of spoils have wrought havoc with economy, order, and justice.

Looking back to pre-Civil War days Chicago was an anti-slavery town, in fact a point on the "underground railway" of that day. One of the characteristic events of the '40's was the trial of an escaped slave in Chicago, in the course of which the fugitive was passed up over the heads of the crowd and disappeared in the confusion. Nor was anyone punished for the "negro riot." Stephen A. Douglas, a resident of the city after 1847, was a general favorite, but in 1854 he was pursued through the streets by an angry crowd, indignant because of his compromising tendencies. Van Buren carried Chicago, running on the Free Soil Ticket in 1848, as did Fremont on the Republican ticket in 1856.

Even at this early time some of the later characteristics of Chicago appeared. The city was strongly for freedom and much against slavery. But it was at the same time for freedom in the use of liquor. The Lager Beer Riot of 1855 was an illustration of this tendency, for in this case a throng of citizens made a riotous protest against the enforcement of the Sunday closing law regarding the sale of intoxicating liquors. And again no one was punished although there were several casualties.

The ideals of Lincoln were not without their influence in the formative period of Chicago's life, and doubtless left their impress upon the political character of their time in the city where he was so well known and so popular. The German elements of the population followed the flag of the Union as did the Scandinavians in general and many of the Irish. It would be too much to say that "Honest Abe" saved Chicago in his generation, but still he was a part of the picture and cannot be left out of an honest account of the situation. In no one was this spirit better expressed than in "Long John" Wentworth (Mayor, 1857-60) whose six feet six and three hundred pounds were matched by as generous a mental mold.

Another gallant figure of the war-time was Joseph Medill, editor of the *Chicago Tribune* and a valiant champion of the cause of the Union as well as of high standards of political conduct. Elected mayor of Chicago in 1871 on the "Fireproof" ticket, he made an admirable chief. But the enforcement of the Sunday closing law alienated the support of the people of the City and opened the way to the election of an inferior mayor on a wide-open town basis. Medill was the last dry mayor knowingly elected by the voters of the City of Chicago down to this day.

During a period of widespread American municipal corruption, Chicago avoided the excesses of Tammanies in New York and Philadelphia under the long protracted Harrison "dynasty" which ruled the city for no less than ten terms in the period from 1879 to 1915. The elder Harrison reigned from 1879 to 1887, and in '93 to his assassination; his son and heir from 1897 to 1903, and from 1911 to 1915.

Carter the First bridged the gap from the Fire to the Fair, and while his rule was often bitterly criticized by the press, the reformers and the clergy, he maintained Chicago at a level above that of other cities in the United States at that time.[1] The picturesque figure of this amiable Kentucky gentleman fell across the way of Chicago for a generation. There were petty bosses, but no great boss could spring up. There were minor peculations and there were gamblers and prostitutes, not pursued if they kept to the rear, but there was no room for a thoroughly organized system of political corruption of the type that had become familiar in American cities.

Johnson says of him in characterization: "He was supported by the majority because he had no boss and would tolerate none, because of his capacity for friendship with every class, race and creed, because of his liberal views on social and political questions, and because of his frugality, integrity, and strict attention to the duties of his office." Well adapted to the cosmopolitan character of the population and to the style of the times in the Middle West, Harrison maintained a certain political "character" in the community, and gave a bent to political attitudes and leadership which had an enduring effect upon the city. His final honor was his election as World's Fair Mayor in 1893, and his assassination during the exposition was one of the tragic events of the time.

On the death of Harrison the forces of the spoils system

[1] See the *Life of Carter H. Harrison I,* by C. O. Johnson, a brilliant analysis of a striking leader. Compare W. H. Stead's, *If Christ Came to Chicago* (1894).

came to the fore and under the leadership of the Yerkes-Lorimer group, the city was delivered over. The City Council fell into a period of incredible corruption while a docile Legislature at Springfield proceeded to enact measures depriving Chicagoans of their rights over the control of the streets. But the enraged citizens were not without a remedy. A revolution occurred in the House at Springfield in the course of which the Speaker was driven violently from his chair and allowed to return only on terms imposed upon him by the rebels.

Before this a revolution had broken out in Chicago, headed by the newly organized Municipal Voters' League, under the unterrified "King" Cole (George E. Cole). In this uprising the Council was raised to a cleaner and sounder basis by a well-planned and well-executed effort, which gave the City for twenty years the best local legislative body in the country. Out of this came a civil service law, an improved mechanism for the conduct of elections, a reorganization of taxing machinery, a new type of municipal courts, a new spirit in the council, a new mayor in the chair, abler judges on the bench. And the city took courage and went forward on its municipal course.

It was during this period that the younger Harrison had succeeded his father, and presided over the City Hall from 1897 to 1903, and from 1911 to 1915. Like his father, the younger Harrison was not an idealist, but a political realist, hostile however to the growth of a boss-controlled spoils and grafting machine, and antagonistic to such formidable spoilsmen as aspired to the complete domination of the city. While he did not follow the lead of the reform forces, he did not as a rule antagonize them, and on the whole prevented the drift of the city into the hands of the spoilsmen of the worst type. Interpreting the spirit of a cosmopolitan community and largely supported by cosmopolitan elements, he did not "clamp down the lid," although in his last administration he broke up the organized "red light district," to the chagrin of many of his supporters.

With the War, calamity descended upon the city. The Yerkes-Lorimer combination of the '90's was recalled in the Thompson combination of the 1915's. The spoils system swept over the city like a noxious blight, and the city hall became a symbol for corruption and incompetence. From the high point reached by Harrison at the end of his term in 1915, Chicago descended to the lowest depths in its history, as the civic idealism of the community was for the moment put to rout. The Council was wrecked, the administrative services looted, the election machinery captured, and vicious hands reached out for the schools and the courts. The prejudices and passions and greed of the city were thoroughly exploited to the accompaniment of a rich pyrotechnic display of the inevitable type, ranging from tawdry "pageants of progress" to bloody race riots in the Black Belt.

The culmination of these scandals came in wholesale indictments of school trustees, and the city was relieved by the election of Mayor Dever, whose notable record was a distinct improvement upon Chicago's civic standards.

The return of Thompson on a wet platform with a camouflage of "America First" marked, however, the beginning of another saturnalia of corruption, more disgraceful, if possible, than any that had preceded it. In this new outburst of municipal greed almost nothing escaped, beginning with the plunder of the schools and extending to almost all branches of the municipal service. The attacks upon the schools conducted by a set of scoundrels wearing the masks of patriotism were an especially notorious feature of this brilliant modern restaging of political piracy. Out of this came the Revolution of 1928 in which the voters overthrew an apparently invincible machine in the primaries, and followed up their victory with an effective conclusion in the fall. The election of an aggressive state's attorney ended the reign of open graft, and began the restoration of public confidence in the local government. Substantial advances began to be made in every direction, as the municipal morale was restored and courage and competence were found for the city's reconstruction and reorganization.

And this is the point at which a more intimate view of Chicago politics may appropriately begin.

CHAPTER II

THE BIG FIX

NEITHER the activities of gunmen nor the exploits of imperial city builders occupy the chief place in the interest of the average of the 800,000 families of Chicago, whose minds are dwelling upon much less dramatic events. They are living in the gray light of daily reality. They are thinking, as are other humans, of their food, shelter, clothing, adornment, and recreation, and looking, perhaps all too complacently, upon the political events going on about them. But the brighter and the darker sides of the city's life may better interpret the life of the city that lies between these interesting extremes. It is proposed to look first at the Big Fix on the one side, and then at the City Builders on the other.

There is in Chicago as in other great cities of the United States an inner organization directed against the greater Organization known as the Law. This inner organization has Graft for its goal, and Protection, a hallowed word, for its god. The name of the inner junto varies with the argot of the day. It may be called the Ring, the Inner Circle, or other term devised by the ingenuity of the moment. In Chicago the Big Fix was its last alias. This organization may be highly centralized or may be widely scattered among many barons who work independently, like feudal lords of old. One may say that there can be no organization among those who are against the government, but this is not true. Indeed in many ways the organization of those who are against the Organization is better than that of the Organization itself. Leaders, policies, administration, codes and customs govern this other world, and discipline is as remorseless as in the world of organized justice, simpler perhaps and more swift. It has its regular members, its honorary members, its affiliated members, and its wide circle of retainers who rally to its support upon special crises.

Looked at from one point of view, this Organization is an outlaw and a predatory stranger, but from yet another, it will be found to be a child, if not legitimate, at least a bastard child of modern society. It may bear the bar sinister, but its parents are well known. They are the situations and attitudes of a busy and newly made civilization. We may not be willing to recognize these trolls, but they recognize us. Probably they are amazed that we are amazed at them, and view us more tolerantly.

At the outset, allow me to register a protest against the attitude that makes of vice and crime and graft a thing apart from our own human life, as if they were not an integral cross-section of the life of our community and our society. There would not be bribe-takers, if there were no bribe-givers; there could not be collections from prostitutes if there were not a wide market for prostitution; nor from gambling if there were not many gamblers, great and small; nor from bootlegging if there were not patrons of the industry; nor grafters in government if there were none in business or labor.

It is too simple, and often too hypocritical, to assume that all graft and crime are the acts of wilful and wicked persons entirely set apart from the superior rest of us, and by the same logic that the simple remedy is the rigorous application of the criminal law. Upon this very attitude, unreal as it is, the underworld has thriven. Vivid pictures may be drawn of the breakdown of the law under certain urban conditions, and they may be truthful, but the real picture must be that of a world in reconstruction, under new conditions; and not merely that of the old lines fading in the new surroundings.

I am going to show the Underworld, but I am also going to show the points where its boundaries overlap those of the Upperworld, and how its deeds are those of our own inspiration or of our own neglect, how we share in responsibility for them. What we see is ourselves, not them.

What is the Big Fix? It is the combination of influences and agencies designed to control the political situation, and to be able to give immunity from the law. Never quite complete, it strives for completion, reaching out constantly for new connections and protections. Prosecuting officials, police, sheriffs, judges, mayors, governors, were among the many meshes in the great net, recently designed to entwine and entangle the law. It was presumed that the Big Fix could fix anything sought by the hordes of fixers, little and otherwise. The Big Fix could protect grafters and gunmen, gangsters and thugs, of high degree or low; could protect theft and fraud and violence, and murder, even, if killings and killers were necessary. Graft and spoils spread before the Big Fix, in an endless series of golden opportunities for the faithful who followed the sign of the Fix, obeyed its system of Drag and Pull, and fought its battles if need be. Its revenues, running into the tens of millions, were dazzling in their lavish richness, and attracted a motley army of retainers with insatiable appetites for loot. It was thought that all lines of attack were "fixed," except the United States District Attorney's office.

Its philosophy was well stated in the very recent case against election frauds and murder. The conspirators were told: "You've got the governor, the state's attorney, the sheriff, and—if you need him—a judge with you. If anybody gets in your way, push him out. Come prepared, come well armed."

The Big Fix is broken now and only the little fixers remain, more furtive and hesitant in their ways. Greed outstripped all bounds of discipline and restraint, and brought about the inevitable downfall of the Kings of Graft at the very moment when all seemed most secure.

The greater Fix may never form again, but its methods, objectives and spirit linger, and may perhaps rise again to power and wealth.

A bird's-eye view of the Big Fix shows that its budget is an ample one.

The revenue of the System is derived from a great variety of sources, some of which may be regarded as standard and others as special.

The standard sources include a list something like this:

Personal Services
: Assessments of public officials, split salaries, half time and no time men, appointments and promotions and the perquisites of the party service of public servants.

Public Deposits
: The placement of public funds, with possibilities of split interest, lines of credit, political banking.

Contracts and Purchases
: Letting and enforcement of contracts for services and purchase of materials, with rigid or lax enforcement of specifications if any.

"Protection"
: Includes bootlegging as its largest item, gambling, prostitution, various types of criminals and their defense.

Taxation
: Tax fixing and adjustment, legitimate and illegitimate.

Public Utilities

Contributions for services rendered.

Legislation

Sundry payments for enactment and blocking of ordinances.

Control of Election Machinery

The equivalent of 50,000 votes in a primary or election.

Good Will, Favors and Adjustments

Covering a wide variety of profitable governmental actions, for which the beneficiary is willing to pay, as in building operations, and many other cases where favorable interpretation, speed, priority, differential advantage are useful.

Perquisites, *honoris causa*

Emoluments arising from official position, such as loans, market tips, real estate information, and business favor and patronage of miscellaneous and varying forms; law practice, contracts, and good turns, of a legitimate or quasi-legitimate nature.

The city's pocketbook is always an object of magnetic interest to the Big Fix. Even a small commission on an annual expenditure of $300,000,000 is attractive, and modesty does not always limit itself to a reasonable rake-off. As a rule city expenditures are not too large in proportion to the income and wealth of the community, but the service rendered may be too small and the distribution of the burden unjust.

I was once indirectly approached by an incoming official and asked for my chart of the possible and usual forms of leaks in public expenditure. While flattered, it seemed wiser to decline in view of the special situation. Nor is this the occasion to spread out a list of all the varied types of loss in the outlay of the taxpayer's funds, and the reader need not be alarmed at any such prospect; nor need the expert scan these pages for anything new at this point. It is enough to show the chief sources of revenue for the Big Fix in the letting of contracts, the handling of public deposits, the purchase of materials, the padding of payrolls, and assessments upon the payroll list.

The army lives upon the country, so to speak, for the soldiers of the system are mainly paid by the public. The first move of the invader is to scan the list of the payroll and either fill it with old friends, or compel enemies and neutrals to take a new oath of allegiance. The organization checks the ward and precinct of the official and keeps close track of who is back of him, a consideration of paramount importance.

Chicago has contributed nothing new in the development of this old system. Assessing the employees, splitting salaries, paying those who do not work or not enough;—these are standard devices, and little originality appears in the construction of new types. It is true that the city was once amused at finding that "L. C. Smith" who was carried on the payroll for many weeks was a typewriter and not a typist, and it may be conceded that this showed a sense of humor as well as a dash of audacity.

One exception may be noted, and that is the employment of the real estate experts of million dollar fame. The City Plan required the widening of many streets and for this purpose condemnation proceedings were necessary, and on a considerable scale. Some ingenious rogue hit upon the idea of compensating experts for this purpose, not by salary or per diem, but by a payment of 1 per cent of the value of the property on the streets affected, reconstruction value at that. The net result of this innocent device was that over $2,000,000 was paid for services estimated by the real experts as worth not one-fortieth the sum. One of the experts received $577,000, another $577,000 and another $577,000, another $460,000, another $544,000, averaging $1900 per day for each expert. When the facts finally came into the light, the city gasped. But more, the *Tribune* [1] brought suit for the recovery of the money, named as defendants the experts themselves and still larger fish, the comptroller, the president of the board of local improvements and his honor the mayor. At first this seemed a merry jest, but the wheels went slowly round. Another turn of the wheel and the court held the mayor and his colleagues liable for the sum of $1,732,279.

Some of the experts plead that they did not keep the money but passed it in to the organization for campaign purposes. Of course, the officials disclaimed responsibility with facile protests and shrugs of official shoulders.

But, said the Court: "It is a well established rule that a court of equity will assume jurisdiction to try charges against persons taking or expending money of a municipality in violation of constitutional or statutory provisions. Courts regard corporate property as public trusts, and public officers as trustees of such property, and equity has inherent jurisdiction, not only to prevent the unlawful dissipation of corporate funds but to decree restitution of money unlawfully paid out by those who are by constitution or statute intrusted with the care of such funds." A perilous doctrine this for the Big Fix and for the little fixers as well!

In the Sanitary District there was performed the athletic feat of increasing the payroll from $2,000,000 to $10,000,000 in the course of seven years, but no special inventive ability was displayed in this process. The audacity of the procedure was notable in its breadth of imagination, but the technique of grafting was not materially enriched. The army of spoils was equipped with more artillery but not with new types or

[1] The Tribune Company v. William Hale Thompson and others. Opinion by Judge Hugo M. Friend of the Circuit Court (1928).

new tactics. The citizen of New York, Philadelphia, or Boston would merely yawn as he turned the sordid pages of crude theft.

Interests upon deposits of public funds is one of the great centers of political and financial piracy. In fact the rate of interest on funds is not a bad index, taken with others, of the political health of the community. The spectacular case of Governor Small, while Treasurer, and the final settlement by which he returned the sum of $600,000 to the State, has attracted nation-wide attention, but it is only one of a long series of cases which have never come to light. The Chicago system has included from time to time the revenues from split interest, a method by which one rate, say 2 per cent, is paid to the public and another rate, say 1 per cent, is paid to the official personally. The "split interest" committee of which I was chairman (1914) once investigated this question, and presented a series of recommendations which when carried out resulted in a large annual saving.

In one case a bank had loaned the sum of $2000 to a local politician who, when the note came due, did not pay, nor would he after repeated pressure. He finally issued his ultimatum: "If you make me pay, I'll withdraw every cent of your city deposits." And so he did, $100,000 at a time, until the end was reached, and almost the end of the institution.

Most important and far reaching, however, are the alliances between banker politicians and regular politicians for the control of large sums of public money, in ways just inside or perhaps just outside the law, lucrative and elusive. Most banks are not ready to coöperate in such enterprises for the pirating of public funds does not help sound banking practice. Ex-Senator Lorimer's invasion of the banking field with public deposits in his ample pockets was resented, and in the end brought him to financial ruin. But the power to deal with perhaps $50,000,000 of public money on deposit is still an important element in the organization of local spoils.

An important factor in the control of Chicago is the taxing system. Under the law all property, both real and personal, must be assessed at its full cash value. Equitable methods of valuing real estate have been devised and might readily be applied. But no one has found a way of fairly ascertaining the value of personal property in a modern city. No one knows what stock or bonds or mortgages the citizen may have either in Chicago or some other part of the United States, and no one has thus far been able to invent a workable and tolerable way of answering this question.

The practical answer in Chicago has been chaos. In one sense the personal property tax is like passing the hat for a collection, but in fact it becomes a great mechanism for perjury and corruption, under the least favorable conditions, and for favoritism and adjustment under the more favorable. For in faith who can administer such a law. As an assessor once said, "I am damned if I do not enforce the law, and I would be driven in the Lake if I did." The personal property tax thus becomes mightily useful in the hands of the political magicians, who find in the ridiculously antiquated formula of the law a magic incantation which they may repeat to conjure votes and sometimes more from the bewildered citizens.

For years the voters of Chicago and of the state have been ready to change this old constitutional provision, but the Constitution-makers in their wisdom, or their egotism as one may look upon it, made it impossible to amend the Constitution without a majority of all those voting, at the election, not merely on the question. In consequence of this interesting provision, it has been found impossible to strike out the obnoxious language of the law.

The assessment of real estate, which might easily be placed upon a fair basis, has been allowed to fall into the ruts of favoritism and inadequacy. Recent studies showed the average valuation at 40 per cent of the legal 100 per cent, and startling variations in the valuation of similar types of property. Efforts are under way to remedy this situation, and there is no legal reason why immediate improvement cannot be made.

In any case we may conclude with John Marshall that the "power to tax is the power to destroy," and with the practical politicians that the power to value property for taxing purposes is just as important a weapon in political warfare. With sound and vigorous administration, these difficulties are by no means insurmountable, but if the hand of the Big Fix attempts delicate readjustments, the results will not be encouraging.

A well-organized political machine likes to count the votes as well as to cast them. In fact the power to count may offset many a weakness in the casting. It is estimated in Chicago that election frauds in a poll of 1,000,000 votes may reach as high as 50,000 to 100,000 and if the central machinery is in friendly hands would go much beyond this generous figure. A state law requires that the local precinct election officials shall be residents of the precincts in which they serve. In some sections of the City, especially where there has been collusion between the party machines, this has made extremely difficult the choice of impartial election officials. In these cases the usual devices have been used to defeat the purpose of the voters—the padding of the registration lists, the impersonation of absent voters, the assistance of "helpless" voters, and finally the fraudulent counting of the ballots. Striking as some of these cases are, they offer little that is of interest to the student of electoral frauds, for much progress has already been made in the centers of Eastern political culture, notably in New York and in Philadelphia, but by no means limited to these cities. It is only in the quantity rather than in the quality of the fraud that the "20th Ward" experts may be given a high rating. Kidnaping of opposition agents and murder of some of them are shocking but not novel expedients in spirited election controversies, where much is at stake. It may be a matter of chagrin that more inventive ability has not been displayed in cases where necessity was so plainly in a maternal mood, but the Big Fix is not always original, and in Chicago indeed has shown more aptitude in slogans than in mechanical devices, in the judgment of students of comparative political pathology.

Organized crime is one of the most spectacular aspects of urban life, and one of the most difficult to deal with technically. The problem is not merely one of repression and punishment of crime, but of definition and description of crime under urban conditions, of treatment of offenders, of modern methods of crime prevention. Manhunting and murder trials are of absorbing interest to readers. The study of the sources of crime in social conditions and in the individual are far less interesting, but fundamentally more important.

Urban difficulties are not caused by the fact that the populations of cities are more disposed to criminality than those in other groups, or that the foreign population is more criminally inclined than others. Edith Abbott conclusively showed long ago that the American-born are as likely to be found in the criminal lists as others, and this evidence has been corroborated by other inquiries in other cities.[1] Our system

[1] *Chicago Council Committee on Crime*, p. 52.

of justice breaks down in cities for a variety of causes which cannot be discussed here, but which have been partially set forth on several occasions.[1]

My first contact with a serious phase of the crime problem came when I learned that the conditions in the Bridewell were such as the community would not tolerate, if it knew what was going on. The labor of between 200 and 300 inmates of this institution was let without competition to certain favored political contractors. Indeed no contracts ever were awarded, but the labor of these men was simply turned over to firms with a strong political pull. Some were employed in making brooms for contractors at 50 cents a day. This contract which should have been worth $50,000 a year, went to a firm with a political pull.

Others were employed in making little tufts of scrap leather with the use of a mallet and a die. For this the city received 25 cents a day. The daily task of the man committed to this labor was from twelve to twenty pounds of the little tufts. If he fell short, he was sentenced to solitary confinement in a dark cell. This contract went to another favored firm. Others were employed in the making of leather purses and for their labor the city received an average of 18.2 cents a day. Presumably only pickpockets were allotted to this work.

I introduced into the City Council a resolution, calling for an inquiry into these conditions and by the Council. As a result of turning on the light, contract labor in the House of Correction was abolished. Thereafter inmates of this institution were employed by the city.

Later we undertook a much more elaborate inquiry into the crime situation. This took the form of a Council Com-

[1] See *Survey of Criminal Justice in Cleveland; Report of Illinois Association for Criminal Justice*, 1929.

mittee appointed on my resolution "for the purpose of investigating and reporting to this Council upon the frequency of murder, burglary, robbery, theft and like crimes; upon the official disposition of such cases; upon the causes of the prevalence of such crimes; and upon the best practical methods of preventing these crimes." Competent legal counsel was employed, working with the aid of the Burns and other detective agencies. Edith Abbot, an eminent statistician, was engaged for statistical studies of various types and others, including a psychologist and a physician, were engaged. We made what was, as far as I know, the first attempt at a scientific study of the crime problem in an American city.

Since that time the Chicago Crime Commission has been organized upon a permanent basis, and now closes ten years of activity. In 1927 the Illinois Association for Criminal Justice came into being and has employed competent attorneys, crime experts, statisticians, to prepare an elaborate and many-sided study of crime conditions in Chicago: a mine of information upon existing conditions.

Some facts regarding the criminal world are not difficult to discover. We once found one hundred hangouts of criminals. As a rule it appeared that these resorts were not molested, and in some cases criminals boasted that they could not be taken out of one of these "cities of refuge"—the name is mine. A list of five hundred professional criminals not pursuing any lawful occupation was also assembled by investigators, not as a matter of original research, but to show the ease with which such facts might be secured. They included pickpockets or "dips," burglars or "prowlers," shoplifters or "boosters," hold-up or stick-up men, confidence men of all classes from high class "con men" to low class safeblowers, known as "peter men" or "yeggmen," gamblers of all descriptions from crap shooters to those in the big games, and so-called "all around crooks."

Of these the pickpockets are the best organized, and the most adequately defended. At times an inquiry is received at the police station as to whether Brown is being held there, before Brown has actually arrived. One of the mob has been arrested and one of those who have escaped has rushed to the telephone to inform the attorney for the gang, and see that the necessary steps for bail or release are promptly taken.

Burglars and hold-up men are regarded as lower class criminals; for there are dukes, counts, and lords in the criminal group, although there is no king who rules over the entire population. The closest approach to centralization is found in the lines of political influence that converge toward a small group of men, characterized as the man, or sometimes the men, "higher up." While this criminal group is by no means completely organized, it has many of the characteristics of a system. It has its own language; its own laws; its own method and technique; its highly specialized machinery for attack upon persons, and more particularly upon property.

In order to show the system in detail we once tried experiments of an unusual type. Two of our investigators were arrested for loitering around a railway station, and were held in the police station. Their release was obtained through a professional bondsman. They then went to a hang-out where they posed as professional criminals. They made the acquaintance of certain police officers, who finally offered to protect them in their business of picking pockets. They actually picked pockets (mine) and then divided their loot with the officers. Richer fields were then pointed out to them, and one of the officers expressed a willingness to escort them on their explorations, so that if they should be arrested by mistake, the protecting officer might secure their release. These officers were dismissed from the force, but were subsequently reinstated many months after, with full pay for the time of their vacation.

Hold-up men are not as a rule organized, and often are run-down professionals who no longer are competent for the crimes requiring greater skill. They are extremely dangerous to meet, for the reason that many of them are very young and nervous, and some of the older ones may be temporarily braced up by whisky or drugs. A trembling finger on an easy trigger has been the cause of many unintentional shootings and murders.

Even if a criminal is apprehended, there are many blocks in the way of conviction. In fact, the opportunities for escape are very great. Collusion or connivance or incompetence of the police, the work of the professional "fixer," the inactivity and incompetence, or worse, of the prosecutors; the high pressure of political influence; the spineless attitude of certain judges, or some other loophole in the intricate mazes of the criminal law may open. We must admit that professional crime is better organized for defense against the law than society is for the apprehension and conviction of the professional criminal.

Perhaps the greatest weakness of all, if comparison is possible in this field, is in the office of the prosecutor. Under our political system, the prosecuting official is changed every four years, and a new staff of men are brought in to oppose the skilled army of the criminals. In fact, the community in some cases trains a man as a prosecutor, and then turns him over to become an attorney for the defense. However good the intentions of the newcomers in the state's attorney's office, however great their natural endowments or their legal skill, they are at a great disadvantage in dealing with attorneys for the defense who have been familiar for many years with the intricacies of our preposterous criminal procedure. In addition to this, allowance must be made for the influence of political pressure and for favoritism that slips over the line into outright corruption.[1]

A related question is that of police efficiency. To what extent do the officers of the law carry out their duties? With lax administration even the process of patrolling may be seriously neglected. Restaurants, pool rooms, laundries, bakeries and other similar places may be found to be convenient "holes" for officers who were presumably traveling their beats and watching over the sleeping public, or that part of them not asleep and requiring watching. These conditions are never characteristic of an entire force, but they illustrate the types of difficulties that arise when the vigilance of the supervising officers is allowed to relax for any cause.

Still more serious is police collusion with criminals, a situation not infrequently encountered in neglected cases. This may originate on the fringe of less serious offenses and be carried over until it touches the gravest crimes against life and property. If superior officers are known to be grafters, it is difficult for the men employed as their collectors to maintain an indifferent attitude and the outcome is inevitable. An honest policeman may find himself punished for his honesty and learn to say nothing, to go along, and perhaps in the end to go out "to get his," to share in the proceeds of illegal actions.[2] Transfers to inconvenient posts, failures in promotion, and in the worse cases "frame ups" against them, go a

[1] See report of John J. Healey, former state's attorney on the lax practices now obtaining in that office, in *Report of Illinois Association for Criminal Justice.*

[2] See Bartley Cormack's vivid study of Chicago police conditions in *The Racket.*

long way to demoralize the best intentioned of the department, and to discourage the men who might save the situation. This is not conjecture on my part but the crystallization of many sad stories in Chicago and observation of others elsewhere. When the "right guy" becomes the "wrong guy," and the rules are the exceptions, almost anything may happen.

The lack of high professional standards is also a factor of weakness in the police forces of our cities and in Chicago. Such standards are only slowly built up, but the process is not a hasty one at best and is made more difficult by the general lack of high standards in American public administration and by the desire of many politicians to maintain the police force as a private preserve for the raising of favors and graft. A few chiefs like Woods of New York and Vollmer of Berkeley will go a long way toward building up the morale of police forces and starting the movement for really well trained and effective police.

In sharp contrast to the laxness of the law, are the many instances of harshness and brutality on the part of overzealous officers. Over 200,000 persons are arrested every year in Chicago, of whom more than half are discharged upon first hearing. In some cases arrests are made for the most trivial causes. For example, J. T. was arrested because "he made a loud noise at 21st and Dearborn, and threw a dog out in the street by the leg"; J. L. for "sleeping in a barn"; others for speaking back to an officer, sometimes for remonstrating in the case of what seemed an unwarranted arrest of another person. The common scolding or "bawling out" of traffic offenders instead of polite warning or firm arrest and punishment is a typical case of vicious police administration, intolerable if it were known that there are other and better methods. But the officer's ready defense is that a "notice" is all too likely to be canceled by a ready politician;

and that oral rebuke is his only recourse. Thousands of persons are taken into custody and held over night in police stations, who might much better have been summoned into court; and thousands of others are brutally treated by unthinking officers.

In some instances, otherwise kindly persons are apparently transformed by a uniform, and treat their fellow-men in a manner quite uncommon to them in their ordinary relations. This is not true in the large majority of cases, but there are enough instances to make material and necessary improvement possible. One of the most interesting and significant changes is the very gradual transformation of the police, through the development of the sanitary police, the park police, the policewoman, into an agency in which the club pays a much less important rôle than in the past. We may reasonably look forward to a time when the duties of the police will be much more of the preventive than of the repressive type.

Some of the saddest cases in my observation were those of criminals who have served their terms, were living decent lives, and were still hounded by the police and their road to recovery made more difficult. A middle-aged man came into my office one day and requested an interview. "Years ago," he said, "I don't know how it happened, but I slipped. I forged a check, and I finished a term in the penitentiary of a neighboring state. I learned my lesson, and since that time have been honest and industrious and in a measure successful. I occupy a position of trust in a business firm. But a certain officer has unearthed my record, and demands money, or exposure of me to my employer. Unfortunately I once gave him money, and now he keeps coming back for more and more."

In the case of newcomers, ignorant of the English language, the operation of the law is sometimes very severe. One case was called to my attention in which a man was sent to the Bridewell, served a term of 30 days, and returned to his home again before he found out what he was sent there for. He had been unfamiliar with the language, but had said he understood English, as many do, meaning by that a few simple phrases; had answered the questions put him wrongly, and hence been convicted.

On the other hand, in another case, a Polish girl was assaulted by a restaurant keeper, who was freed because of a misinterpretation of the Polish word for sleep. She was asked what she had done after the attack, and had answered, "I went to bed at once," but bed was translated as sleep, and hence the conclusion that she was not much disturbed if she could at once go to sleep without further ado.

Two judges have related to me cases in which a knowledge of the language was essential. In one case the Judge detected the interpreter in the act of deliberately altering the answers of the witness, in this instance in order to obtain the freedom of the accused. In another case, the Judge understanding Yiddish, overheard the conversation between a witness who had testified and a newly arrived witness, on the subject of what the former had told about the case. The unfortunate conversationalist when detected by the Judge, said finally, "And how should I know that an Irishman could understand Yiddish?"

Hundreds of men are sent to prison every year because they do not have a small sum of money necessary to pay their fine, and hundreds are confined in jail because they have no friends to provide bail for them.[1] For the first of these cases, the man who has not the money to pay his fine, we provided a remedy through the passage of a law authorizing the payment of

[1] See A. L. Beeley, *The Bail System in Chicago.*

fines on the installment plan, in the discretion of the court. At one time 80% of the inmates were in confinement for inability to meet small fines.

It frequently happens that the fine inflicted upon a prisoner operates most unjustly. If A, being a man of means, assaults B, a laborer without any property, real or personal, A may be fined $25, which he promptly pays. If, however, B, a laborer, should assault A, a man of means, and the fine of $25 should be inflicted upon B, he would be obliged to go to the House of Correction, and remain there at hard labor for sixty days. In this situation, clearly the so-called equality before the law is entirely destroyed. In many instances it happens that men are sent to the Bridewell as convicts, with the humiliation of such a sentence for the time being, and the after effects of it lasting through their lives for no other reason than that they do not have the $5 or $10 necessary to pay the fine inflicted. In order to cover these cases it is necessary to amend the statute in such a manner as to provide for the payment of fines on the installment plan. If Mr. B is fined $10 and has only $5, it would be just as well to allow him to pay the $5 he has and go out and work to secure another $5 as a second installment. Such a regulation is entirely lawful and would relieve a great amount of injustice now done to individuals sentenced to a penal institution because they have no ready cash, and would also serve to protect society against the criminals who are often manufactured by this very process.

Few persons who read tranquilly of crime inquiries realize that those who deal in detail with underworld conditions must work under extremely difficult conditions. It is easy to make an error in the facts in a world where perjury is common. Civil and criminal libel suits are on every hand. The "frame-up" by perjured witnesses is often encountered, and no matter how flimsy in its material, is likely to have an immediate effect. Misrepresentation and counter-attack are bound to arise if the work is thoroughly and effectively done. In this connection, the apt phrase is more than usually appropriate; "Woe unto thee, when all men speak well of thee." All the standard methods were applied to prevent the progress of our work at various times. All kinds of traps are set, and all sorts of obstacles interposed, from crude threats of death, to far more subtle schemes more artfully finessed.

The problem of official collection of tribute from crime and vice is one of the most serious questions in modern municipal administration. The Chicago Vice Commission reported in 1911 that the profits from prostitution alone were estimated at $15,000,000 a year, and that probably one-fifth of this amount should be classed as police graft. Subsequent inquiries under the Harrison administration, and by the state's attorney, by local papers, and latterly by the crime inquiry of 1928, indicate that this sum is too small. And to this must be added the revenue from crime, gambling, and drugs.

These interests are incessantly active in legislative halls, and especially in administrative circles. Certain influences actually held up the mailing of the Vice Commission's report for some time, on the alleged ground that it contained obscene, and therefore unmailable material. Following the appearance of this notable report the old redlight district was broken up, and open prostitution materially reduced, but by no means wholly suppressed, as is evident from the reports that come out from time to time.

The repressive treatment of the social evil has been vigorously followed in Chicago, as elsewhere in the United States, during the last ten years, with notable effects on the outward show of things; but it became clear long ago that the mere application of drastic severity of the Puritanical kind would not carry us through. More and more the medical aspects of the problem, the organization of recreation, prevention and substitution, the subtler psychological and biological phases of the problem have been emphasized. In other words, modern science is advancing to deal with the ancient evil in its modern forms, in modern ways. The removal of the taboo upon free discussion of sex problems, although not complete, has helped to create an atmosphere in which real progress can be made.

We are beginning to inquire into the factors that contribute to professional prostitution on the one hand, and into the large demand for such services on the other, and to deal with many other phases of the problem in addition to those of the police question of punishment. The physician and the social worker will have more to say upon this question in the future than the politician or the policeman who has used the situation to enrich himself, or the moralist who has exhausted his efforts in spasmodic crusades.

The latest models in the world of graft are racketeering and bootlegging, both profitable and both dependent upon the protection of public officials. They are in a sense not new, but variations of an old tune, set to new words.

The XVIII Amendment imposed the prohibition of the sale of intoxicating liquors upon an unwilling metropolis. In 1919 Chicago voted 406,000 wet and 147,000 dry, and though the battle was uncontested, the result is probably typical of the general sentiment; in 1922, 501,000 wet and 111,000 dry; in 1926, 427,000 wet and 166,000 dry. The pressure for public sale and for private manufacture has been tremendous, and has broken through the walls of the law, which finds itself without the support of public opinion.

The amount of protection paid runs into staggering millions annually, a sum sufficient to warrant the amplest organization and equipment, administrative, legal, financial, and political. A new aristocracy of wealth and power has arisen for the management of this revenue, the amount of which is unparalleled in the history of graft and startled the imagination even of the most inventive minds of the ancient regime. Little wonder that prostitution and gambling have been relegated to a secondary position, and wonder even that cruder forms of contract and payroll graft have been allowed to continue, menacing as they are to the maintenance of the organization. The flow of liquor into the city from the outside, the control of its sale in the rich Loop district, its distribution in the several wards, the control of the manufacture of liquor within the city, both wholesale and retail, must be organized, operated, and supervised by someone, and protected as well, for Protection is the magic word in this world upon which the Law may descend at any moment with padlock and prison in its hand, and Trouble in any case.

Little wonder that gang wars have broken out and that bloody struggles for power have been fought out in the streets of the city by competing gangsters with their eyes on the fabulous profits of the game. Until the advent of Mayor Dever, bootlegging was fairly well centralized, but when Dever disavowed control over the sale of liquor and demanded the enforcement of the law, savage war broke out among contending factions, no longer restrained by the compelling hand of the City Hall. Bloody struggles occurred between rival gangs of bootleggers with local police and other public officials taking sides. The return of Thompson failed to restore central control and the contest went on for the great prize of Protection. Indeed the war zone spread out, reaching the areas of gambling and the new world of racketeering in small industries. In four years 215 gangsters were killed and no one punished. The police, however, took toll of 160 gangsters during the same period. In short, the war was not localized but spread through many different strata of social life.[1]

In one instance policemen cruising about the street in ostensible pursuit of evildoers, but in reality with an eye upon incoming trucks laden with liquor, fell afoul of each other and opened fire as if upon the high seas in time of war. The ranking nobility find it necessary to step cautiously, perhaps to wear steel vests, to ride in cars with bullet-proof glass, to cultivate sitting with the back to the wall, to go abroad attended by faithful servitors with assiduous attendance such as a potentate might receive in old Russia. For in this shadowy world there is no property, since no one may legally possess contraband of war, and no personal safety, for the law of the land is that no one shall squeal even if guns crack and victims fall. One lives in a strange realm wherein the protection of persons and property under the law no longer exists. It is an adventurous world, where life is uncertain and often short, even if rewarded by profits such as few workers in the vineyard are able to reckon at the end of their day's work. A force of gunmen, killers, crooks at one end, salesmen and polite customers at the other, and genial officers of the law in between. Perhaps the golden stream is gained, and perhaps the swift stroke of the assassin.

Experience showed however the difficulty of drawing the line when once protection had been bought. If the policeman, uniform and all, is purchased by the bootlegger, must he distinguish and divide between bootlegging in the narrower sense and other violations of the law more commonly supported by the community. Theft and violence certainly in defense of liquor are legitimate under this agreement, and perhaps more. An officer is paid to ignore the sale of liquor

[1] *Report of Illinois Association,* already cited.

in a café. Enter a man and his lady. Enter two toughs, demanding the girl. Refusal. The man is kicked into a corner, the woman dragged to a taxicab and assaulted. The officer paid to ignore, still ignores. The bootlegger's staff is selected with results in mind, and is not always composed of tender-minded individuals. Often they are tough rascals, recruited from the underworld where jungle law prevails. And the officer whom they buy may be obliged to turn his back upon many things, not directly involved in the sale of liquor. Likewise the prosecuting attorneys and the influential politicians when sold find themselves enmeshed in a net from which it is difficult to escape; in fact have actually found themselves entangled; and thereby hangs a tale.

Bootlegging then introduces a new complication in the already complex metropolitan situation. There are laws which no one should break by immemorial custom and enactment, and there are laws which any gentleman may break if he can. And in the twilight zone, there are hatched many puzzling problems for the guardians of the law and the responsible custodians of the community.

Another new figure in the dramatis personæ of the underworld is the racketeer. In a broad sense, anyone is a racketeer who has a "racket," just as anyone is a grafter who has a special "graft." But in a more special way the racketeer is a regulator of competitive business by means of pressure of an illegal and violent nature. In the dry cleaning business, for example, the cleaners' scale of prices is established, or dealers warned to keep out of certain territory. In case of refusal, discipline may be enforced by breaking windows, by damaging the goods in the shop or in transit, by beating up the proprietor, and in some instances by the use of bombs exploded on the premises. The owner finds it difficult to protect himself either because of the activity of the racketeer or the inactivity of the regular officers of the law. If offenders are apprehended and fall in the toils of the law, they are vigorously defended and if only half-heartedly prosecuted, may escape; in short they may be guaranteed immunity from the beginning. Industries such as the candy dealers, the laundries, even the bootblacks, have been caught in the grip of the racketeer and often found themselves helpless. Ostensibly, regulations are put forward to prevent cut-throat competition, but in actual practice the aim may be sheer extortion. The line is drawn somewhere between business consolidation and blackmail. Labor agents, jobbers, small proprietors may all be variously involved in the tactics employed and in the accruing advantages.[1]

Racketeering may then be established as a lucrative enterprise, on the borderland between blackmail and organization, largely in the hands of thugs and gangsters, relying upon the god of Protection for their salvation. It may and does extend into many lines of business, especially those that are not previously highly organized. It is estimated that as many as 90 different lines of racketeering are found in Chicago at one time. But no estimate has been made of the amount of revenue collected in the pursuit of this enterprise.

An interesting development in the underworld encounters has been a new technique of warfare. The sawed-off shotgun is a relatively ancient weapon, often found useful under urban conditions where convenience of transportation and shortness of range make a gun of this type peculiarly attractive. And of course it has the advantage of conclusiveness and finality. The Great War has made the further contribution of the machine gun, which has been employed in a selected class of cases where rapidity and width of range

[1] "The gunman and the gangster are at present actually in control of the destinies of over 90 necessary economic activities." *Illinois Assn. Criminal Justice.*

have been important factors in the problem. In one case a machine gun was planted in the window on the second story, effectively commanding the post eventually occupied by the enemy automobile, and at the right moment took its deadly toll.

The use of bombs is by no means peculiar to Chicago, as bombings occur in many cities under various conditions. In Chicago there have been over 300 cases in twenty years and a large majority of these within the last four years. These pineapples range from the terrifying but relatively harmless type of "firecracker" bomb, to the more deadly high explosives which aim not merely at intimidation but at destruction and death as well. The bombings may be traced to a variety of causes: to feuds between rival sets of gamblers; to black-handers; to interracial clashes between blacks and whites, Italians and Irish; to labor quarrels; to the racketeering among the smaller merchants, and sometimes to political antagonisms. So wide indeed has been the demand for "bombers," that professionals seem to have arisen, whose services are available for almost any reasonable kind of bombing. Detection is difficult under the most favorable conditions and even the worst punishment seems remote to those who are within the circle of Protection.

But is it possible that these outlaws can prevail against the intelligence and organizing ability found in a great modern commercial city, priding itself upon efficiency and managerial capacity? And surely the majority of the community are not pimps, and bootleggers, and grafters and racketeers. And if the voters elect Thompson, do they endorse all of his policies, or only prefer him to his opponent?

How does it happen? is the question often asked regarding the sprees of the cities. Broadly speaking the answer may be found in the combinations and balances of social forces operating in Chicago and in other cities, and of these more anon. More directly the specific causes may now be examined. Perhaps "cause" is not the term to use, but rather the situations under which these developments are found.

Two of these conditions are of prime importance. One is the alliances of the Underworld with the Upperworld. Another is the level and nature of public attitudes. One who is interested in a more intimate view of urban politics may well examine these situations with care, for in them lies the understanding of this problem.

The lords of the Kingdom of Graft do not live apart. They move among men, men of substance and affairs. They know magnates and powers in the world of efficiency and organization, and they do business with them from time to time, with some of them. In the world of things as they are the passport is Power, and those are received and recognized who have it, regardless of how they came by it. Bank accounts, property, and the stream of power; these are influential in a world of industry and business.

If you control public funds to the extent of millions and may determine where they shall be deposited and on what terms (within limits) and for how long, you can deal with some bankers; and you will find allies among them. Not with all but with some, and they may render you powerful assistance. You may yourself become a banker.[1]

If you control the machinery of taxation, and if the system is an impossible one, there are those who will make terms with you, as best they may, and perhaps better than others, not so enterprising. And here again you may find friends or at least neutralize foes—silence and complaisance, deepest where darkest.

[1] See Steffen's amusing tale of "The Honesty of Honest Tom," *McClure's Magazine,* Vol. 45, No. 3.

If you control the police force, those who are concerned with strikes in times of industrial unrest will inevitably seek your aid, and they will not be concerned with whether your captains are grafters but with what their attitude will be in the time of storm. They will prefer a dishonest officer who is friendly to an honest one who is unfriendly. And this will be as true of labor as of business. They will prefer the open shop or the closed shop or the winning or the losing of the strike to the nature of the "force." And you may make or lose friends here, and find tolerance where otherwise there would be denunciation. Unless you carry your blackmail and extortion too far.

If you control the political situation, you may make friends finally with certain public utilities who may unite with you in an offensive and defensive alliance for the mutual interest of the high contracting parties. Whether the chicken came first or the egg, whether utility companies corrupt the city government or are the victims of blackmail and extortion is often disputed. Whatever the answer, the lords of the grafters will find opportunity for alliances with some of the great corporations who administer the quasi-public services of the city. These groups have ready money, avenues of publicity, a long arm in the business and labor world, a large interest in the community, astute and practical legal counsel, and they are not unaccustomed to intimate relations with public officials and politicians. They watch with solicitous care the elimination and election of aldermen and legislators, not neglecting mayors and corporation counsels. Nor are they unmindful of the many minor cogs in the machine, important for its final control.

Their trustees and directors will be men of great business capacity and of high social and perhaps religious standing in the community. They are in a position to lend effective even if quiet support to a machine or an individual who is friendly, or to castigate those who are recalcitrant; to lend, even more than cash, legal advice, subtle counsel, a certain form of respectability in the circles of business where the oddities of politics might be explained in terms of the exigencies of the utility situation, and where graft might take the politer form of extortion or blackmail or the sweeter term of "legal expense," without detail.

To the public much of this may sound terrifying and fearful, but not so in certain regions of the Upperworld of business, where affairs are placed upon the hard and realistic basis of engineering. Obstacles must be swept aside at whatever cost in the interest of the greater efficiency, and among them are the obstacles of politics and the politicians whose whims and eccentricities and financial appetites are subjects of alternate irritation and amusement.

But is it not a far cry from the elegant office of the efficient to the haunts of racketeers, panders, grafters and grifters, gatherers of jewels in the muck heaps of the City, to these political perversities that outrage and humiliate us in public affairs? Yes, but the alliance between the Underworld and the Upperworld is a part of the total situation, and perhaps one could not exist without the other. At any rate one cannot be explained without the other and in terms of the other, for they are both parts of the picture, if it is a true one.

Now by no means all business agrees with this interpretation of things political. If it did, then graft would be institutionalized. It would become the "regular thing," and everyone would know how to deal with it, as we do with taxation and tips. 10% would be added and we should all accept the situation, with regret but yet with understanding. Graft is the unfair advantage given to one over the other and herein lies its substantial differential to those who use it as against those who do not. Thus most business does not pay tribute and properly resents the imputation against industry as a whole, or all utility corporations. The mores of the business world do not require open condemnation of traders in political graft, but they do not approve them, and build toward a higher level of integrity and public responsibility. Sharp lines divide the responsible and the irresponsible in the world of business, but the line moves over toward the field of social responsibility.

Yet the existence and position of the Underworld cannot be understood by blaming "the interests" alone and without looking at the Public itself. This is too simple and flattering a solution. The Public does not will the Underworld, but the Underworld reflects certain attitudes or, if we choose to call them so, the moods of the great god Demos in a modern city like Chicago. What are these?

Some of them are characteristic of democracies, some of them characteristic of human nature itself, and some of them doubtless are peculiar to Chicago. But most of them will be recognized by observers as found everywhere in greater or less degree of development. One of these is the community's confused attitude toward the enforcement of divers types of laws; or more accurately the lax attitudes of various groups regarding diverse sorts of laws.

It is plain that many different types of offenses are jumbled together, and while the law is in each case venerable, it is not in all cases equally venerated.[1] There are offenses which have been condemned from time immemorial, such as murder, assault, and robbery; there are offenses which have been contrary to law for many years, but not contrary to widespread custom, such as gambling and prostitution and drunkenness; there are other offenses freshly created under the

[1] See E. A. Ross' brilliant study of *Sin and Society*.

stress of new urban conditions, as by speeding ordinances, health regulations, and building laws; there are offenses arising out of the industrial conflict of the time, as anti-trust laws, tax laws, types of labor laws on which struggling classes hold divergent views. These are all Laws, but they are differently regarded by the community or by large groups of it, although in theory all are administered upon exactly the same basis. Practically the result is confusing when the red-handed murderer, the citizen taken in a game of stoss, the automobilist who forgot his tail-light, the merchant guilty of a technical violation of the anti-trust law, are all taken in the wagon or put in the bull-pen, or at least held up to public scorn and put, so to speak, in the stocks at the same time.

In the whole field of municipal relation with the morals of the community, I have been struck with what may be characterized as the unreality or the hollowness of the general attitude. In the field of crime, except as it touches the industrial conflict on one side or the other, the public is in deadly earnest. There is no mistaking the determination to deal with ordinary crimes against persons and property. But in dealing with vice, gambling, Sunday laws, and liquor laws, tax and trust laws, the community clearly sets up a double standard of morality, which is puzzling for the administration and the government. In the abstract, every city is against gambling, and would vote strongly against the repeal of existing statutes forbidding it, but in the concrete, the citizens are not deeply interested in strict enforcement of the law against games of chance. In low dives and in splendid clubs, in little stores and in private houses, in churches even, games of chance are constantly going on, and if the law were drastically enforced, an army of inspectors would be necessary, and additional judges in the local courts. No one has ever taken a census of the number of persons gambling on a given day or a given week, but I do not doubt that the figure would be generous.

The same situation is found in dealing with the social evil. If the Vice Commission was correct in its estimate of $15,000,000 a year as the vice toll in a city of 2,500,000, evidently the practical opposition was not as strong as the theoretical. In the case of liquor laws where the violations are most widely spread, the difference may be accounted for by the fact that these laws are imposed upon the urban center by the state or nation, but this is not so in the other instances.

The community is not keenly interested in the strict enforcement of all of its many regulations, and the representatives of the people will not be any more severe or unrelenting than those who choose them, in a representative system of government. There is a great mass of laws and ordinances which are either openly or tacitly broken with relative impunity. It may even happen that ordinances are enacted with the express explanation on the part of their sponsors that enforcement is not expected, but that the rule will have a useful hortatory value.

When the anti-expectoration ordinance was passed in the Council, objection was made that it would be impossible to enforce such a rule. But, said the proponent of the ordinance, at any rate it will serve as a warning, and sometimes it will be enforced. So the police in the exercise of the large discretionary power which we will not give them in law but with which we endow them in fact, limited the enforcement of the rule to the Loop district and issued an order for its enforcement on Tuesdays and Fridays.

If all the laws and ordinances were suddenly and literally enforced the community would be thrown into an uproar, and the law enforcers would be recalled to their senses by the outraged citizenry. Speeding, gambling, bootlegging, are against the law, but how serious is the public in its expectation of the general enforcement of these rules? Does the state expect the literal enforcement of a tax of 5% on the full value of personal property, or the nation the literal enforcement of the anti-trust law?

Now this does not signify that Chicago is not a law-abiding community, but it indicates that there is much confusion as to which laws we are to abide by, and which we are to take less seriously, and it is in this twilight zone that the Underworld may flourish. Its kingdom is not a thing apart, but a realm with feudal jurisdiction spreading over many subjects nominally under other flags. A kingdom of murderers, or of robbers and thieves and pickpockets, or of swindlers alone, would have to live by itself in modern society, but the addition of bootleggers and speeders and gamblers and violators of a thousand minor ordinances makes the lot of the lawbreaker less lonely, and the organization of a demimonde feasible.

Thus the Organization outside the walls against the Organization inside the walls finds aid and comfort from those who make visits outside and those who remain inside but are friendly and tolerant. It is only when these outside the pale become too bold and insolent and undertake to rule instead of suffer toleration that a hue and cry is raised and they are driven back to the outer fields of the semi-darkness again, just as a prostitute who trespasses too far on the premises of convention may be thrust back violently and ostentatiously.

At all times the distance between the criminal and the non-criminal is not a gulf but a gentle slope, and when the law undertakes to make too many persons criminals, the level of the slope is even easier, and the god of Discipline confronted with the task of punishing almost everyone, becomes confused, and alternately lashes out and folds his arms in despair.

A high level of wisdom and firmness combined on the part of officers of the law and a sense of moderation in the enactment of laws reduces the criminal underworld to its lowest terms, and prevents the union of all the forces of disintegration. This may be seen in Berlin, in Paris, in London, and with the growth of a different type of police administration and a more mature sense of the practically possible on the part of the community and its overlords will come about in Chicago.

As preceding paragraphs have shown abundantly, the Chief High Lord among these disturbing elements is John Barleycorn and that for many years back. Two great groups are found in Chicago, each willing to subordinate all other governmental values to the desire for a drink or the virtuous determination to keep the other man from getting one. When this becomes the Great Issue the happy days of government are gone and hours of trouble are sure to enter. If the wets are willing to support an incompetent wet, and the days an incompetent dry, the making and enforcement of law will come upon parlous days.

In Chicago the wets were for home rule and a referendum on the Sunday closing question, but were against these devices for the other six days of the week. The drys were against a referendum on Sunday closing, but were for it the other days of the week. But when the 18th Amendment became a fact the drys discovered that there were grave dangers in the referendum, and the wets discovered its eminent soundness. Each tended to subordinate all questions of public policy and administration to the overshadowing issue of the sale of liquor. Each side played into the hands of crooks. The "liberals" in obtaining a "liberal" representative might get more than they bargained for in a candidate whose record was liberal toward crookedness and thieving. In obtaining a dry candidate in like manner there might be landed a reactionary disposed to look with complacency upon the higher forms of loot and plunder. State's attorneys, sheriffs, aldermen, and mayors were elected upon this one test.

Singularly enough, no systematic investigation has been made of the liquor problem in any American city. In 1915 I proposed such an inquiry in the Chicago Council. The resolution was adopted and a commission of nine wets was named, omitting the author of the resolution. At that an excellent report was made embodying many sound suggestions. But it was pigeonholed, and nothing happened. I also introduced an ordinance providing that, subject to a referendum vote, the sale of spirituous liquors should be prohibited, and only light wines and beers allowed. But this was not agreeable either to wets or to drys. And my ribs were sore on both sides.

I said one day to a leader of the wets: "I don't quite understand your policy. Do you think you can resist forever all suggestions for the regulation of the liquor traffic?" "No," he replied, "but if we concede one point, another will be urged; and then another, and so on. We have figured out that we have only a short time, perhaps ten years to go, and we have made up our minds not to compromise, but to make what we can now and then die in the ditch"—a short-sighted policy, dictated not by the smaller saloon keepers, but by the larger brewing and distilling interests who by this time had obtained substantial control over the retail business and were squeezing out the last drop.

The liquor question had its light side as well as its tragedies. Sitting on the License committee, where I was placed in order to make it necessary for me to vote on all wet and dry proposals, we were entertained at one time by a mysterious ordinance requiring the abolition of the once famous free lunch. This turned out to be a desperate struggle on the part of conflicting groups of saloon keepers. Those who dispensed beer chiefly, favored the free lunch and the long, long drink. Those whose chief business was dispensing a quick shot of whisky thought the free lunch an expensive nuisance and wanted to be forbidden to serve it. I do not recall any other hearing in which the respective positions were presented with such fervid conviction, and certainly no other in which my own opinion was so eagerly, almost prayerfully sought, by all the liquor men. For the moment I became the Judge of Booze. But we never seemed to have enough evidence to make the decision.

It might be supposed that there were other more important phases of city government than liquor, which might prove attractive to the voters of the community; let us say transportation, housing, recreation, taxes, schools, health. But not so. Is there more kick in a drink and in the crusade against the Demon Rum, than anything else in local affairs? It must be conceded that Thirst and Conscience are powerful motives in human behavior, and the other needs of the city must wait upon them, if and as they really are.

Almost no known dry has been elected mayor, prosecuting attorney or sheriff of Chicago or Cook County, and many campaigns have turned chiefly upon the problem of comparative wetness. Thus the active administrators of law must be recruited from among the wets, and the City will be fortunate if it finds an honest and capable wet, of the type of Harrison or Dever.

THE "BIG FIX"

THE GENUS GRAFTER

In looking at the genus grafter and the worst of it, we must recognize the truth that the line between what everyone regards as a legitimate adjustment or favor and what everyone regards as outright graft is not always a sharp one. It is inevitable that those in power should possess a certain amount of patronage, preferment, favors,—an array of perquisites and emoluments. Some of these will be looked upon by everyone as entirely legitimate and others will be considered doubtful. To appoint a friend or an ally to office, other things being equal, is not condemned but commended. To appoint any incompetent raises a question, while to appoint an incompetent to a position where he might endanger the lives or safety of others at once becomes criminal. So there is a limit within which rulings and interpretations may be made and still be considered entirely legitimate, although favorable to political allies; there is a point when this passes over into dubious practice, and then into outright and indefensible violation of the spirit and perhaps the letter of the law. In class or party struggles much greater liberties may be taken with the law than in other types of cases. A Republican interpretation of the law, or a Democratic, in an election case will not arouse criticism at least from the party favored, while an interpretation of the law favoring labor or capital will meet with the approval of one party if not of the other.

There are types of spoils and types of "honest graft" that are commonly regarded as tolerable, even though not desirable.[1] and it is easy to slip over the line from these perquisites of power to regions where the action is universally condemned, and is not even defended on direct grounds by

[1] W. L. Riordon, *Plunkitt of Tammany Hall,* on "Honest Graft." Frank R. Kent, *The Great Game of Politics; Political Behavior.*

the offender himself. No one will justify taking cash out of the public till, except on the very general ground that others are as bad as he is. But an unjustifiable public price for land or a soft job might not be so regarded by the beneficiary or by many of the community. In the one case the individual concerned admits that he is a rogue, but in the other he may pride himself upon his business astuteness or congratulate himself upon his luck. Some persons fall into a perfect maze of confusion in dealing with this problem. I recall a citizen who was once bitterly denouncing municipal corruption and graft. His water rates he thought were exorbitant, owing to a grafting government, and he went on to say that he found it necessary to give the inspectors a ten-dollar bill every time they came around to read the meter as they were "such persistent grafters." He spoke as if his own part in the transaction was entirely innocent.

The grafting spirit is given strength by several aids which are not commonly very closely scrutinized. For example, the party attitude of rewarding workers by a huge system of patronage and favors very readily slips over into condoning outright jobbery and thievery. A very prominent statesman once said to me: "A lot of jobs and quite a bit of graft are necessary to run an organization." Even the most honest men in public affairs are forced to work with others whose thievery they may not know in detail but have reason to understand in general as well as a credit man in business knows his men. In every organization there is something like this going on all the time, but in the party the tendency is much stronger.

The transition from friendship and the clan spirit is also involved. Much that starts as friendship of a fine type gradually becomes, almost before it is realized, flagrant violation of the law. And when it is realized, still the friend must be protected or aided. Now loyalty to friends is a fine quality and is never to be despised or underestimated, and in politics there are many fine flowers of friendship. I have never known any relation in life, outside of war, where men would make so many genuine sacrifices of personal advantage for another or for a group. To lose one's livelihood or refuse a better one; to keep silent while one's reputation is torn to pieces in order to protect another; to face the silence of the prison cell even in serious cases is no easy task to carry out in reality. Yet these are commonplace incidents in the history of every political group. In some cases this is prudence or long time sagacity waiting for a reward, but in many others there is no prospect of ever regaining what is lost, and yet the loyalty of the man is not broken.

Of course the party world is not made up of martyrs, but neither is it composed entirely of Machiavellis. There is much pretense of friendship and loyalty where there is none in reality. Yet underneath all the external bluff, there is an immense fund of friendship and loyalty of the most genuine sort. Often I have wondered why society could make no better use of the fine qualities of courage, honesty (within the circle), loyalty, and devotion so often observed by everyone in contact with the men who are actually grafters, and how it happened that their talents and qualities could not be applied to the public service. If standing by their friends could be translated into standing by the public at the same time, or the two could be reconciled, a great advance might be made in the character of public service. In time of war or public calamity these persons often catch the spirit of the greater group and work for its triumph, but in the piping times of peace, the state, the government, seems to fade away, and its rights and requirements to become dim and meaningless.

Finally, the class spirit operates to encourage graft of various kinds, and in a way to furnish a justification for it. It is idle to say that business and labor are not ready at times to win their way by force or corruption, as the need may be; and each condones the offenses of his agents for such purposes. At least they do not condemn them very emphatically. Just as the clansman stands by his friends, so the director of the corporation may "stand by his stockholders," protecting their interests by bribing public officials, and salving his conscience with praise for faithfulness to trust even under trying circumstances. And the representative of labor will often do "what is necessary" to clear his coworker, even though the way be a malodorous one to travel.

Undoubtedly a considerable amount of graft has been paid in Chicago during the last thirty years. We usually ask, who got it? But equally important is the question, who paid it? Were they men of wealth and standing and respectability? In all probability many were, and still are, if they still live. Undoubtedly they were among our first citizens, entered perhaps in the blue book, with the entree to Society, with their names heading lists of donors to all kinds of worthy benefactions, to art, charity, education. If their names were printed and the amounts they paid, we would refuse to believe, I presume. The king can do no wrong, and they would be publicly pardoned as they are privately condoned now. Bankers and lawyers know the secrets of grafting rings and conceal them as if secrets of some confessional; stenographers, clerks, cashiers, accountants know them, but make no sign; wives, children, friends know them, but give no aid to public prosecutors when the safety of the city is at stake.

Whatever may be said in public, it is true that in private many men of high standing excuse, apologize for and even defend the payment of graft to city officials whether as blackmail in case of a legitimate enterprise, or as "grease" in an undertaking that cuts the corners of the law or even of common custom. When "respectable society" speaks of war upon grafters, it usually has in mind the pursuit of the bribe-takers, rather than the bribe-givers. We do not advance far by refusing to meet these facts, and by acting as if they were not in existence. I am not saying this in a spirit of cynicism, but merely as a realist examining the actual situation.

The question is often asked, is there as much graft in cities as the columns of the newspapers would seem to indicate? I should answer, yes and much more in many places. The more searching the analysis of the municipality, the more are new and undiscovered types of graft revealed, and the larger the number of persons involved. But if we go far enough we prove too much, and what we really find is a state of easy-going tolerance in a great part of the community toward practices theoretically condemned. In other words, we find the law partly repealed by custom. Which represents the standard of the community, what it says or what it does? Is the law what is or what is written? I do not mean to say that all men are grafters, for that would be like saying that all men are subnormal. But there are more persons involved in disregard of the law than we commonly think.

At one time during a crime investigation we undertook to study the fences or receivers of stolen goods; and among other devices we set up a shop with various kinds of goods, which we undertook to sell to purchasers who understood that the goods had been stolen. The investigators came back with a smile of triumph, showing a long list of prospective purchasers and seeming to think that they had clinched the case. I laughed and said, "Boys, you have proved too much." Too many were willing to buy. We encountered something too nearly approaching a custom.

I do not mean to say, as some of the sophisticated and cynical may conclude, that there is no hope then in the present situation. Quite the contrary, we should make the most strenuous and determined efforts to raise our standards of political practice. Progress is being made in that direction, but I am also confident that merely mechanical changes and man hunts will not prove sufficient to reach the goal. And those who loot the public treasury should be punished effectively. But the cause of the conditions is not individuals altogether, but a system, itself the result of a public attitude, of failure to organize appropriately the intelligence of individuals and of the community, of failure to take the long look instead of the short look ahead, to develop common watchfulness over what belongs to all of us—our common system of government and justice.[1]

And, further, graft is not peculiar to government, but spreads through business and labor alike. Large corporations especially are liable to grafting troubles, and the revelations regarding railways and other great institutions read much like those of municipal corporations. But private companies usually cover up their losses from peculation except when an occasional suit brings the facts to light, while public frauds are duly advertised on the front pages of the press as affairs of community interest. The full story would require that business records of loss from graft and fraud during a Chicago year be published and with them all the cases of labor extortion, graft, and violence, together with miscellaneous examples from quasi-public institutions and associations.

If we were not engaged in a struggle to advance, graft would by this time have become an institutional system, gen-

[1] In my *American Party System,* Ch. VII, I have treated this problem more fully.

erally accepted as a form of indirect taxation. This is now the case in certain Oriental countries, and might conceivably become so here, but it is repugnant to our standards of democracy and of justice and we struggle against it, realizing that a graft system is at once unintelligent and undemocratic. When the question of government is seriously considered, the bulk of every community is against the graft system, and in the end their sober judgment will prevail. They will root out the grafting practices that now weaken and demoralize the governmental system. Of course, they will not entirely eliminate the element of preferential treatment for personal or other reasons, but they will make clearer the predominance of uniformity of treatment in accordance with a rule or law, and the importance of universal responsibility for the preservation of the common property.

When a private park is newly opened it may be littered with waste and its beauty perhaps defaced. Offenders may be arrested and punished. They should be. But the real victory comes when the community appreciate that the park is theirs and the responsibility for its care theirs, and when unofficial persons begin to remonstrate with the greedy or careless and perhaps to rebuke unofficially the reckless and persistent; when it becomes bad taste not to look after the people's property, and draws the frown not merely of the policeman, but of the fathers and mothers and even the little ones who use the people's playground.

So it is with the social inheritance called government. For generations the property of the few, it has become the property of the many and we are developing the attitude of responsible owners.

The ultimate grafter, less commonly recognized, yet the father of the whole brood, is the parasite citizen who evades his share in the common responsibility for the maintenance of the common government. Any man is a grafter who is willing to take the inheritance of free government handed down to him from the past, use it and enjoy it for his selfish purposes, and then pass it along to posterity wasted and impoverished. This man or woman reaps but will not plant and tend. He takes but will not give. He is literally grafting on stock supplied by someone else.

But it may be said that these problems are not all peculiar to Chicago and have elsewhere been solved without so notable a breakdown of law and justice. Liquor and vice and underworlds and upperworlds and confused public attitudes are found in many places, and yet order prevails in the main. What is the difference in Chicago?

We might perhaps answer in terms of governmental structure and plead the multiplicity of governments; or the failure of the city limits to include the population of the real Chicago; or we might point to the newness of the city, the heterogeneity of its population, their mobility and their disorganization; or other combinations of political, social, and economic causes might be advanced in extenuation, and not indeed without some grain of truth.

But it is also possible to conclude that a few bad days do not make a climate. On the whole, the sun shines most of the daytime in Chicago, or as much as elsewhere, and these bad days are passing away or are passed. They are not types but dark times when storms settle and the sky is overcast. The civic quality of Chicago is no whit worse than that of other communities, and its ideals of order and justice rise above the highest tide of graft and spoils.

In what city is there no similar chronicle of woe? Is it New York, or Philadelphia, or Pittsburgh, or Cincinnati, or San Francisco, or St. Louis, Los Angeles, or New Orleans? Happy the municipality where graft and greed have not reigned for a time and flaunted their perversions of civic right in the face of justice.

Chicago outlived the terrible scourge of the Great Fire; and it will outlive the pestilence of grafters and racketeers. As Chicago now celebrates the anniversary of the dreadful day of the fire, the city may one day celebrate the passing of the Big Fix with appropriate ceremonies, commemorating recovery from this civic plague.

CHAPTER III

CITY BUILDERS

THERE is another Chicago than that of gangland—a city of builders, a city in which arise types of architectural beauty and strength, some of them of world importance in the urban domain of recent years. It is one of the anomalies, yet one of the realities, of American city life that municipal vision, intelligence, courage, organizing ability, have been able to rear beautiful and stately designs of city structure even in periods of ill-smelling fraud and corruption.

The Chicago Plan is one of the miracles of recent urban progress and holds a place of international importance in the growth of modern cities. The present development is already notable, and its approach toward completion will reveal one of the most striking and beautiful types of urban planning anywhere to be found. The opening and widening of miles of streets and boulevards, the artistic reconstruction of the Lake front, the reorganization of harbor and railway terminal facilities, the straightening of the Chicago River, constitute a notable addition to types of city planning.

The park system of Chicago is likewise one of the community's great treasures. The small parks of the city, the middle-sized park development, together with the outlying forest preserves, attract the interest and arouse the enthusiasm of students of recreation the world over. An intimate view of urban politics requires a look at these triumphs of physical development alongside of the darker phases of the city's life. What are these projects, and how did they come about, and what is their civic significance?

The Chicago Plan in its broadest and most recent sense contemplates a radical reorganization of the physical structure of the city. Somewhat more limited in its earlier phases, the Plan now includes a comprehensive development of a fundamental nature. The details of this undertaking would require a volume for description and analysis, a task obviously impossible within the limits of these pages. The larger features of the Plan alone may be considered here. Broadly speaking, the Chicago Plan includes some 200 miles of street widenings, extensions and improvements, looks to a reorganization of the passenger and freight terminal facilities, considers the city's harbors, and envisages as one of its central features a striking development of the Chicago Lake Front, a bold and artistic design, already justified by its beautiful results.

Reclaiming riparian rights once in the hands of private owners, the local authorities proceeded to execute a masterly design intended to transform the Lake Front from an eyesore to a municipal beauty spot. Great stretches of the Lake's border have been filled in and reclaimed. An outer belt of islands has been constructed in the Lake and an inner series of lagoons, 600 feet wide, between the outer belt of parkway and the mainland. This unique plan covers the Lake Front from Jackson Park on the south to Lincoln Park on the north, with a boulevard ranging many miles, along the edge or on the outer drive. Figures are relatively unimportant in a design of this civic consequence, but since some statistics have been given in consideration of gangland, it may be said that the total cost of city plan projects thus far completed is in the neighborhood of two hundred fifty million dollars, and additional projects already approved by the official authorities contemplate the expenditure of fifty millions more. It is probable that the completion of the Plan will require another two hundred fifty million dollars in addition to the amount already expended.

The full force of this municipal development is not realized, however, unless it is taken in relation to the surprising transformation of the architectural development of the central part of the city. The home of the steel sky-scraper, Chicago's architects in recent years have been able to develop striking designs of modified skyscraper construction, illustrated in such buildings as the Tribune and the Wrigley Towers, to mention only two in a fascinating series. The beauty of the Lake Front development may be more keenly appreciated when it is viewed against the striking mass and the impressive skyline of this new architectural appearance in the commercial world.

The Plan is not completed and perhaps never will be but important units have reached their conclusion. The widening of Michigan Avenue and of Roosevelt Road, the construction of Wacker Drive, the opening of Western and Ashland avenues, are accomplished facts. The Lake front projects near completion and it is expected will be finished within a period of five years. Great railway terminals like those of the Northwestern and the Pennsylvania have taken their place in the city's plan; the Illinois Central terminal is in process of construction, the suburban service of the Illinois Central has been electrified, and other large terminal projects are pending. The great task of straightening out the kink in the Chicago River between Polk and Eighteenth streets has passed the difficult stages of law, finance, and politics, and work upon it is in progress.

Of parks and housing a little later, but in the meantime,

how did the Chicago Plan come into being during a period of civic depression?

Chicago, like most other cities of the world, was not the outcome of a definite plan, but the product of a haphazard process, in which real estate speculation, industrial expansion, street railway extension, and chance played a large part. The city authorities had little power to regulate the development of the municipality, and less desire to do so. Both government and people were intent upon other objects, and would have regarded anyone who proposed scientific study and rearrangement of the lines of city growth as a visionary and if he had pressed his ideas as a meddler, or still more probably in Chicago, an anarchist. It was my good fortune to witness the awakening of city interest in the community plan and to play some part in the movement. As a member of the City Plan Commission, as the author of the zoning law, as the originator of the Railway Terminal Commission and the Regional Planning Association, I was placed in a position where it was easy to observe the rapid growth of intelligent handling of urban problems of this fundamental character. The Chicago city plan was initiated by the Commercial Club and is a worthy memorial to the intelligent foresight of its promoters. As originally drawn by D. H. Burnham it was a magnificent design of a more stately city and slowly fired the imagination of the people of the community as its possibilities were more and more clearly seen.

The struggle for the realization of the city Plan was not an easy one. Legal obstacles must be overcome, financial difficulties must be surpassed, and the objections raised by ignorance and self-interest must be circumvented. A notable pioneer in the movement was Charles D. Norton, and later Charles Wacker, for many years chairman of the Plan Commission, a devoted and effective advocate of the plan theory and practice; and they were supported by many others who were no less earnest in their advocacy of the reconstruction of the city. Newspapers and commercial interests generally supported the plan, and helped to override the objectors who were many. The City Council was an active force in explaining the system to its constituents throughout the city, and in lending legal and financial aid at all times without hesitation. An occasional alderman would demand that the "frills" be cut out of the appropriation, but in the main they were proud to be a part of a great constructive movement, in which, for many years at any rate, politics did not intrude. A school primer was prepared and the school children learned about the plan.[1] Illustrated lectures and newspaper publicity were incessant in their appeal.

What happens to the best laid plans is nowhere more clearly illustrated than here. Supported by a splendid community sentiment, with the imagination of the city aroused by the prospect of a greater Chicago, the way was clear for a notable advance in municipal planning. But the city's idealism fell into the hands of expert architects of thievery. Grotesque gargoyles with forked tails and devilish faces began to decorate the plan for the City Beautiful. The City was aghast at the spectacle and uncertain whether to go forward or back, realizing the heavy loss by either move, but went on toward the completion of a plan of world significance. The intolerable odor and exorbitant expense did not stop the movement.

The Regional Survey of New York has this to say of the plan: "In this century and on this continent Burnham's plan of Chicago stands out as a great presentation of a grand architectural conception of city building and extension. Probably

[1] Wacker's *Manual*.

no other plan, as a plan, has achieved more than this as an inspiration to a people."

The fully developed city Plan, one that includes not only the automobilist's boulevard but regards the living conditions of the whole city, is of prime importance. Its adoption indicates a long step forward toward a higher level of municipal life. The advantages to be gained by the community are difficult to measure, or to overestimate.

"We may measure our gains in square feet of land saved by the more ecónomical use of space. We may calculate them by the clock in terms of transportation time. We may gauge them by the reduction in the ravages of disease and the grim reaper's toll of death. But we cannot measure by rule, scale, or computer, the gain in human values, the warmth and brightness of more abundant life, the happiness and joy of larger living, in those personal values which transcend all others and whose protection and promotion is the supreme end of government." [1]

In 1914 I prepared the ground for the zoning system by working out a study of the conditions in the city, and publishing it in the form of a special report.[2] In this inquiry, we developed the abuses arising under the present system which permits the mingling of industrial and residence districts. We showed the inadequacy of the system of private agreements, under the Illinois decisions regarding such cases; and we suggested the remedies in the way of necessary legislation. It was not necessary to go far for illustrations of what happens. The ice-plant on the corner in the center of a residential section, a nuisance to the neighborhood and a detriment to property values in the vicinity, is enough. Hundreds of like cases were to be found all over the city. In Chicago,

[1] City Planning Conference (1917, Kansas City) on "City Planning in Chicago."

[2] *Building Districts of Chicago.*

as elsewhere, there are acres of property ruined for residential purposes, but not yet ripe for industrial. These twilight zones are often used for cheap and unsanitary tenement purposes, and may become the home of redlight districts where easy tolerance is the rule. The Chicago fire was not more costly to the city than the heavy losses caused by unregulated building conditions.

Support came to this movement from many quarters, the health department, the fire department, the insurance companies, the coroner's office, and from the real estate interests which were not slow to see the point. The Manufacturers' Association at first opposed the measure, but on more mature deliberation found that zoning would not tend to hinder but to help legitimate industrial expansion. The health department was ready to show that better sanitary conditions would be found where residential and industrial centers were separated; the fire department to show that fire risks were less in such territories, in which they were confirmed by the fire underwriters; the coroner's office presented figures to show that the number of children injured by automobiles was much greater in mixed residential-industrial districts than in districts devoted to either one or the other purpose.

And so we were able to accumulate a mass of testimony tending to show the desirability of urging the Legislature to provide a law authorizing the Council to enact a zoning ordinance. At first the aldermen were indifferent, but after the day of the first public hearing they were convinced of the importance of the measure. The small property owners from all parts of the city, most of them members of various local improvement societies, stormed the City Hall, and overwhelmed us with the eagerness of their demands. They piled up instances of their grievances and would not be denied. The larger real estate boards, the Association of Commerce and the Federation of Labor were likewise in favor of the plan. And the Council, it may readily be conjectured, became the friend of the measure.

The park policy of Chicago, and especially the small parks on the outer-belt park system, are notable features of modern park development and have attracted the attention of specialists in park organization all over the world. An elaborate system of small parks and playgrounds has been set up and equipped, with field houses in some cases and playground apparatus in others. Some of these are maintained by the City, some by the Board of Education, and some by the three large park boards.

Outside of the city limits the forest preserves have been developed under the auspices of the County government. This development includes over 30,000 acres, encircling the city from Lake Michigan near Glencoe on the north to the Lake on the Indiana line on the south, and constituting one of the most remarkable features of the recreation development of any community. The foresight of this action will be increasingly evident.

The park plan owed its beginnings to the admirable report on the whole problem made by Charles E. Zueblin, George E. Hooker, and Dwight H. Perkins, many years ago, surveying the whole field and outlining a masterly policy for the next generation. The regular park authorities remained indifferent to the special features of this plan, but the aldermen became interested in the provision of small playgrounds for their constituents, and began experimenting to their great satisfaction. Subsequently the movement was taken up by the South Park Board and a remarkable development followed. The outer belt parks system was the creation of the Cook County Board under the original impulse of its president, Henry G. Foreman. Later, a Recreation Commission was appointed by Mayor Dever for the purpose of making an elaborate study of the recreation problem and preparing appropriate suggestions, but the work of this committee has never been completed, and it remains one of the city's problems.

One of the largest questions confronting Chicago or any other city for that matter is the question of adequate railway terminal facilities. Especially in a great railway center like Chicago the proper arrangement of terminals and the adjustment of their facilities become a matter of very vital interest to the entire city. As an illustration of the advance in municipal point of view, when the Northwestern terminal project was presented to the Council, a lone citizen, George Hooker, appeared to raise the question whether the City should not consider the relation of this proposed terminal to the other facilities of the town. He was laughed out of court, and his query went unanswered. Of course it was no concern of the City where the companies placed their stations. What had the City to do with that?

Both in the Illinois Central and in the Union Station cases in 1913, the City took an active part in the consideration of the whole matter, and reached conclusions in coöperation with the railway authorities. A Railway Terminal Commission was appointed, on my resolution, and the eminent engineer John F. Wallace was engaged for the city. At the same time a remarkable study of terminals was made for a group of citizens by the well-known engineer, B. J. Arnold. Legally these cases came before the city, because they necessitated vacations of streets or alleys, which could not be done without the consent of the municipality. Both companies were politically strong, and at first endeavored to sweep the city from its feet by audacity of attack, but proved unable to intimidate the Council. In the end, important concessions were gladly made to the city. The plans proposed were squared with those of the City's Plan Commission, and electrification was ensured on the south side lines.

The passage of the Pennsylvania and Illinois Central ordinances, the outcome of long investigations and struggles between various interests, together with the work of the Railways Terminal Commission were in fact landmarks in the history of the community. Their full effects will not be seen until the plans and requirements of these projects have been concretely worked out and made plain in actual construction. At that time the enormous advantages gained for the city will begin to be evident. The Lake Front improvement, electrification, the huge development west of the River, will loom large in the physical outline of the city. Further, the future development of the remaining terminals of the city will be materially affected by what has already been accomplished in the way of establishing intelligent municipal control over municipal development. It would be idle to work out a picture of a city plan as was originally suggested and omit the direction of the railway development of a city in which railways are as important as in Chicago.

Finally, Chicago has set up a Regional Planning Association, headed by the son of the Burnham who made the original Chicago Plan, and brought together the various planning and zoning schemes with a view to their application to the Region as a whole. The Region is conceived as the area in every direction within 50 miles of State and Madison streets. It includes an area of 5000 square miles and a population of almost 5,000,000. I originally suggested the idea to the City Club of Chicago and on their initiative a conference was called and an association organized. Under the vigorous leadership of Daniel H. Burnham II and his energetic staff significant progress has been made toward the solution of one of the most important problems of the community. The Chicago Region is on its way toward organization, whatever the final type of it may prove to be. Important steps have already been taken toward more intelligent programs of highway construction, of zoning and planning, and of study of the fundamental features of regional development.

The development of more adequate housing conditions is also a part of any well-considered city plan. Hitherto, it must be admitted, this aspect of planning has been somewhat neglected, but in more recent years important developments have been undertaken in this field. Notable among these are the Marshall Field project for the development of model houses in a region north of the Chicago River and, still more recent, the Rosenwald project for the provision of model housing in the colored section of the city has come into being and is on its way toward execution. It is altogether probable that these two undertakings are the beginning of a wider expansion of a housing program that will ultimately transform many of the shabby, unsightly, and unsanitary sections of the city into more comfortable and attractive surroundings. A Housing Commission was appointed by Mayor Dever toward the end of his term, but in the twilight zone the movement came to an end. It will rise again.

THE COURTS

In previous paragraphs, some of the darker aspects of Chicago's judicial system were set down. There is another side to this story, however. The municipal court organization of Chicago has been a model upon which many other courts have been built, and the Juvenile Court, now past the twenty-fifth milestone of its existence, has been cited in many places as an example of notable adjustment of legal principles and practices to an important problem of behavior.

Prior to 1907 the judicial system of Chicago was characterized as the "justice shop" system, because justice might be bought and sold in the old courts maintained by the justices of the peace elected in the old towns, which still had a surviving nuisance value. This desperate situation was ended when the Municipal Court Act was adopted and a centralized system of judicial administration established. Under the guidance of a presiding chief justice, Harry Olson, the court has developed many striking advances in judicial administration. Among the more notable are those dealing with Small Claims, Traffic, Renters, the Morals Court, the Domestic Relations Court, the Boys' Court:—in all of which special treatment is given to special types of cases, following the names just indicated. In recent years there has been a marked tendency toward deterioration of the personnel of this body and likewise a lowering of the earlier standards, but nevertheless the court still stands a notable type of municipal administration of justice.

Likewise the Juvenile Court of Chicago has attained nation-wide fame in the period since 1900.[1] It established the important principle of the specialized treatment of minors, to the age of eighteen, and the practice of special professional advice to the court. First under Judge Mack and later under the leadership of a series of faithful justices, the last of whom is a woman, Mary Bartelme, this judicial institution has made long strides ahead in the treatment of younger delinquents. The work of Dr. John Healy in developing the research facilities of this court has attracted nation-wide attention and led

[1] See proceedings of 25th Anniversary of the Juvenile Court with review of its activities and achievements.

to notable advances in this domain. Around the court there has sprung up the Juvenile Protective Association, the Institute for Juvenile Research, the Behavior Research Foundation, and other similar institutions.

PUBLIC WELFARE

Significant as are plans for the physical reorganization of a city, they are surpassed in importance by those for the social reorganization and development of the community. The health of the people, their schools, their living and working conditions, the fundamental causes of poverty, unemployment and crime are questions of direct interest to the city; and in their intelligent disposition lies the welfare of the community. In large measure these problems lie outside of the domain of ordinary politics, and therefore may be considered more calmly. It is true that the Department of Public Welfare, set up in accordance with an ordinance I introduced and sponsored, has never functioned effectively except for a short time. But in other fields distinct advances have been made.

From the nature of its work, no department is usually more nearly free from politics than that of health. Its methods are essentially scientific, a powerful profession is associated with its work and there is no special property interest opposed to it. On the contrary, as in the case of the Fire Department, there is a strong commercial interest reënforcing its requests —the interest of the insurance companies. Furthermore, the general tendency of the times is in the direction of considering a larger number of questions as medical matters than ever before. Preventive health measures as against repressive police measures are in growing favor with the community, as the advantage of dealing with fundamental causes rather than the superficial results becomes clearer. The professional standards in health departments also tend to inspire greater confidence than elsewhere.

Under such conditions the Chicago Bridewell has in large measure been transformed into a hospital, and in the future will be still more so. The Psychopathic Laboratory has become an important adjunct of the judicial system, and will be still more useful in the future. The treatment of the social evil is passing into the hands of the physicians rather than the police, and the public is the gainer by the change. Retarded development of children in the schools is now treated by the doctor rather than by the old time punishment administered by the teacher. Statistics show an interesting comparison between the declining percentage of expenditure for police and the increasing percentage for the purposes of health, remedial and preventive. Schools, health and social welfare are in fact slowly absorbing the budget of the municipality.

Even in the darkest areas, the health department of most cities has been conspicuously better than the others. This has been true in Chicago. Of course there is politics in the medical profession itself and health departments are not immune from their own social toxins, but relatively they are slight sufferers. There are always technical standards within the profession by which their work may be fairly judged. There are sharp rivalries between old school and new school, between "highbrows" and "lowbrows," but these are comparatively insignificant, when taken in the large. It is much easier to get a fairly general agreement on the question whether the health commissioner is efficient than whether the police chief is. In the one case there is no local body of police experts to whom appeal can be made, and the decision on the part of the public is distorted by considerations affecting parties, classes, and public policies. In the other there is a large body of certified physicians who may pass judgment or assist the public to form an intelligent opinion on the competency of the incumbent. We cannot give the physicians a clean bill of health, but we know that on the whole their judgment is unbiased.

The greatest weakness of the health department thus far is the failure to insist upon the basic conditions of health, rather than the cures and palliatives. Dr. Woods Hutchinson said some years ago that in early days a physician might give the patient a prescription which the nearest pharmacist might fill easily enough. But now the prescription which we must make for many of our patients is something the corner druggist cannot give him. It includes fresh air, sunshine, an abundance of pure food, pleasant surroundings. These things only the community itself can supply. It is this fundamental truth that health departments have not sufficiently emphasized, with many notable personal exceptions of course. They have lacked the courage or the vision to ask for the amounts really necessary to lay the foundations of municipal health, adequate medical care for the population, adequate housing, attractive surroundings, the minima of all effective social organization and of government itself, under modern conditions.

Chicago has scored one notable triumph, in the battle or rather the warfare with disease. In 1891 the death rate from typhoid was 172. In 1927 it has been reduced to .7. The Drainage Canal was the instrument by which the attack was directed, an undertaking in which the flow of the Chicago River into the Lake was reversed, sent down the new canal and eventually into the Mississippi River at a cost now reaching $150,000,000, with greater expenditures still to come. This was an elaborate and expensive engineering feat, but it went a long way toward accomplishing the desired result.

Along with the Canal went an elaborate campaign of an educational and preventive nature against typhoid, and the efforts of the campaigners were crowned with success in the remarkable reduction of the deaths from this once dreaded cause.[1]

SCHOOLS

Spectacular events in the history of the schools of Chicago have doubtless led some to think of this institution as a storm center of educational controversy. But in point of fact the development of the school system is the greatest triumph of the municipality, an evidence of intense interest in this organization and profound belief in its usefulness to the community. With no aid from a national ministry of education or a state department, as would be the case abroad, the city has built up locally a marvelous educational development and jealously guarded its progress. The immense influence of the public schools in cities made up of all nationalities and creeds is difficult to emphasize. One may say that without this force our cities could not exist in anything like their present form. The complexity and difficulty of the task of administering a great school system has not prevented the city from carrying through the undertaking in remarkable fashion. Unquestionably the system might be very materially improved with the application of all that is now known about education, although the science is only in its infancy; but if we are viewing the failures and successes of a metropolitan community, we cannot ignore the far-reaching importance of the educational development under the direct charge of the city, and without supervision or direction from the outside, of the type that would be found in most European cities.[2]

[1] The campaigns against tuberculosis and later against venereal disease are notable, but are not discussed in this study.

[2] The school question is fully treated in G. S. Counts' *School and Society in Chicago,* 1928.

CHICAGO

What is "news" about the Chicago schools and what is significant from the point of view of education and of the community are not the same thing. The attack upon Superintendent McAndrew by Thompson is news; the charges of British propaganda in the schools is news; the threat to burn the British books in the Public Library on the Lake Front is news. This is front page material, and is eagerly read by thousands of persons, amused or outraged by the grotesque proceedings.

But the construction of beautiful school buildings at an expense of $100,000,000 is not sensational. The new temples rise slowly and one by one take their place in the great system of which they are a part. When a school falls it is news, but not when it rises. The steady growth of attendance now nearing 600,000, the doings of 12,000 teachers, the improvements of the curriculum, the expansion into higher ranges of instruction, special and technical schools, experiments in novel types of instruction:—these are not "news." They are not spectacular enough to arouse general excitement, although in fact they are of far-reaching importance.

This is not the fault of the press, but the outcome of a human situation in which steady growth awakens less interest than the unusual, the irregular, the exceptional. What is actually going on, notwithstanding the thunders and lightnings of political storms, is the steady development of an educational system, surpassed in importance only by that of New York City.

Finally, and it cannot well be too often repeated, Thompson was not reëlected because of his school policy, except as it referred to McAndrew; and McAndrew was not dismissed because of his lack of patriotism, but because of his controversy with the teaching force in regard to junior high schools, the platoon system, intelligence tests and teachers' councils. When Thompson began the literal application of his platform utterances on schools he was given the beating of his life at the first opportunity, in the primaries of 1928.

The Civic Agencies of Chicago are as numerous if not as well organized as those of gangland. They reveal another side of the City's life, in which personal profit and greed give place to the interest of the neighborhood or the city. More than five hundred such organizations are found in Chicago, 130 city-wide in scope and some 400 local in character. Their total membership is more than a million and their annual budgets run into many thousands of dollars.

The purposes of these numerous groups cover a great variety of objects, ranging from Americanization to Transportation, and including among others, citizenship, housing, parks, public improvements, race relations, public safety, sanitation, and schools. Together they constitute a somewhat disorganized but in the long run effective group of forces, tending to offset the predatory interests of other types.

In the field of social agencies many groups have been brought together in a Council of Social Agencies, admirably designed to provide a common organization of welfare work, but the larger group of civic agencies have thus far not been linked together except for specific purposes.

More recently the Cook County Board has initiated an important movement for the purpose of bringing together the disorganized financial public agencies in Cook County and endeavoring to find some common plan for all of them —a long-distance but intelligent plan for common action. Neither the outcome of this particular undertaking nor of the more general and difficult effort to integrate the metropolitan region can safely be predicted. But in any case it is clear that the community is becoming conscious of this problem and has started on the way toward a more workable arrangement than the chaotic contrivance under which it now operates.

On the borderland of political activities stands a wide range of quasi-public institutions interpreting the life of the city as truly as gangland and the underworld. The cultural life of the community has developed important institutional forms, some of them significant not only in the local life of the community but in much wider fields. Three universities are centers of training and research, the University of Chicago, Northwestern University, and Loyola. In the special field of social sciences, the University of Chicago has its Local Community Research Committee and a far-reaching program of study of community and municipal affairs. Many important studies have already been produced and others are in process. Northwestern University has its Institute of Land Economics and Public Utilities by which important contributions have been made to the understanding of the life of the city. In Loyola, Father Siedenberg particularly has interested himself in the social development of Chicago from the scientific point of view.

Numerous Chicago foundations are devoted to cultural and humanitarian purposes. Two of these, the Wieboldt Foundation and the Community Trust, are particularly interested in the study of local situations and have made notable contributions in this area. The Julius Rosenwald Foundation is concerned with a far wider range of undertakings but is not without deep interest in the local community. The Behavior Research Foundation and the Institute of Juvenile Research are important centers of scientific investigation in these specific directions. The Harris Foundation in the University of Chicago is concerned with the study of international affairs and plays an increasingly important rôle in the discussion of international problems.

The Field Museum has long been a widely recognized center of anthropological and archæological research. The Rosenwald Industrial Museum is to be a notable organization of industrial material and presumably a center of industrial research. The Chicago Historical Society quietly carries on its labors through the years. In the study both of music and of art, many thousands of students are enrolled in the various Chicago institutions and must be reckoned as a part of the city's cultural development.

There is then a Chicago of the Big Fix and a Chicago of The Builders, two opposite sides of the same people, two moods of the same community. Each is wont to deny or forget the other, but both are an unavoidable part of the whole and true picture. It is easy for friend or foe to look only at one or the other, but in grim fact neither can be omitted from a study directed neither at eulogy nor anathema.

CHAPTER IV

GOVERNMENTS: VISIBLE AND INVISIBLE

There is a formal government of Chicago, and there is also an informal government. Both are highly complicated, and the interrelations between them are still more intricate.

The formal government is chaos. There are eight principal governments, at this moment, and many more minor ones, at this time twenty-five of them. The chief governments have each independent taxing and other financial powers, each its own set of officers and its own right to make rules and regulations, each in short is seated on its own little throne. These are the Feudalities.

The City Corporate—with its mayor and city council.

The Board of Education, appointed by the mayor and council but after that independent.

The Public Library Board, likewise appointed by the mayor and after that independent.

The Sanitary District, including all of Chicago and some territory outside, a body with its own independently elected board of nine, now expending some $60,000,000 a year.

Cook County, including Chicago and outside territory, with a County board and a long series of independently elected officials.

Lincoln Park Board, appointed by the Governor of Illinois.

West Park Board, appointed by the Governor of Illinois.

South Park Board, appointed by the judges of the Circuit Court of Cook County, some 20 in number.

In addition to this formidable list there are twenty minor

governments, most of them independent park systems, and some seventy-five elective judges, Circuit, Superior, Municipal, and County Courts. The burden of the Chicago voter is the election of 161 officials during a six year period.

But this does not tell the whole story. There is a Metropolitan Chicago, far greater and far more complex than the corporate Chicago which happens at the moment to fall within the corporate limits as they now stand. Metropolitan Chicago includes the territory within 50 miles of State and Madison streets, with a population of some 4,000,000 and an area of some 5000 square miles.

Within this region there are some 1600 independent governments, presiding over the destinies of the community of Chicago. They are classified as follows: [1]

States	4
Counties	16
Cities	203
Townships	166
Park Districts	59
Sanitary Districts	10
Drainage Districts	188
Miscellaneous	1027
Total	1673

This enumeration of course takes no account of the branches of Federal and State government, operating in the Chicago Region. The United States government has an official Coördinator, but the others are uncoördinated.

The overlapping and confusion of these governments presents a very serious problem of political control. How can 4,000,000 people manage 1600 governments and attend to

[1] See S. D. Parratt, *The Governments of the Metropolitan Area of Chicago* (unpublished mss.); also R. F. Steadman, *Government and Health in the Chicago Area* (unpublished mss.).

their own affairs or 3,000,000 deal with 30? Even in the more limited field, how can they keep their eye on eight principal governments with their eight sets of officials, eight budgets, eight sets of rules and regulations? An eight ring circus is difficult to follow for even the most alert and untiring eye. While the mayor and council are battling in the city hall, the county board and the sheriff may be in a controversy, across the way the Sanitary District may be adopting plans for the expenditure of another $100,000,000, the Board of Education may be involved in a struggle with the Superintendent of Schools, and the three large park boards may be engaged in any enterprise you like.

There is no consolidated report or summary of the activities of these governments which a diligent and responsible citizen might be moved to examine in some leisure moments.[1] The press is generous in its comment on the doings of our rulers, but after all the newspaper reports are necessarily brief and discontinuous, and incline toward the presentation of the more vivid and exciting moments in governmental life; and these are not always the most important. State and national, to say nothing of international, affairs also loom large, and may be more dramatic in their appeal than the local and familiar.

Is it not true, then, that the formal government is chaos?

But there is another informal and irresponsible government back of the formal, and this must be understood in order to comprehend Chicago. There is a network of social groupings with continuous or intermittent activities of a governmental or partly governmental nature. Similar groups in other combinations are of course to be found in other cities of this and other lands.

The informal government may be set up in this way:

[1] See Herman C. Beyle, *Governmental Reporting in Chicago.*

Political Parties and Factions
Civic Societies
Business
Labor
Racial Groups
Religious Groups
Regional Groups
Professional Groups
Woman's Groups
The Press
The Underworld

In the interaction and balance among these forces is found the secret of the political control of the city. These ten or a dozen main groups with their many subdivisions act upon the eight or so main governmental agencies, with their hundreds of pettier governmental groupings.

All these groupings, both formal and informal, are crossed and recrossed by many-hued attitudes, we may call them, binding sets of persons in more or less intimate bonds, some permanent and some ephemeral. These attitudes may spring from the traditions of the city or from its prophets and its hopes. They are made up of reasoned or unreasoned attractions and aversions to personalities and toward principle in the political firmament; trust in and distrust of the politicians;[1] trust in and fear of the newspapers; divergent attitudes toward diverse aspects of the problem of law enforcement; varying attitudes toward the expenditure of public funds; fundamentalism and modernism in the political world. These and many other currents cross and recross the formal and informal groupings in the great web of political control, which from time to time, notwithstanding its

[1] See L. D. White's interesting study of *The Prestige Value of Public Employment* for illustrations of the ways in which public officers are variously esteemed in different social groups of the community.

tenuous character, must take on a very definite form with specific relations to life, liberty and property.

Vivid personalities are woven through the complex scene, binding together or tearing apart social groups and attitudes, and giving them expression for the time. The Harrison dynasty with the elder and the younger each mayor for five terms, Roger Sullivan, Democratic boss, and his successor, George Brennan, William Lorimer and his successors, Lundin and Thompson, Deneen, Lawson and the McCormicks, Dunne, Robins and the radicals, Walter Fisher, Jane Addams, Mrs. Bowen, Janet Fairbanks, well-known industrial and labor and professional leaders, clericals of various faiths. These figures flit in and out of the formal and the informal government, in a kaleidoscope of endless combinations and recombinations. The national party system is bankrupt in Chicago. Its great organizations have neither local principles, nor programs, nor tendencies.

POLITICAL PARTIES

The two major parties have occupied the center of the stage in Chicago's government, although independent groups have been active from time to time. The Socialist Party prior to the War possessed no little strength, but was able to muster only 8000 voters in the election of 1928. At present it has little strength. The Workers' Party exists, but its voting strength is very small (1879 votes in 1928). The City Council is elected upon a non-partisan ballot, and in this field the independent forces have been active for many years. Their efforts are later discussed under the head of civic organizations.

In the Republican Party there have been for some years three powerful factions. Of these the Deneen group, headed by Senator Deneen, was strongest in the outlying districts, with a special appeal to business, to middle class, to reformers, and the press, but with a firm belief in and a shrewd knowledge of the value of political patronage, and not averse to disconcerting combinations with distinctly opposite elements.

The Lorimer group, originally organized by Senator Lorimer, was strongest on the West side, but developed a powerful organization all over the city, and in general built upon patronage, graft, privilege, and all sorts of political alliances of whatever character seemed useful for the moment.

The Lorimer organization and methods were taken over by Lundin and Thompson, although the Lorimer influence is still evident in the management of the Thompson mayoralty campaign of 1927 by the ex-Senator.

The North side developed the Mayor Busse group, controlling a string of wards in this section of the city. On the death of Busse this following was taken over by his former Corporation Counsel, Edward J. Brundage, later Attorney-General. Still later Senator Medill McCormick joined forces with the Brundage group, but upon his death Brundage again is left as the sole heir. This faction has alternated in its alliances between the Deneen and the Lorimer-Thompson armies, and has seldom aspired to independent domination.

The present Thompson faction is built upon the old Lorimer following, reënforced by occasional combinations with the Brundage group as in 1915 and in 1927, and with the Deneen group as against Medill McCormick in 1924, and nominally in 1927 for the mayoralty. The Lorimer downstate following and part of it in Chicago was taken over by Len Small (in 1912 Lorimer's candidate for Governor on the Lorimer Lincoln League Ticket), and under the direction of the astute Lundin elected Small as governor in 1920 and again in 1924, going down to disastrous defeat in 1928 in alliance with Thompson and his Chicago forces. It is interesting to observe, however, that since 1923 the original Thompson organizer and boss, Fred Lundin, together with Dr. Robertson,[1] have split away from Thompson and allied themselves with Governor Small.

The Thompson organization was at all times heavily reenforced by Democratic battalions, and by understandings and alliances with Democratic aldermen and committeemen, culminating in 1927 in a thinly veiled alliance with Brennan the Democratic leader. A striking feature of the Thompson forces has been the support given by the colored voters to this group. Originally small in number the colored immigration to Chicago beginning with the outbreak of the War has continued with the restriction upon immigration. The negro vote has reached a substantial figure estimated at 75,000 and in recent campaigns has tended to support Thompson personally and to some extent the candidates of that faction. Since the War, the Thompson following has received powerful support from the German elements in the City, owing to his attitude during the late hostilities.

For nearly a generation the Democratic factions centered around the rival personalities of Roger Sullivan and the Carter Harrisons. Sullivan (succeeding Hopkins) was a dominating figure in party organization, and usually controlled the machine, but the personal popularity of the Harrisons made it possible for them to capture the City Hall on ten occasions, and to maintain a constant warfare against the Sullivan organization. Sullivan was identified with the gas company and other utility companies and his vigorous personality and influential connections enabled him to maintain great party strength. In later years he acquired large

[1] Thompson's Health Commissioner and candidate for mayor against him in 1927.

wealth and aspired to the United States Senate in 1916, vainly awaiting however the support of President Wilson. On the death of Sullivan his dynasty was continued by George Brennan, a former lieutenant, who maintained the same general line of political tactics, but reconciled some of the Harrison irreconcilables. The death of Brennan in 1928 left the organization leaderless for the time.

The Harrison tradition was reënforced in 1907 by Mayor, and later Governor, Dunne and his adjutant O'Connell with a program of municipal ownership of traction lines. Brennan's choice of Dever, an important figure in this group for mayor in 1923, effected a temporary truce between Democratic factions, which lasted however only a short time.

These various factions divided federal, state, county and other patronage, and rose and fell with the currents of political fortune. Their connections and combinations constitute an intricate tangled skein which I should not undertake to disentangle, even if I could. At times they rallied to the support of their respective parties, and at times they crossed party lines and fought together, especially in local contests where the national party lines were shot to pieces. Almost any combination of these elements was possible and actual. There was no boss strong enough to control all of these factions even in one party, and as a rule each man fought at the head of his own faction, except that Mayor Thompson at one time delegated many of his functions to Fred Lundin as chairman of a patronage committee. All the others, however, ruled, so to speak, in their own right, and stood on their own feet. A good artist with an eye for color might draw a picture of these groups, properly applying the appropriate shade to indicate the spoilsmen, the statesmen, and the showmen, but I shall not undertake to do so, although there were important differences in the groups. Nor shall I estimate the number of men and amount of metal at the disposal of these factions. In general the Deneen faction was strongest in Republican times, and the Brennan in Democratic times, and these two factions were most generally supported by the press. Deneen made a special appeal to reformers, and Dunne to radicals, while Harrison relied upon his hereditary strength and the weight of the Harrison name, an estate managed with great shrewdness by the thrifty heir.[1] Sullivan, at first disposed to be merely the power behind the throne, as time went on became more anxious for honors as he took a broader view of political life and became himself a contender for senatorial and social honors. Brennan followed in his footsteps and was also a candidate for the Senate in 1926.

The political factions of Chicago remain in a feudal system, corresponding to the feudal organization of the community itself. Just as there is no centralized control of community affairs, but a division of authority among eight principal and many minor governments, so there is no Chicago boss, but a series of four or five major factions and innumerable minor ones distributed among the 3000 precincts of Chicago and Cook County.

Among all these independent agencies of government, the defeated faction usually finds some place of refuge where it may still hold some remnants of patronage, which it may reënforce by pleasant memories of better days and persistent hopes of better things to come. There are 161 elective offices within Chicago, and in addition to these state and Federal positions, elective and appointive; and these are elected and appointed for varying terms of years, well adapted to the waves of popular approval and disapproval which must be met by all factions. If the City is lost, some part of the

[1] See C. O. Johnson, *Carter Harrison as a Political Leader.*

county may be held; or the Sanitary District trustees chosen for six years may offer some provender; or the South Park Board chosen for five years by the judges of the Circuit Court who are elected for six years; or the Lincoln Park and West Park Boards appointed for five years by a governor chosen for four years; or some of the elective or appointive state offices; or some crumbs of federal patronage may fall from the table; or some stray aldermen, legislators, judges of the municipal court, congressmen or others may help to maintain the army in time of need. Or there is the possibility of alliance with a "cause" and the recruiting of volunteers for good government, an open town, or municipal ownership or its extermination. In last resort there is always the courtesy of the opposing party even when factions within one's party are stern and forbidding in their attitude. All of these factions see Valley Forge in retrospect and they are not disposed to be wholly inhospitable to party foes, who may for the moment be in straits. One must practice his profession, even at some sacrifice of party principles, which it must be admitted may often become somewhat attenuated.

In the modern city in America there is little left in local affairs of the national party except a tradition and an appetite. The lines that divide men in national affairs do not run in the same direction in local questions, and the attempt to force them to do so has been a conspicuous failure in this country. The issues separating men in city elections have usually been questions of the relative fitness or adaptability of candidates, or a struggle between some frankly predatory group and the less perfectly organized community, or a policy of expenditures, or some problem of the wide-open town, or some phase of the question of municipalization of property, or occasionally some racial or religious strife. National issues as such have found it difficult to find a place, particularly within the last 25 years. The days when Senator Thurston of Nebraska might be imported to address the voters of New York in a city election on the virtues of the tariff have gone by.

The feudal organization of Chicago and its feudal party system may perhaps be cause and consequence. Be that as it may, they exist side by side and the political behavior of Chicago must be interpreted in the light of these varied factors, and their reciprocal relations. From this point of view it is not readily comparable with the centralized governmental and party system of New York, or the overwhelmingly Republican system of Philadelphia, or the non-partisan system of Detroit or Cincinnati. It presents a unique picture of political organization and control, a background upon which strange political events might well be thrown.

There is no great mystery surrounding the power of an organization to control and deliver votes. It lies in large part in the influence exerted by a continuing series of small favors and accommodations, some of them necessary and others neither necessary nor legitimate. Favors produce obligations and these obligations are turned into votes at the critical moments, when they are required. Except where underlying issues are outstanding, most men's votes are lightly held, and a good turn by the local politician will be rewarded by the ballot if he asks it. To the newcomer, unfamiliar with the environment and economically dependent, the outstanding issue may well be a job given him, or some favor or adjustment important in his world.

To do this work effectively both the disposition and the opportunity are necessary. The organization recruits men for this purpose, adapted to the services they are to render to the community and to the organization itself. Most men have no leisure for this work, and hence the workers are paid from the treasury of the organization. This is the public payroll in the main, which is supplemented by miscellaneous graft of divers types, depending upon the locality. Tribute may be levied upon the predatory rich for distribution among the needy poor, and what might otherwise be regarded as betrayal of trust be put in the light of a Robin Hood adventure in which those who have are robbed for the benefit of those who have not.

Where class lines are more sharply drawn, as in many European countries, the working class and the poor cannot be mobilized by the local politicians through local attention and favors. They respond to the appeals of those who champion the larger interests of their class as a whole, probably to the Socialists and the Communists; or at times are captured by the prestige and the plans of the conservative. In a few American cities a like position has momentarily been held by some notable figure in the community. Types of such an appeal are Golden Rule Jones in Toledo, Tom Johnson in Cleveland, Potato Patch Pingree in Detroit, Hoan in Milwaukee. These figures are rare, however, and a continuous series of them does not develop in the average city. When they do come the precinct politicians are hard pressed to hold their constituency against the more dramatic appeal of the champion of the mass. The appeals of reform, however, unless presented by some very striking figure do not carry with them the same attractive quality, and as a rule are likely to run upon the rock of a mass appeal against the rich and the upper class, in which case the task of the local captain is made all the easier.

Intelligent students of government and affairs have been fertile in suggestions for the improvement of the mechanism of government, but they have not been able to provide a substitute for this anomalous system of local government by local favors. It seems most probable that the answer will be supplied by the development of group organization and group activity in which the poor and needy will find readier recourse for the righting of their wrongs. A labor, or radical, or socialist party would of course take away the special position of the precinct committeeman, unless he preferred to ally himself with the new organization, which in many cases he would be likely to do. Most cities have recognized this situation by changing the date of the local election so that it would not coincide with the choice of national or state officials, and by adopting the non-partisan form of ballot in local affairs. To be sure, changing the form of the ballot does not eliminate national political parties, but the action indicates a situation and a sentiment of great significance.

CIVIC ORGANIZATIONS

Non-party organizations have often sprung up and are doing the work of the national political party in local affairs, including both the task of selecting personnel and that of formulating and administering policies. They are sometimes classified under the general head of Civic Organizations, which while not a very happy term may perhaps cover the case.[1]

These organizations coöperate more closely with the press than with the party organizations, although they have a definite influence with almost all types of party leaders from time to time. They represent a body of sentiment which, while weakly organized, may at any time under sufficient provocation or with sufficient inspiration become effective in the direct political sense, both in elections where votes count,

[1] See *Chicago Civic Agencies* by the Union League Club and the University of Chicago, 1927, analysing the activities of some 526 organizations with a more or less definite local civic purpose.

and in the meantime when steady pressure is often evident in securing results.

This group of societies and organizations includes the Municipal Voters' League, the Citizens' Association, the City Club, the Civic Federation, the Bureau of Public Efficiency, the Woman's City Club, the League of Women Voters, the Chicago Crime Commission, all of which are exclusively devoted to the consideration of local questions. They are reenforced by the collateral civic activities of a great host of other organizations not primarily interested in governmental affairs, but in many instances developing notable activities in this domain. Conspicuous among these is the Union League Club.

The Commercial Club and the Association of Commerce, elsewhere discussed under industrial organizations, are often closely affiliated with this group, although primarily interested in business activities. Likewise the numerous improvement associations, primarily made up of property owners interested in the physical development of their communities, have much in common with them.

In most cases these groups do not endorse or oppose candidates for office, but they do commend or criticize the conduct of officials from time to time. In local affairs they initiate many public policies, which they endeavor to put into law or administration. In Chicago, as in many other cities, they have largely taken over the policy-formulating function of the political party, and to a considerable extent the initiating function of the municipal administration itself.

Concerted action by all of these groups in any city, especially if strongly supported by the press, is very likely to meet with success, although this does not uniformly follow. In other cases they provide a public forum where pending questions of public policy are discussed and given wide publicity. With the exception of the Thompson faction, no party group has cared to antagonize them openly, however little disposed to follow their suggestion.

These groups are recruited from, and largely supported by the middle class and the benevolently minded well-to-do. On many measures their lead is followed by the community, unconsciously, perhaps. Several factors prevent their more effective leadership. Among these are the frequent lack of an aggressive attitude on public utility questions, on which their members are divided; the avoidance of, or relative indifference to, the interests of the labor group; their relatively weak representation among the nationalistic groups; their lack of technical intelligence in the scientific sense. Business interests are likely to look upon them as radical; labor interests as conservative; politicians as meddlers and cranks; graft interests as dangerous foes. Thus the Civic Organizations, while they are strong at many points, are weak at others, identified in most quarters with sincerity and zeal, but also with narrowness and class affiliation.

Many members of these groups are fully conscious of these limitations, and struggle against them, but they have not thus far broadened the base on which they rest. Their forces may easily be split by a hot or a cold traction attitude; or a hot or cold liquor stand; or a hot or cold labor position. They have done much, however, to fill the gap caused by the lack of efficient administration, of permanent prosecuting officials, of effective political parties, of thoroughly aroused, discriminating and informed public opinion. They have had to combine the qualities of the technical engineer, Scotland Yard, the Republican (or Democratic) party and the Roman forum, a propaganda bureau and a lobby, all upon a slender capital.

And as Billy Kent once remarked at a famous Beefsteak dinner of the Municipal Voters' League:

"Fellow Reformers:

"Our problem is how can we make the other fellow better, without being too damned good ourselves."

The organization and activities of such groups of citizens have become a common characteristic of American cities, and Chicago presents nothing unique or distinctive in this respect. A similar array of societies with similar efforts and achievements might be made in any city of metropolitan size. The Municipal Voters' League, however, has been notable in its methods and results, and may well be examined more closely than the others. This organization came into existence in the stormy days of 1896. At the behest of the traction interests and against the protests of Chicago, the Allen Law had been passed, giving to the City Council the power to extend existing street railway franchises for fifty years. Public indignation ran high; mass meetings were called; and a committee was organized to protect the public interest by the election of an honest council. A preliminary investigation showed that of the 68 aldermen there were only six who were suspected of being honest. There was no doubt about the others. In a vigorous and intelligent campaign of two years duration the Council was purged of its venal majority and a reliable group was placed in power. With the rise of Thompsonism the power of the League has declined, but it still remains a notable civic instrument of a non-party type, and perhaps the most significant of this description in the United States, by virtue of its long continuance, its unique tactics and its spectacular successes.

The methods of the League have been simple enough. It has maintained a permanent assistant secretary who has been "the eyes of the people," reporting what was going on in the Council, and in the committees, and particularly scrutinizing the capacity of the aldermen. The secret of the League's influence really lay in the courage of its members and the intelligent observation of its active secretary and assistant secretary. Its leaders have numbered many effective personalities, including George Cole, commonly known as Old King Cole, Charles R. Crane, later adviser to Wilson, Walter Fisher, later Secretary of the Interior, Dr. Henry Favill, William (Billy) Kent, later Congressman from California, Allen Pond, Graham Taylor, Edwin B. Smith, Kellogg Fairbanks, Lessing Rosenthal, Bruce Johnston, George Sikes, "Doc" Davis and "Si" Watkins. It is in the integrity, courage and practical capacity of these men rather than in the form of organization or method that the cause of their success is to be found.

It has not been the policy of the League to nominate candidates for the City Council but to make recommendations for the nomination and election of suitable personnel for these positions. Encouragement, advice or occasionally financial support has been given to or found for desirable candidates, but there have been no aldermen in the field as the nominees of a party. The theory of the League is that if the public is fully and accurately informed of the proceedings of the Council and the records and qualifications of particular candidates, it will make wise and sound choices in the main. Significant are the League's bulletins summarizing the records of the candidates and making recommendations where a choice is manifest. It encourages the desirable and discouraged the undesirable candidates, all of whom are invited to call upon the League and sign the League platform.

Of course the success of such publicity depends on accurate knowledge of the facts; general fairness and honesty and judgment; the practical political sagacity of the leaders many of whom know the "game" as well as the politicians. The League has impartially endorsed Republicans, Democrats, Socialists, Prohibitionists, Independents, radicals and conservatives, wets and drys, men of all faiths and races and classes. Errors have doubtless been made, but all things considered, they have been surprisingly few when the possibility of error is considered.

In its earlier battles the League fought for honest men and obtained an honest council as a result. Later it endeavored to obtain efficient as well as honest men, declaring that brains are as essential as legs in the equipment of a useful alderman, and seriously trying to develop initiative, competency, constructive ability. On one occasion a weak committee had allowed a powerful corporation to dictate terms to it. Thereupon the M. V. L. denounced and helped to defeat aldermen who were supine and helpless, even if not corrupt. They realized keenly that well-intentioned stupidity could not protect the city's interests against clever exploiters, and that mere personal honesty is quite compatible with complete loss of municipal rights and prospects.

In later years the League lost ground chiefly because of the attacks of Mayor Thompson coupled with the absorption of the people of the city in the War and the reaction following that event. Connected with this was the failure of the League to publish the names of the directors and to include women in the list, both of which difficulties were overcome.

For twenty-five years, however, the League has been and it still is, a powerful agent in concentrating public interest and attention and in crystallizing public opinion upon council representation. The life of a reform organization, like that of a machine, is likely to run its course in ten years or so. Mistakes happen, enemies accumulate, friends are estranged or indifferent, personalities are worn out, or lose their fighting edge, and the whole institution must perpetually be revived and renewed. The M. V. L. exhibits unusual vitality after a quarter of a century of existence, and, like the Citizens' Association, founded the year before the Chicago fire, may well modify the rule regarding the life of such agencies.

The organization of the League and its activities have been imitated in other cities without the same degree of success, a circumstance indicating the force of the personal element in political organization as well as the mechanical. The leaders of the movement have been men of unusual political acumen, quite capable of dealing effectively with the current party leaders and with the general public and the press; and it was the interest and devotion of these officers of the League that made its most spectacular triumphs possible. Thus the Legislative Voters' League of Illinois serving a similar purpose for the State Legislature has been reasonably successful, although operating under greater difficulties because of the cumulative system of voting. The National Voters' League organized to render a similar service for Congress has not shown the same measure of success.

The activities of the League stand as an interesting phenomenon in the evolution of representative government, illustrating the possibilities of adaptation to new and unforeseen conditions. The fundamental principle of action in this case is the value of timely information regarding the records and qualifications of public servants, assuming disinterestedness or a reputation therefor, and the responsiveness of the electorate to analysis of candidatures.

BUSINESS

Of the economic groupings in Chicago, as in other cities in the United States, by far the most effectively organized are the business elements. In comparison, the labor organizations are relatively feeble, the professional organizations ineffective, and of course the middle class is notoriously unorganized. When they care to act unitedly, the business groups are the real masters of Chicago, but in the main they are likely to be indifferent and if interested disunited. Along with the larger financial magnates go a mass of smaller business men and merchants whose interests may not in fact be identical with those of the larger operators and engineers of finance, but who in political struggles are likely to be found upon the side of the greater financial leaders. Some informal steering committee or group may be organized and mobilize a large force for rapid and effective action, or more commonly may use the machinery of one or more of the party factions. Newspapers, campaign funds, propaganda, services of political leaders and bosses, are readily available, and all of these forces may be thrown with great effectiveness into the midst of some campaign, or into the consideration of some specific issue between campaigns.

In Chicago, the Association of Commerce, the Commercial Club, the Commonwealth Club, the Chicago and Cook County Real Estate Boards, the Department Stores, the manufacturers, the bankers, the Industrial Club are strong factors. These groups are extremely powerful, but as a rule do not fully control and rarely assume complete responsibility for the conduct of the government. The business group dominates when it will, but it does not will to rule continuously as a responsible class might commonly be presumed to do. The government is at its beck and call, but this class has not thus far been willing to assume unquestioned responsibility for the conduct of public affairs in the municipality. Commonly, it shifts direct responsibility for the city government to the "politicians," whom business men are always ready to denounce, but who are usually at their service when summoned. At the heart of the city problem, therefore, we have this anomalous situation, that the most powerful group does not govern. Power and responsibility are divided. Those who can rule, will not. Those who would rule, cannot.

James Bryce once said: "In America as elsewhere in the world, the commonwealth suffers more from the apathy or shortsightedness in the richer classes, who ought to lead, than from ignorance or recklessness in the humbler classes, who are generally ready to follow when wisely and patriotically led."

Admirable "civic work" has been done by many of the business organizations, particularly in the field of public improvements, of charities, and finance. But there are cases where their interests do not coincide with those of the bulk of the community. Here they find themselves frequently at odds with the many and in bitter and deplorable struggles with the mass of the people on the question of franchises, public ownership, strikes, schools or other similar problems involving the respective rights of the many and the few. And in these contests it is that they are likely to lose much of the prestige they otherwise enjoy as public-spirited servants of the community.

One of the striking phenomena of American public life in recent years has been the fact that in a wide range of affairs various groups have been active in the initiating and development of political programs.[1] This does not signify the decline of politics, but its vitalization with vigorous social forces which provide its real content. Politics is a cross section of human life, and not a thing apart, either dominating

[1] See my chapter on "Unofficial Government" in *American Political Ideas;* H. S. Childs, study of the Chamber of Commerce of the U. S. and the American Federation of Labor (unpublished mss.).

the rest of society or always utilized by others as an occasional and convenient tool. Modern cities were built by men who came together to better their life conditions, and in the earlier stages of development preoccupation with economic affairs led to the serious neglect of responsibility for common conduct of governmental conditions. Later it began to appear that municipal health, municipal beauty, municipal order were assets of an industrial as well as of a strictly governmental type.

Nowhere has the recognition of this fundamental fact been more notable than in the last twenty-five years of American urban life, and nowhere more interestingly portrayed than in Chicago. It would be hopeless and useless to catalog all the numerous and detailed ways in which business organizations have shown an interest in the civic development of the community, but some of the more spectacular may be discussed. The Commercial Club of Chicago contributed the design of the Chicago City Plan, through the services of Burnham and through long sustained support of the plan projected by him. The full development of this design is undoubtedly one of the most striking events in the municipal history of the last generation, and will abide as an enduring monument of municipal enterprise. The Industrial Club fathered the valuable report on the crime situation in Illinois. The Union League Club has repeatedly championed the cause of honest elections and through its committee on public affairs contributed in countless other ways to the development of the civic life of the community. In particular the Chicago Association of Commerce has in organized manner developed a civic program of far-reaching interest and importance.[1] The metropolitan traffic survey is a strik-

[1] See annual reports for 1925-26-27, especially *A Record of Progress and Achievement* for 1927.

ing example of one of the more recent of these undertakings but is only one of a wide variety of similar constructive elements in the program of the Association.

On the other hand, and with an analysis of political control in mind, it must be observed that the legislation committee of the Association reports opposition in 1927 to the following measures: eight-hour day for women, old age pensions, firemen's pensions, income tax bill, two bills providing for complete home rule over all public utilities; all of which had wide popular support among the masses of the City. The battles between the Association and the Federation of Labor are also notable illustrations of divergent purposes.[2] It must also be noted that the campaign against the Thompson bond issues and against the election of a notoriously incompetent state's attorney was made in 1928 without the aid of the Association, although these were among the most important issues of a generation, certainly in the latter case.

As in almost every city, the public utility groups are closely concerned with the organization and exercise of political control. They may be desirous of obtaining new grants of power from the municipality, or of protecting old ones. They may fear blackmail or they may have positive piratical designs of their own. Whatever the cause, they are found deeply interested in party machinery and in all the mechanisms of political mastery. These interests have large funds available for instant use, they have as many employees as the city itself, they understand the arts of publicity and propaganda. They are well-equipped for active participation in community affairs, and as a rule they must be reckoned among the dominant factors in the city's scheme of political control. In Chicago they are incarnated in the person of Samuel Insull, well-known public utility operator and

[2] Fully discussed in Counts, *op. cit.*

organizer, with his staff of publicity experts headed by the competent Mr. Mullaney, and his intimate contacts with the Republican and Democratic organizations.

Although the city government may remain divided these utilities tend toward rapid consolidation and unification. The Commonwealth-Edison electric company brought together two large and many minor concerns; the Commonwealth-Edison electric acquired control of the People's Gas Light and Coke Company, itself a consolidation of the Ogden Gas and many minor companies; the Commonwealth-Edison acquired the Elevated Lines, again a consolidation of three major systems. The diverse traction lines are united in an operating agreement.

The intimacy of utilities and politics was well illustrated in the union of the gas company and the Sullivan Democratic machine. The boss was also a high official of the gas company and provided the connecting link between these two important agencies. The head of the Democratic organization was also heavily interested in the securities of the electrical industry, a subsidiary company of which he was himself an owner. And thus this organization became in a general way the official representative of the utilities, looking after their interests not only in the city, but also in the state Legislature where many important measures were presented from time to time. Of course, this organization was deeply interested in the election of aldermen and of the mayor. They would be found active in the preliminary maneuverings, in conventions or primaries, in the conduct of elections. They would have a number of public officials affiliated with them; a number of committeemen and party officials and a large number of men on their corporate payroll, some of whom could be relied upon to do political work for them, especially the lawyers. In later years the lines shifted somewhat, and the gas, electric lighting and some other interests affiliated more closely with the Thompson machine, although not abandoning their earlier connections with the Democratic party.

Of course these interests did not control the parties without a struggle. In the Democratic party they were opposed by both the Harrison and the Dunne faction which were particularly strong in local affairs—at the very point where the utility interests desired no opposition. In the Republican party there was a very large progressive element opposed to their domination of political life.

The utility groups were not in a controlling position at all times, but they were very strongly represented in public bodies and in the press, and were at all times a significant factor to be reckoned carefully in all political calculations. They were by no means uniformly united. Doubtless they preferred to gain their ends honestly and peacefully, through the processes of persuasion and publicity, but if necessary some were ready to use coarse methods which they would justify on the ground of business necessity.[1] They wanted a Council favorable to their interpretation of their rights, and ready to give them more, and they wanted a mayor who was disposed to look at their problems from their point of view. They perhaps preferred respectable alliances, but if necessary would join hands with whatever element was available to provide the votes, and on the whole they found the corruptionists their most steadily reliable friends. If they were expensive, still the market price was fairly definite, and the wise ones knew whom to pay and when and how, and legal expenses were a relatively small item in the huge annual budget. The high personal charac-

[1] See C. N. Fay, *Big Business and Government,* for an exposition of the position of a man intimately connected with the political side of utility activity.

ter of many of their directors had nothing to do with their political methods when politics was in question, and their public spirit did not stand in the way of the most greedy and desperate undertakings in the special field where franchises and other political favors were to be obtained.

The Senatorial inquiry of 1926 revealed like a lightning flash the possibilities of this system, and a local affair became a nation-wide event. The chairman of the body regulating the public utilities of Illinois and Chicago was a candidate for Senator. Mr. Insull, chief among the public utility operators in Illinois and in the nation, contributed to his campaign fund the sum of $150,000, supplemented by other grants from other utility operators. Upon the finding of facts by the Committee, it is well known that the U. S. Senate twice refused to seat Mr. Smith, notwithstanding his election by the voters of Illinois in the campaign of 1926.

LABOR

It goes without saying that by far the most powerful group, numerically speaking, is that of labor. Chicago is commonly characterized as "a union town," and its formally organized unions are large and active. Their total membership is difficult to estimate but may be placed at 500,000. These forces are centralized in the Chicago Federation of Labor, with powerful bodies in the Building Trades Council, the Women's Trade Union League and the Amalgamated Clothing Workers. If united in political action, they would of course be masters of Chicago. Their leaders, however, have not encouraged union participation in political contests, fearing the effect upon the unity of their trade union organization. This policy was abandoned in the mayoralty campaign of 1919 which proved wholly unsuccessful, however. The union groups have possessed ample funds for political battles, but they have lacked solidarity in the spectacular struggles that have aroused the city, and thus far they have not been able to overcome the wiles of the old-time party organizations and the force of party traditions. They have also suffered from the lack of a labor press to carry on continuously their propaganda and their special interpretation of political events between campaigns.

At any moment, however, the labor group may come to power as its leaders acquire more skill in elections, as its press becomes more effective, and as its members become more and more impressed with the importance of political control for the advancement of the labor cause. In England and continental European countries this time has come, and in many smaller cities of the United States, both east and west, there have been similar developments, but thus far they have not been effective in the domain of Chicago political life.

Laboring men have not been deeply interested in the efficiency side of government, often identifying it with their own struggle against private employers and therefore viewing the movement with suspicion if not with open hostility. Honest government they have supported effectively except where members of their own organizations are involved in dishonest political transactions, not unknown in cities. The grafter does not hold their support, except for class reasons, and is likely to be most severely rebuked in the workingman's territories. So-called "business government," however, they fear may carry with it only the relief of the larger taxpayers with whom they have little sympathy. It is to be noted, however, that labor groups when actually in power have often done better than they promised, and have instituted significant changes promoting efficiency in the local government. A striking example of this is found in the city of Milwaukee, under the Socialist regime, when remarkable strides in municipal progress were made.

Labor's chief type of activity for the purpose of improving working conditions and wages has been the mechanism of collective bargaining, with the incidents of negotiation, conference, joint committees, and in last analysis the strike. The attitudes of the city police and of the state's attorney (Cook County) are of course factors of significance in the industrial struggles. The kind of picketing, if any, allowed, the limitations upon freedom of speech, the tactics of the police, the prospects for arbitration, restrictions on blackmail, extortion and violence; all these are fundamentally affected by the attitude of the local authorities. From the point of view of labor this sector of the front far transcends in importance any aspects of the efficiency and economy problem.

My first governmental experience with strikes was the case of the Amalgamated Clothiers. 40,000 garment workers, recently organized, had gone on strike and remained out for many weeks. Among the workers and their dependents there was great distress and almost a complete suspension of the industry—an important one in Chicago. I introduced a resolution calling for the appointment of a conciliation committee, of which I was made a member. We found the situation a typical one at that time (1910). We were not able to bring the contending parties together, and our negotiations were carried on in three adjoining rooms, one for the Union, one for the Council Committee, and the third for the Employers. The latter refused to meet with their employees as union men, and declared that there were no substantial grievances. Finally, Mr. Schaffner, of Hart, Schaffner and Marx, said he would check up some of the alleged grievances that we transmitted to him, and on examination found conditions of which he had not been aware and of which he did not approve. Mrs. Raymond Robins and Mr. Schaffner came together and in a short time an agreement was reached. This was approved by the local union, by the national and the international officers, but on presentation to the men was rejected. It seemed as if the whole work was a failure. Hart, Schaffner and Marx, however, negotiated a separate agreement, which became the basis of the notable plan now generally adopted in Chicago and in other clothing centers as well. The other firms made no agreement but within a few years another strike came, and during this time the business of Hart, Schaffner and Marx went along at a rapid rate. In recent years the garment-making industry has been placed on a basis which has attracted attention throughout the industrial world, as a model of intelligent coöperation between unions and employers, a triumph of industrial statesmanship.

Distressing features of these industrial wars are the tendency toward violence on the part of the strikers or their sympathizers, toward brutality on the part of the police, and toward the employment of unreliable private police on the part of the employers. Strike leaders may and usually do deplore violence as a substitute for peaceful persuasion and economic coercion, but their followers are not equally careful and furthermore in a struggle of this kind the riffraff of the community may take advantage of the occasion to run riot in their madness.

The attitude of the police, while often marked by great patience, is on other occasions extremely brutal. This was notably the case in the waitress' strike when pitiful tales of wholly unnecessary physical cruelty were related to the Council Committee. The irritating possibilities of women are well known to mankind, but this did not justify treatment that would not be given even to cattle by intelligent handlers of kine.

At the same time many private police are brought in, and often they add fuel to the flames. Indeed this seems to be their purpose in some cases where it is clear that their function is that of *provocateurs.* The fact that they are not in uniform makes it difficult to identify them, and they may escape responsibility for their conduct in a way that a uniformed officer would be unable to do. My personal contact with them on visits of inspection showed that there was grave danger in turning over the people's police power to men not in public employ, not in uniform and without any official badge or designation. Any person not a public or a private policeman may of course declare himself to be one if there is no way of identifying him, and in this way make endless trouble. Observing one strike I was roughly told to get out of the way by a tough looking person. "By what authority?" "I'll show you at the station," he said. "Well, where is your star?" "Under my coat." "Well, so is mine." He looked at me like a mad bull, and I looked at him as we are told to look at mad bulls, right in the eye. And he did as mad bulls are supposed to do, but do not always, he walked away. He was not a real "bull," but an imitation.

Labor touches the city at the point of wages and working conditions of employees who are unionized. Chicago long ago adopted the union scale of wages and working conditions. The adjustment of these scales we finally left to conference of a subcommittee of the Finance Committee and a committee of the Federation of Labor, and on the whole this was a satisfactory arrangement, at least as satisfactory a plan as we could devise considering the disturbed condition of industry. The greatest difficulty was encountered in cases where there was no other employer than the city, as in the case of calkers in the waterworks department or sewer cleaners. The union scale in such a case would be whatever the city paid.

Strikes against the city did not occur during my service in the Council, although there were threats on the part of the garbage handlers and the street-lighting employees. Later these disturbances actually occurred, however, in the fire department and the water pumping stations. It should be and is possible in all such cases to provide for genuinely impartial arbitration of the points at issue, and to avoid any open breach. This is in part a problem of the law, but still more is it a question of a standard of public opinion and a sense of responsibility on the part of the employees themselves. The difficulty with the latter situation is the analogy between the governmental and the industrial services, and the transfer to one of all the hatreds and prejudices of the other, together with a feeling on the part of the employee that the government is usually in the hands of the employer group, or at least in sympathy with them.[1] The cities will not be able to solve this difficult problem apart from its relation to the industrial struggle now playing so significant a part in the nation's development. Intelligence, patience, toleration, firmness will accomplish more in the long run than drastic methods which may bring quick results in the short run but prove disastrous in the long time period. Neither the labor leader alone, nor the employer group alone, and certainly not the demagogue alone, should be allowed to have a free hand in the solution of a question of such wide concern to the entire community, and one where compromise and agreement are so indispensable for the attainment of an equilibrium.

[1] No adequate study has been made of this important problem in the United States although sorely needed at this time, as the basis of an intelligent public policy, and still more of the popular psychology which must underlie any successful policy.

GOVERNMENTS: VISIBLE AND INVISIBLE

The darkest spot in the relation of labor to the city is seen in the region where labor crooks, political crooks, and business crooks confederate and jointly rule. The government through its police force may enable a crooked gang to control an honest group of laboring men, and these crooks then combine with business pirates to hold up industry and the public often on a gigantic scale. The revelations of the Lockwood Commission in New York and the Dailey Commission in Chicago (1921) show the detail of this far-reaching combination against the general public. Where to start in such a case is a problem. Usually the start and the finish also is made with minor labor crooks, a few of whom may be punished, while most of the principals escape. The other parties to the program are usually forgotten by the time the general interest in the situation has died down, and are never punished, or perhaps never even exposed in their true light.[1] This dark jungle—perhaps the darkest in city affairs—is never explored and it goes without saying that adequate methods of bettering the situation are never suggested or put in effect. Until this swamp is cleared, however, it will be impossible to maintain the political and the industrial health of the community, and constant epidemics will sweep through the urban centers, carrying with them the most debilitating and destructive effects.

The program of the labor group is further revealed in its legislative plans, dependent in large measure on the locally elected representatives in the General Assembly and on the man who sits in the Governor's chair. Here the ambitions and efforts of the labor and the commercial groups come into sharp conflict. Specific questions such as the hours of labor for women, the use of the injunction in industrial disputes,

[1] See the interesting concrete study by R. E. Montgomery, *Industrial Relations in the Chicago Building Trades.*

the control of the schools and other similar aspects of the great industrial conflict that is incessantly going on, become lines of battle for the opposing forces typified by the Association of Commerce or the Illinois Manufacturers' Association on the one hand and the Federation of Labor on the other. Precisely here is the danger spot for local government, the point where machines and spoilsmen maneuver for advantage, and where obligations and commitments of the most important nature are made, both by business and by labor. Here may occur the tragic crossing of the lines, where the spoilsman may become the friend of labor and the reformer his foe; or where the friends of efficiency may make terms with the apostles of extravagance in order to carry through their industrial program. These are great days for the mercenaries who may sell their valued services to the highest bidder, in terms of cash or opportunities to coin money, through power and position. And sad days for those who witness the confusion in the ranks of urban progress, and realize its meaning for the civic future.

MIDDLE CLASS

In Chicago as elsewhere the middle class is unorganized and relatively ineffective. This group includes the clerks, the smaller merchants and employers, the unorganized wage workers (white collar) and the professions. They do not have the compact organization either of labor or of capital. They are constantly losing to the organized wage workers on the one side and larger capitalists on the other. Many of the middle class take on the color of those by whom they are employed, as a sort of political uniform. There are no powerful and impressive organizations of Renters in a city where most of the population rents, or of Consumers, important as they are. These groups have no special form of class or group press, as do labor, business, the nationalities, the religions. Their leaders live a precarious existence as the middle group alternately turns in rage against big business and now swings against the unions, or those who favor either too little or too much as the case may be.

There are many groups of smaller merchants and dealers in the outlying districts, whose interest is somewhat more closely identified with that of the middle class in general than the business class in particular, at least of the downtown and larger business group. Likewise the local improvement societies of which there are scores—are important as small home owners much interested in certain aspects of the city's policy, with special reference to public improvements. Building and Loan associations constitute a similar group of great importance in some phases of the city's development and are very powerful where their special interests are immediately and clearly affected as in the case of taxation and improvements.

The middle class have many municipal interests and ideas. They are concerned about economy and efficiency, about honesty and morality. They are against boss rule and do not like machines or spoilsmen. They are afraid of big business and trusts. They are broadly speaking friendly to reform, but frightened by anything that may be considered radicalism or socialism or in latter-day terminology bolshevism. They are the conservators of conventionality in a more real sense than business or labor, both of whom are readily open to adventures in unconventionality where it seems advantageous. They will insist that progress be respectable, dignified, decent. They are often responsive to the appeals of progressive leaders, such as Roosevelt or Wilson in the national field, but they are likely to be stampeded by the press, or by appeals to religious or racial prejudice.

On the whole they are the most consistent supporters of such progressive programs as do not involve primarily either business or labor. They support the assaults upon graft and the organized criminal groups; they demand regulation of public utility concerns; they are the rebels who precipitate political revolutions from time to time, like that of the pineapple primary of 1928, or the election of Judge Jarecki, head of the election machinery, in 1926, the impressive triumphs and defeats of franchises and bond issues. In combination with the more progressive and responsible elements in business and labor and with the support of the independent press, they are likely to determine the trend of the political situation.

In Chicago as elsewhere, however, the middle class tends to be a diminishing quantity for two reasons. One is the general movement toward organization of labor, business and professional groups, and the other is the constant emigration of the middle class group to constantly new suburban areas outside the corporate limits. Both of these factors are of the first order of importance, and have a direct bearing upon the prospects for improvement in municipal conditions. One of these, the first, is constantly being offset by the increasing trend toward responsibility on the part of the labor and the business groups; and the other by the trend toward regional government, a movement destined to alter fundamentally the character of the municipal unit of government.

In more recent years powerful vocational groups have sprung up in Chicago and elsewhere. Of especial strength are the physicians, the engineers, the lawyers, the teachers. All of these groups have their special vocational or occupational interest, but they have also a larger interest, and their solidarity tends to give strength to the middle-class position in general.

All of these groups have been active from time to time in local affairs. The Chicago Medical Society has concerned itself with the department of health, and the Western Society of Engineers with the department of public works, although it cannot be said that either of them has been very successful in imposing its program or its ideas of personnel upon the departments concerned. Factional disputes among the physicians have stood in the way of effective coöperation with a general health program, while indifference among the engineers and the preoccupation of some of them with public utility interests have reduced the helpfulness of this society.

By far the most active and energetic group has been the Chicago Teachers' Federation, for many years under the picturesque leadership of Margaret Haley a storm center of Chicago enterprises. The association, including some 6000 teachers, has for the last twenty years played an important rôle in the determination of questions of personnel and of policy in the Chicago schools. For many years the Teachers' Federation was affiliated with the Chicago Federation of Labor until driven from this position by a rule of the Board of Education, but since then it has remained in close contact with the leaders of the labor movement.

The Teachers have taken an active hand in the election of local officials and members of the Legislature, in struggles for equitable taxation, for the regulation of franchise corporations, in the prosecution of delinquent school officials, and in many other ways have made themselves felt in the conduct of local affairs. Their long and spectacular battles over the control of the schools of Chicago are perhaps best known, but their program has been a general one and has included many fronts. In this connection their chief emphasis has been upon educational democracy and upon the unitary system as opposed to the dual, suggested by the Commercial

Club, and in the case of McAndrew when he undertook to dissolve the Teachers' Councils, the symbol of teachers' opposition to educational autocracy.

From the point of view of the balance of social interests, it is plain that their most intimate relations have been with the labor group and that their chief antagonisms have been against the business group. As a well organized and aggressively led group the Federation has had no superior among all the social groupings of the City, even among the professionally political organizations. If all groups were similarly organized and deployed for action the politics of Chicago would take on a colorful hue and the problem of non-voting would become a memory.[1]

Underneath the surface of the school question run the deep currents of fundamental prejudices, involving such important working factors as the press, the conflict of religions, the industrial class struggle. What happens on the surface is only a reflection of these struggles going on down below and ruffling the upper regions. A brief explanation of these factors is indispensable to any intelligent comprehension of what has been going on in Chicago, and it will be found that many of these questions are not local to our city, but typical of many urban communities throughout the United States.

The press has been involved through the lease of school lands. Years ago Chicago was given some sections of school land upon which is now built the loop district, the industrial center of the city. Most of this land was sold, but some of it was leased for ninety-nine-year periods. Among the lessees were the Chicago *Tribune* and the Chicago *Daily News* whose buildings then stood upon the school lands. These leases were originally subject to revaluation at periods of ten years,

[1] The positions of the Federation are fully stated in Margaret Haley's *Bulletin;* for discussion of the school problem see Counts, *op. cit.*

but in 1895 at a midnight session, the revaluation clauses were stricken out. As a result there was a wide discrepancy between the later value of these properties and the amounts paid under the old leases. The leases were subsequently upheld by the Supreme Court, but there was a general feeling that while the change may have been lawful it was unfair.

The inevitable consequence has been that the comments of the press as represented by the *Tribune* and the *Daily News* have always been the subject of caustic reply on the part of their opponents. It would have been better for the community if these papers, both of which have long since acquired new sites, had waived their privilege and accepted revaluation.

A second factor has been the element of religious prejudice. Contest between opposing religions over questions of school control and policy has been unavoidable, although usually covert rather than open in its manifestations. Catholics and Protestants have charged each other with the desire to dominate the school system and turn it to their own uses, and doubtless there is some truth in the mutual recriminations, but much more of exaggeration and misunderstanding. Protestants have charged that the majority of the teachers were Catholics and that others were unequally treated, and Catholics have felt that the general control of the schools was Protestant in its tendencies. Doubtless some have been hostile to the public school system, and have looked with jealous eye on its advance as compared with the parochial schools. No impartial body ever inquired into any of these charges and countercharges, for when religious questions come into politics reason usually goes out. Nothing is ever investigated, because all is known, and the man who does not agree with you is not merely mistaken; he is wickedly and intentionally wrong. Whisper, gossip, innuendo, and rumor take the place of inquiry and judgment. Thus the attack on the Teachers' Federation was inspired as much by religious prejudices as by labor prejudices. Curiously enough it was led by a Jew from Kovno, Russia, who, born in bitter religious and class intolerance, lent himself to this movement. One might have thought that his experience would have suggested tolerance and sympathetic attempt at understanding of his fellowmen.

A third factor is the element of class antagonism in the industrial world. Here as elsewhere the problem of training for democracy has been a bone of contention. Specifically the question once arose as to whether the industrial training of pupils should be organized in one unified system or whether there should be two systems of schools, one the regular and the other a special type of trade or industrial school. It was alleged that one set of schools—the industrial under this arrangement—would be under the jurisdiction and control of business, which it was feared might develop apprentices who would combat the unions, and might also assign the poorer children automatically to the trade schools and tend to restrict their general training for citizenship and society. The Commercial Club stood for one policy and the bulk of the teachers and the labor group stood for the other. Sharp clash was inevitable, not only at home but with more dramatic setting in the state capitol before the Legislature. Here was a fundamental issue regarding the character and range of education upon which opposite views have existed and still exist. The undemocratic implications of the dual plan were not, it should be said, conceded by its advocates.

Another aspect of the same problem was the affiliation of the organized teachers with the Federation of Labor. It was ordered that this connection be ruthlessly severed. The teachers and the labor group insisted upon its continuance.

The teachers had disclaimed the right or intention to strike for the purpose of making their demands effective, but aside from this there were many to whom the idea of affiliation with the labor unions seemed offensive or even dangerous to the community and the schools. They could not view such a situation with equanimity. Furthermore the Teachers' Federation was a powerful and compact body led by a skillful and unterrified woman, Margaret Haley. They had brought suit against the utility corporations to compel higher taxation, and had carried on vigorous battles in other fields. If they had been less aggressive and less competent, doubtless the question of their status would have been less acute, and less of an open warfare would have been precipitated. In 1915 it was determined to destroy this organization at any cost, and eliminate the Federation and "Maggie" as factors in the Chicago situation.

I was waited upon by a gentleman of the very highest standing in the business and philanthropic world who unfolded to me the plans of "his group" for the control of the school system; and was informed that it was the unanimous opinion of the group that I was the one to take the leading part in this movement, and the parliamentary steps to be taken in Council were indicated. Some doubt as to the facts was impatiently received; suggestions that certain eminent experts, the leaders in their field, should be consulted as to facts and procedure were swept aside. "We don't want any facts; we have made up our minds, and we are going ahead. Those who are not for us will be against us." Willingness to coöperate in the very fullest inquiry into the facts, and in a policy based upon these facts, and upon sound expert advice, was conceived to be hostility. And so the dogs of war were loosed.

At times these factors are combined, and then we have a

type of Catholic-labor-foreign complex, as over against a Protestant-capitalist-native American complex. Here the unreason of religious prejudice is multiplied by the class prejudice and the total of these two multiplied again by the foreign prejudice. The result is momentary municipal madness, in the midst of which corruption and incompetence take their heavy toll of the community, and often of the school system itself. Any city whose inhabitants choose to go on a spree upon religious-racial drugs will pay the penalty, and it will be a heavy one in the form of corruption and graft. The Thompson regime which began in an alleged campaign to save the schools from the Catholics, went on to turn the town over to outright crooks, and ended by selecting a Catholic as Superintendent, is perhaps the best illustration of this in the whole land, but it is by no means the only one. It is only typical of what happens everywhere when men cease to reason about the actual community problems and substitute bickerings over their religious reliefs and their racial prejudices. Fortunately the common sense of the bulk of our citizens makes it possible to rise above these aspects of the case; otherwise our public schools, after all the foundation of our democratic system, would be wrecked or destroyed.

The important thing is not that there have been battles in and around the school system, but that attacks upon the integrity and progress of the schools have brought ruin to their sponsors, as Thompson twice discovered.

The other professional group emerging in the life of Chicago is the Chicago Bar Association, with which may be considered also the Lawyers' Association. The former, however, has played by far the more active rôle in the conduct of local affairs. In a sense, trustees for the conservation and development of the system of civil and criminal justice in a great metropolitan center, they have been in this respect as inert and backward as the bar in general throughout the United States, although individual members of the Chicago bar have rendered distinguished service to the adaptation of ancient procedure and law to new situations. From the point of view of local political equilibrium, however, the Bar Association has taken on a definite function in the nomination and election of the judges in the community.[1]

In Chicago an unusual situation is found. The judges of the Circuit and Superior Courts, 48 in number, are named by the ward committeemen of the political parties, and these committeemen through their party leaders enter into a bipartisan combination for a union ticket. Two conventions sit simultaneously and make a slate of agreed nominations. The official filing of the names agreed upon may be held back until it is too late to obtain the necessary number of signatures for independent nominations, if any are to be made.[2] The importance of this situation for the control of local politics cannot escape the attention even of the most unobservant. It places the control of the higher judiciary in the hands of ward politicians.[3]

Under these circumstances the Bar Association take a poll on the fitness of candidates for nomination in direct primary or in convention and for election as well. They have gone farther and campaigned for the election of members indicated as desirable from the Bar poll; they have watched the count of the votes in many precincts and taken a hand in the prosecution of election frauds. In a few instances they have even

[1] A full and interesting account of this function of the Bar is given by E. M. Martin, one of my students, in his manuscript on the influence of the Bar on nominations and elections.

[2] The number necessary is 2% of the vote cast at poll preceding general election, which ordinarily means at least 20,000 to 30,000 signatures.

[3] This system does not apply to the municipal court judges, 37 in number, or to county judge or judge of the probate court. These are selected in the direct primary.

placed in the field independent candidates of their own. In the primary of 1928 the Bar Association came to the conclusion that the office of state's attorney was within the scope of their action, and took a poll of their members upon that important position. It happened amusingly enough that while Crowe, the incumbent, made public a list of 4300 members of the Bar endorsing his administration of that office, in the Bar primary the vote was Swanson 3000, Crowe 600, a factor of no mean importance, not in discrediting the good faith of lawyers, but in defeating Crowe.

These examples illustrate the possibilities of vocational development and activity in a modern city. Undoubtedly they are the forerunners of other groups who will also become active elements in the social and political control of the city, both for special and inevitably also for general reasons. Their full fruition will present interesting problems in the evolution of the civic order. And there will be both figs and thistles. There will be more compact and determined defense of special interest, and in the end a deeper sense of responsibility for the common weal as well.[1]

The social groupings are then important in the political control of the city, for its government after all is only a balance of their conflicting or concurrent interests, an instrument for their use and not a master to drive them. Individual groups may of course seize and exercise arbitrary power for the moment, but not for long, and only until the others perceive, and have time to organize and overthrow.

It must not be assumed that these groups present by any means a united front. On the contrary they are often wide apart in their group interests and still farther in their political interests. There are widely varying types of business men

[1] See the suggestive comment of Graham Wallas in his *Social Heritage* on the tendencies of guilds.

with widely different civic attitudes like Insull and Rosenwald; there are clashes between the Loop and the outlying business districts; between railroads and bankers and manufacturers and real estate operators and department stores and public utilities and within each of these smaller groups again. The labor movement is still less a unit, with clashes between the Federation and the Building Trades Council and the Amalgamated, and the Socialists and the Workers party, with fundamentally different points of view regarding graft, violence, coöpération with other groups, between opposite types like Fitzpatrick and Olander and Murphy and Boyle. The middle class is still more disunited, and with great difficulty mobilizes for action either at election time or between times. Its trends and its policies are either timid or vacillating as a rule and difficult for a political leader to build upon.

Nor are economic interests the only ones that determine political action; or if so, they are interpreted in widely different ways by different individuals under the same circumstances. Racial, religious, sectional, personal, traditional influences come in to upset economic calculations at a thousand points, and to perplex and confuse the observer who stresses one chord of human nature too strongly, forgetting the infinite complexity of human life.

CHAPTER V

CROSS CURRENTS: RACE, RELIGION, SEX

RACE

THE racial complexity of Chicago is one of the characteristic features of its social composition, and is directly related to its processes of political control. No other great city of the world has a like problem of racial heterogeneity, with the exception of New York. Two-thirds of the population of Chicago is either foreign born or of foreign-born parents. Of the remainder perhaps 200,000 are colored. The number of persons actually born in Chicago is of course very small.

Here is a major problem in adjustment and adaptation, in reconciliation of attitudes and objectives, in the rapid development of that common understanding which is the basis of all government. Here is also a field in which tares may easily be sowed; in which clever and unscrupulous persons may play upon prejudices, hatred, and ignorance to the detriment of the common weal.

The bare figures outlining the racial composition of Chicago (city only) are as follows:

Native White	1,783,687
Native Parentage	642,871
Foreign Parentage	888,496
Mixed Parentage	252,320
Foreign-born White	805,482
Negro	109,458

FOREIGN BORN POPULATION

Nationality	*Number*	*Per Cent.*
Poland	137,611	17.1
Germany	112,288	13.9
Russia	102,095	12.7
Italy	59,215	7.4
Sweden	58,563	7.3
Ireland	56.786	7.0
Czechoslovakia	50,392	6.3
Austria	30,491	3.8
Canada	23,622	2.9
England	26,422	3.3
	805,482	

The following figures represent the various nationalities of Chicago (as computed by the Chicago Association of Commerce) in 1920, second generation included:

Nationality	*Number*	*Per Cent.*
American	642,871	23.80
Polish	319,644	11.81
German	285,216	10.55
Russian	230,668	8.55
Swedish	154,051	5.72
Irish	145,919	5.40
Italian	129,815	4.80
Czechoslovakian	116,115	4.30
Negro	109,456	4.05
Austrian	72,531	2.70
English	67,907	2.51
Canadian (other than Fr.)	62,006	2.30
Hungarian	61,847	2.29
Norwegian	53,891	2.00
Lithuanian	43,274	1.60
Danish	29,450	1.09
Greek	27,017	1.00

CHICAGO

Nationality	*Number*	*Per Cent.*
Scotch	26,094	0.90
Jugoslavian	22,211	0.82
Dutch	22,163	0.82
Roumanian	11,644	0.43
French	11,379	0.42
Swiss	8,772	0.32
Belgian	7,900	0.29
Canadian-French	6,039	0.23
Indian, Chinese, etc.	3,078	0.11
All other	30,855	1.14
	2,701,705	100.00

But these figures give little impression of the complexity of the actual situation. This must be written in more vivid symbols, must be seen in the contrasts of the black belt, the Ghetto, the Nord Seit, the Polish section, back of the Yards, the Gold Coast, Ravenswood, Englewood, Woodlawn and other outlying residential districts.[1] Only by long and intimate contact with the tragic problems of this the world's greatest adventure in nationalistic adjustment under a democratic system, can there be an appreciative understanding of the human life currents in this rushing stream.[2]

Any sustained experience dispels the illusion so commonly entertained for almost a century that the ignorant foreigner is at the bottom of our municipal ills. Native American communities like Philadelphia and Cincinnati are in no manner superior in political behavior to New York and Chicago with their high degree of complexity, to say nothing of native American communities in certain sections of the South.

[1] See the significant studies of neighborhoods made by the Local Community Research Committee of the University of Chicago.

[2] Important contributions are those of Grace Abbot, *The Immigrant and Politics;* Jane Addams, *Twenty Years in Hull House;* publications of the Chicago School of Civics and Philanthropy, *passim.*

There are no figures to show that the alien crime rate is higher, or that the alien's judgment either of issues or of men is any more fallible than that of the natives, where issues of personalities are outstanding. Considering the exploitation of the immigrant in the United States, the lack of attention to decent housing, to obtaining employment and small credits, to organization of recreation, it is not remarkable that he distrusts the distant and unknown outsider and clings to the Little Father of the Community, who is always there and ready to help as best he can. The newcomer's political allegiance goes first to those human beings who satisfy his immediate and urgent needs, however much they may neglect and betray his higher wants.

Practical experience and observation readily show the causes for the elements of leadership appearing among the newly arrived groups. When he can be actually reached, the judgment of the newcomer is likely to be honest and sound and he does not vote very differently from the old-timers. Referendum votes on questions thoroughly discussed such as a traction franchise or a bond issue, often show substantial judgment and discrimination.[1] The same is true of votes on well-known personalities, such as Roosevelt who carried every ward in Chicago in 1904, or the famous pineapple primary of 1928.

Furthermore, there is no basis of solidarity among the many nationalistic groups, otherwise they would consistently elect their candidates and dominate the municipality. There are sharp rivalries among them, far more acute and permanent than those that divide the old and newcomer. Pole, Irish, German, Czech, Italian, Slav, Jew; these are not the symbols of concord in Chicago any more than they are in

[1] See Maynard's analysis of referendum votes in Chicago (unpublished mss.). On the liquor question alone is there a sharp and continuing variation between the nativist and the newcomer.

Europe from which they came. On the contrary the battles between them are often very bitter.

A story is told of a nominating convention in a certain ward some years ago, where two aldermen were to be nominated. The ward had long been predominantly Irish, but had more recently become at least half Italian. The Italian delegates demanded at least one of the nominations and made an eloquent appeal for recognition. But at the critical moment an Irishman arose and upset the moving plea by demanding fiercely, "Well, ye got the Pope, ain't ye? Wot'n'll more d'ye want?"

Nor are the racial groups themselves a solid block. There are sharp rivalries for leadership here and bitter rivalries developing, often of a wholly irreconcilable nature. There are factions among the Poles, among the Jews, among the Germans, among the Irish, among the Italians, and at times they seem to hate each other more cordially than the outsiders.

After the first generation, the solidarity of the racial vote begins to break up, and while there always remains an attachment to racial candidates the power of the nationalistic leaders rapidly declines, and the solidity of the vote tends to disappear. The nationals can no longer be relied upon to vote blindly as the leader directs, except perhaps for those of the right name. Their territorial basis is gone, when Bohemians, Germans, Italians, Poles scatter through the city, forming business and matrimonial connections outside the pale. Class interests, religious interests, regional differences, soon spring up and become as important as the bonds of nationalistic solidarity, powerful as the latter may be.

In the case of the new arrivals, it is of course inevitable that the important factor in their political allegiance is personal knowledge and contact with others better oriented than they. Here common language, small favors and adjustments made by the local leaders count very heavily. After this stage is passed and the newcomer may stand upon his own feet, economically and otherwise, the cohesive factor will be a type of race pride, modified by a wider acquaintance and by broader contacts, and with a clearer view of the underlying issues at stake. It is the overwhelming desire of most newcomers to become and be regarded as Americans, in costume, language, manners, and of the American immigrants to become urbanized rather than country folks. So strong are these tendencies that they lead to the neglect of the cultural heritage of the group in many cases, notably and lamentably of the language, and of the distinctive achievements and ideals of the group. A part of the same tendency to be regarded as American is seen in the recent efforts to show the contribution made by various groups to the making of America, as in the case of the Irish, the Germans, the Poles, the Italians.

In Chicago there has been a struggle between the Scandinavians and the Italians over the naming of a new driveway turning on the problem whether Leif Erickson or Columbus should be regarded as the real discoverer of America; between the Poles and the Lithuanians as to the racial allegiance of Simkiewicz.

The drive toward American assimilation is then one of the outstanding characteristics of the immigrant group, and colors not merely their politics, but runs through all of their social relations.[1] It is in the light of this intense interest in American institutions that the civic attitudes and relations of the newcomers should be considered. They arrive thinking of America as the land of their dreams, the land of unlim-

[1] On the reasons why men do and do not become American citizens, see Gosnell, "Non-Naturalization," in *American Journal of Sociology,* XXXIII, 930, 1928.

ited possibilities in the economic world, of social equality, of political liberty. They arrive accustomed in the main to expert and honest government, with the exception of some groups. Their exploitation by clannish leaders is often only a short phase of their experience, out of which they soon emerge into responsible citizenship.

When is the full transition in allegiance made? When a man marries a woman of another group; or when he forms a business relation with another group; or when he learns another language than his native tongue; or adopts other food, clothing, and mores; when he marches in a political parade; when he pays taxes or puts on the uniform of another country? Who can name the precise moment when he passes the boundary line of national allegiance and more than that of national emotional loyalty? In a little village among the hills of Slovakia I once talked with a man who had lived in America but returned to his native village to spend his remaining days. But after he had been there a year he found that he was an American; and now, he lamented, "I cannot go back again." In other instances I have been told that the moment of full American adherence came upon return to the native land, when what had seemed familiar in memory now seemed strange and alien.

An interesting shift has occurred in the last half century with the rise of a more vigorous nationalism in many European states, such as Germany, Italy and Russia. While the '48ers were often critical of their native government and fled from its persecutions, now there is a stronger sentiment of adherence not only to the mores of the fatherland, but also to the national political unity itself. This is not only true in the case of the new Germany, the new Italy, the new Czechoslovakia, but to some extent of the new Soviet Russia. The bearing of this upon national politics is easy to see, and upon local politics is also widely influential. The political change involves a shift from the politics of local personalities to the politics of larger group allegiances in some manner even though remotely connected with the local situation.

Among the foreign-born groups, the Irish, now numbering 145,000 in Chicago, as elsewhere, have been most active. They arrived first and clung to the political domains, until driven out by the waves of other nationalistic arrivals. Some of the most fascinating stories of the political world are those of the transition periods when Irish battled with German, or with Italians, or with Poles or with Scandinavians or Jews. Their political *savoir faire* and engaging personalities made it possible for them to hold their own long after they were overwhelmed numerically, and to retire with the honors of war when no longer masters of the field. The struggles of Johnny Powers in a rapidly Italianizing ward, where it became necessary for him to be reincarnated as Johnny de Pow are intriguing, to one who can translate them. But in the end only a gerrymander of the ward saved Johnny, and for his home he sought more elegant quarters outside, from which he still ruled the ward.

The Irish supplied countless local and ward leaders and in recent years Democratic bosses like Sullivan and Brennan and mayors like Dever and Dunne. At one time there were no less than three Sullivans on the bench. In the main affiliating with the Democratic party, they were liberally represented in the Republican ranks, and did not lack office and leadership here too. They were found in fact in all parties, all factions and in the countless combinations across party lines that characterize the modern political scene. Of all the groups they were the most keenly conscious politically, the most capable in political struggle and the most persistently active in pursuit of the political ball.

The Germans, now 285,000 [1] strong, dominated the North Side, but are far less inclined to political activity than the Irish, and were and are more likely to be found in the Republican ranks. The German tradition of efficient public service, the thrift of the small home owner and taxpayer, the emergence of prominent figures in the cultural world and the interest in independent civic action, were significant. The German attitude toward the liquor question and the bitterness aroused by the recent war, are also factors of no little importance in the political life of the community and require careful analysis and study for a full appreciation of the problem of local political control.

207,000 Scandinavians, localized most strongly on the northwest side but scattered widely elsewhere, are a significant element in the government of Chicago. Active in all phases of political life they supply many notable factors and figures. Olson who organized the Municipal Court, Lundin the political boss who organized Thompsonism, Swanson who baited and overthrew the political ring centering around Crowe and Thompson, are types of many others. Largely Republican, they have also been progressive and liberal in their tendencies, and strong supporters of movements for the political betterment of the city, and they have been perhaps more strongly inclined toward political independency than any other group of newcomers.[2]

In the more recent waves the Poles and Bohemians and the Italians are more numerous and powerful and picturesque in their contributions to the colorful life of the city—319,000 Poles chiefly in the northwest (near), 116,000 Czechs

[1] Not including 72,000 Austrians.

[2] Hemdahl's forthcoming study of the Scandinavians in the politics of Illinois deals with this interesting phase of Chicago.

chiefly in the southwest, and 129,000 Italians, chiefly on the west side. Of these the Polish and the Czechs are largely Democratic in their national party affiliation and the Italians likewise though not so uniformly in national as in local contests. These groups passing through the period of the first generation are just emerging into political consciousness, leadership and power.

In the Polish group distinguished positions of responsibility and of leadership as well have been furnished by Judge Jarecki, head of the electoral machinery of the city and county, Anthony Czarnecki of the *Daily News* and Collector of the Port, and John Smulski in earlier days.

One of the most colorful personalities in the City Council in its vivid days was Alderman Stanley Kunz, whose bull-like mien and voice often carried consternation into the ranks of the opposition. One of my most vivid Council recollections is that of the moment when the enraged Kunz threatened to throw an inkstand at Mayor Harrison who was presiding over the deliberations of the Council, compromising on a stream of violent invective. A moment later on my demand and on my reference to the habitual and characteristic politeness of the Polish people, he apologized reluctantly but fully. Later he said, "I never meant to throw it. I was trying out his nerve."

The Czech groups do not have the religious solidarity of the Poles, and include Catholic and Masonic elements of strength. Originally Republican, they were diverted to Democracy by the liquor issue and have remained in the fold since then. When politically awakened they display political interest and capacity of a high order, with a talent for organization and administration, recalling the high level reached by Czechoslovakia in recent times under President Masaryk. Their most prominent representative in the local field has been Antony Cermak, President of the Cook County Board, and an active factor in the control of the Democratic organization, likewise the leader of the wets. Among the Czechs a group of home-owners, business men and professional persons is likely to appear quickly and to assume an important rôle in the life of the community.

A colorful element in the local situation is supplied by the Italians, now some 129,000 in number, located chiefly on the west side but also scattered through other sections of the city. Responsible political interest in this group developed more slowly than in some others and it is more recently that significant leaders have come to the front, and assumed positions of authority, men of the type of Borelli, Barasa and others. In the meantime many of the smaller fry have occupied themselves with minor ward politics and with the organization of bootlegging enterprises with which the name of Scarface Al Capone is familiar. The factionalistic tendencies prevent the appearance of any general type of boss, dominating all the others, and leaves the way clear for forms of feudal control without strong central authority.

Many other groups not so powerful numerically are found entwined in the politics of regions and of factions. The Lithuanians, the Greeks, the various Slavic groups, weave in and out of the political situation, developing national party and factional affiliations. Thus the Lithuanians and the Greeks have been largely Republicans and the Slavs have been Democratically inclined; while in local affairs they have all been inclined in the first generation to follow the lead of the clan heads, with due allowance for personal rivalries and factional disturbances within the group itself—a factor which can never be omitted from calculations.

By far the most striking development of racial politics in recent years has been the new importance of the Black Belt and the colored vote. Originally a small element in the city's population, 14,825 in 1890, in 1900 30,150, in 1910 44,103, in 1920 109,000, it is now estimated at 200,000 to 250,000, while the colored vote is rated at not less than 75,000. These votes are centered chiefly on the South Side in the territory for the moment characterized as the Black Belt. Two solidly colored wards have their own aldermen and two others have a very strong colored element in them. The colored voters are almost all Republicans and if they hold together possess the balance of power in the Republican primaries. With the exodus of voters from the residential areas to the suburbs of the City, the influx of colored voters has materially changed the aspect of the political situation, and has given rise to grave problems of party control. The colored leaders thus far developed have not been of a type to command general confidence. In their own group they may pass as the symbols of race recognition, to them a precious thing, but outside they have been ranked as the allies of a system of political corruption. Other leaders of a more responsible nature begin to emerge, but thus far they have not been able to establish themselves firmly in the political areas where they have been active, although there are many indications that this will constitute the next phase of their development. Nor has the Black Belt shown strong tendencies toward solidarity except in adherence to Thompson for mayor.[1]

With inferior social opportunities and education, economically weak, the colored man has been the victim of far-reaching exploitation by predatory politicians, perhaps not greater than that of other newcoming groups, but shaking it off less easily in the second generation. In return for the

[1] In 1918 Medill McCormick polled 1001 votes for Senator against 6064 for Thompson in the 2d Ward, and 2292 to 2625 in the 3d. In the 1928 primary the anti-Small vote rose even against very great pressure.

recognition of a few racial representatives, for the most part wholly unrepresentative and unworthy of their race, they have returned political allegiance and adherence. Unscrupulous crooks have used the colored vote to establish themselves as collectors of graft from gambling and vice and on the other hand have almost totally neglected the material interests of the colored man in housing, sanitation, recreation, education. His most useful friends have been men like Rosenwald and others who have exerted themselves for the betterment of the living conditions of the negro, but none of these persons possess any widespread political influence among the colored men.

However, to be willing to exchange the substance of living for the illusions of race representation is not a new phenomenon in the history of race relations. It is in fact one of the indices of a rising sense of dignity and responsibility. To be recognized and represented by a crook is better than not to be recognized or represented at all, from one point of view. This is not in fact the only alternative, but if it seems to be, the result is the same.

It would be possible to draw a vivid picture of the political conditions in the Black Belt in which the dark colors of gambling, vice, crime and their political protection would be heavily outlined, but I have no special interest in doing so. Such a scene illustrates the struggles of a once enslaved race on the way to higher responsibilities and possibilities. White leadership is back of it and white hands take in the profits coined from the sordid system which uses the weakness of a race to fatten the profits of the stronger and more responsible.[1]

In time sounder leadership will prevail and the white

[1] See Lowden Commission on Race Relations; Merriam and Gosnell, *Non-Voting,* pp. 39-41, 80-84.

demagogues and rascals will be succeeded by colored representatives of higher ability and deeper understanding of the problems of their race. As types of business and professional leaders emerge, a process now rapidly going on, the material for leadership is improved and enlarged; and the result is inevitable. In the meantime, if some of the brains devoted to the problem of how to help the black man were given to understanding how to deal with him politically, more rapid and substantial progress might perhaps be achieved.

The whole story of the absorption of the newcomer into American political life is not told by the bare figures and outlines above presented; for these are only a shell. To know what really is happening we must know the background from which the Italian or the Slav or the Scandinavian comes, what traditions and political ways he brought with him; how he adapted these older ways to the newer ways of the new country, ways interpreted by local leaders on the one hand and by business and the schools on the other. Here is the material for a great study in political adaptation, yet to be written with a wealth of detail and an understanding of political processes without which all would be in vain;—a great study in political science and an epic without a parallel in political history.

While the local leaders train the newcomer in favoritism and pull, the larger personalities such as Roosevelt, Wilson, Smith, may interest and attract him; the schools are training his children in political attitudes quite opposite to those of the ward, perhaps; employers or business associates are familiarizing him with broader points of view; foreign and native language press are imposing their ideas upon him; the small home owner begins to challenge the tax rate; the family resents the flaunting of vice in the neighborhood; and out of his own temperament, observation, experience, sense of values, personal and group interests there comes an attitude toward the policies and personalities of his city.[1]

From the political point of view, it may be contended that it is better to have some political interest, no matter what its nature, than none at all. Thus the type we call the worst, grafter, crook, may defeat himself. He may become a pillar of society *malgré lui.* Graft and crookedness are parasitic, and if we interest everyone to take a hand in graft, we tend to defeat our own purpose; for everyone cannot be on an exceptional basis. The exception becomes the rule and the graft the recognized institution. In this sense one may often find among grafters a broad view of civic responsibilities and a ready responsiveness to community welfare where their personal interests are not adversely affected. In spite of himself community projects and advances must often intrigue the grafter, partly because of his personal advantage in periods of greater expenditure and power, but also because he unwittingly takes a public point of view. This applies also to the new nationalities.

RELIGION

Religious attitudes divide the population of Chicago widely. There are, roughly, 1,000,000 set down as Catholics, 429,265 [2] as belonging to various Protestant denominations, and 400,000 as Jewish. Read in relation to racial alignments the following are predominatingly Catholic, namely the Irish, the Polish and the Italian; the following are largely Protestant, the native American, the negro, the Scandinavian. The German and Bohemians are divided between

[1] L. D. White's study of the *Prestige Value of Public Employment* shows higher ranking of public employment by the immigrant groups than the native American. Compare Burton's *Civic Content of the Sixth Grade Mind,* for superiority of civic knowledge in immigrant groups.

[2] It is usually estimated that the constituency of Protestant churches is about three (2.7) times its members.

Protestant and Catholic. Lithuanians and Greeks and Jugoslavs are of the Greek Catholic Church.[1]

These religious bodies are not primarily concerned with political control, except as an incident in their wider relations, and they are not a major factor in political action. Yet they are not to be ignored in any realistic study of actual political forces, for both religious attitudes and religious personalities are of fundamental importance in general and in specific instances their influence may prove to be decisive. Certain phases of local government are of especial interest to the clerical groups. The treatment of vice, the maintenance of standards of integrity, the liquor problem, and the school question, are all likely to come under close observation. While it is true that neither religions as a whole nor large groups as a whole unite in political demands, smaller groups often do, and combinations of the representatives of various denominations are from time to time very powerful. The Federation of Churches, a Protestant group, is especially interested in political problems and is not unlikely to take a position upon questions of public importance.

In their individual capacity many of the clergy give advice to their flocks or to the general public either in regard to persons or policies, with widely varying effects. In local affairs they have been more successful in dealing with issues than with personalities,[2] and in issues other than the liquor problem, where the attitude of the Protestant denominations has usually been at variance with that of the community as a whole.

At all times, however, they constitute a formidable array which no sound leader would desire to antagonize, if there

[1] There are no figures available upon the value of property, the annual revenues and expenditures of these bodies.

[2] See C. O. Johnson's *Carter Harrison* for illustrations of the ineffectiveness of the clerical attack upon the doughty warrior.

were another way out. In recent years there has been a higher development of group organization, and in the Anti-saloon League, the Better Government Association, and the Christian Citizenship Council there have been technical organizations and in many instances significant results.

A far less wholesome phase of religion in politics is seen when we observe the influence of religious attitudes or prejudices working in the realm of the political, without special relation to the specific interests of morality and religion. Here hatreds and animosities the origin of which few living men clearly understand come in to determine the problems of the living present; and often with most disastrous results. In my own experience I have found plenty of Protestants who would vote for a known scoundrel to defeat a Catholic of whatever character and ability; Catholics who would blindly do the same to prevent the election of a Protestant; and Jews who would follow the same sad course. When religious bigotry marks the ballot, grafters rejoice. The raising of religious issues without warrant or relation to the actual problems of the time inevitably affects city government detrimentally, and those who stir the embers of religious rivalry and bitterness, whatever their motives, serve the city badly.

I have found, what anyone with the slightest political experience must soon discover, that there are rogues and honest men in all religions, and that a man's religious confession is not a safe index of what he will do when a political crisis comes. Whenever I hear anyone saying or whispering as is usually the case that such and such a man should be supported because he is of some particular faith, I begin to question the qualifications of the candidate or the judgment of the informant. Ald. Dever was a good Catholic, Judge Thompson a good Protestant and Ald. Schwartz a good

Jew, but they all agreed on the major questions respecting the welfare of the city.

Col. Roosevelt once remarked to me: "When a man asks your religion in politics, you may be sure it is for no good purpose." The famous French philosopher, Rousseau, once declared that the only persons who should be excluded from the ideal democracy were those who would not tolerate the religious beliefs of others; "for such individuals," said he, were "incapable of associating with others in a democracy." If intolerance is anywhere justified, it is toward the intolerant. I have often wished that the institution of ostracism might be revived for the purpose of applying it to the temporary exile of those who deliberately stir up the flames of religious warfare in our political affairs. Under our present form of government, I can merely express the pious hope that they may spend at least a season in the regions so graphically portrayed by the great Italian poet.

REGIONS

The territorial groupings are also of importance in the social and political organization of Chicago. North Side, East Side and West Side cut off by the forks of the Chicago River, at one time possessed a considerable degree of solidarity. There is still a degree of local pride among the inhabitants of the town, but this is diminishing in quantity, and tends to disappear altogether. Neighborhood and ward consciousness is much more realistic than the sense of being on the same side of town, and of still greater importance is the antagonism between the Loop, the central business district of the City, and the outlying territories. A chain of business and improvement associations from these outer districts confronts the Chicago Association of Commerce, and may oppose its measures, especially as they may affect the transportation facilities of the city as a whole. The height of buildings, the subway, the central high-pressure system, are at times subjects of rivalry, and underlying this regional antipathy there is of course the deeper antagonism between the small merchant and realtor and the larger ones who constantly tend to absorb or outdo them. Branch departments and chain stores add fuel to the flames, and keep the contest going.

Less conspicuous are the smaller sections and neighborhoods with a degree of community interest, notwithstanding the rapid mobility so characteristic of urban life in American cities;—Englewood, Woodlawn, Ravenswood, Austin, the Ghetto, the Valley, Back of the Yards. These regions have their local history, their old citizens, their local improvement societies, their local business associations, their local schools and churches, fraternal organizations.[1] It is often assumed that neighborhood sentiment has gone from the larger cities, but this is not strictly true, for it is still a vital factor in the city's political control. Many important facilities may be granted to a locality or withheld by the city government, and these interests form a center of organization around which the inhabitants of the neighborhood tend to cluster, first of all the property owners but after them tenants who also have a direct interest in the local school, park, bathing beach or pool, police and fire protection, transportation. If these sections had been retained as wards with representation proportioned to their changing population, they might have continued as even more powerful units of local government; but the rapid change of boundary lines has somewhat interfered with their development as political centers.

[1] See studies made of these regions by the Local Community Research Committee.

In all municipal calculations these intersectional and neighborhood rivalries are forces to be considered; otherwise they may upset the best laid plans. The contacts, acquaintances, interests, accumulating through common dwelling on or near a common spot have their slow and inevitable effect, in the long run by no means a negligible one, even in the hurry and whirl of urban metropolitan life.

It is true that in the city few men can point with pride to the "house where I was born," or associate the old familiar scenes with struggles and triumphs of youthful days. Riding by St. Luke's Hospital one day with a girl who had first seen the light of day there, I said, "This is where you were born." "Well, what of it?" she replied. But this does not mean that impressive scenes do not soon fill the eye of the citizen. He soon adopts the outstanding features of the city's physical development as his own, and claims them as a part of his heritage, parks and rivers or other water fronts, cathedrals and skyscrapers, famous and infamous streets, impressive monuments and spectacular architectural displays are quickly caught and converted into the substance of local interest and patriotism. If the tempo of change is faster and the new is soon out of date, the tempo of adaptation is also by the same logic faster and makes its adjustments accordingly.

SEX

My experience with women in local politics began a number of years ago when I was asked to address a woman's organization on the history of suffrage in the United States. I read a carefully prepared paper on the subject, tracing the various movements through our history. The auditors seemed interested, but expectant. When I had finished, one arose and said, "But he has not stated his position on the question." My apology that the request was for a historical survey of the development of the franchise seemed unanswerable, but somehow inadequate. Whereupon one of them said, "Let us pray for him." The chairman seized the occasion and announced a moment of silent prayer for me. It seemed to me an eternity. A morning paper, with greater accuracy than usual, said that Professor Merriam moved uneasily in his seat and blushed. There is no denying the efficacy of prayer under such circumstances, as any one may determine by experiment.

In 1913 the General Assembly of Illinois gave the suffrage to women, so far as could be done under the Constitution of the state. Offices provided in the Constitution itself could not be included in this, but presidential electors, and all municipal offices, were thrown open to women. In Chicago no women have been elected to municipal offices, although there have been a number of candidates in various wards whose qualifications were notable. Women have, however, taken an active part in the political life of the community, as in fact a number of women had done before the ballot was conferred on them. This was notably true in the Progressive campaign of 1912, and in my campaign of 1911. The figures for the votes of men and women were kept separately until 1920, and therefore may be analyzed more carefully than in most other places.

Two developments surprised many of the citizens, although in line with observations already made in other states where women had been voting for some time. One was the large number of women who voted, and the other was the tendency of men's and women's votes to run on parallel lines. The wide differences expected did not appear. This need not have been the occasion for surprise, for the general testimony has been that votes are not primarily determined by sex lines, but by other social considerations. This cannot be taken to mean that women follow the lead of men, for in many instances the contrary is true, and the woman may persuade or cajole or intimidate the man.

The art of managing man has been studied by womankind for many generations, and as the power behind the throne, the influence of woman has always been great. Now that all are on an equal basis in the eyes of the law, it need not be supposed that woman's intelligence in the arts of guidance and control of the indirect type have been lost. Even in the very many cases where she "votes as her husband does," there is no way of knowing to what extent she may have gently led her husband to will to vote as she had already decided.

In local affairs the interests of women are manifold. Indeed city government has been compared to municipal housekeeping, and it is true that many municipal matters were formerly in the control of the mother as manager of the household. The special interest of woman has been the school system, as the child is much more in the charge of the mother than of the father, who probably knows very little about the actual school conditions in comparison with the information the mother of the family acquires. Women are also especially interested in health, housing, parks and playgrounds, and in the whole problem of recreation as it affects the children and the youth. They also have interest in what are called moral problems, such as the restriction of commercialized vice in its numerous forms, and in the sale of intoxicating liquors. The bulk of womankind, however, does not follow its leaders as compactly as might be supposed, and the attitude of the great mass of women is perhaps more tolerant than is sometimes maintained. There is no uprising of women, as such, against the political leaders who are known to be vice lords, or liquor lords in their respective districts. If so, there would be vacant chairs now occupied by complacent beneficiaries of the exploitation of commercialized vice. Crusades demanding drastic action against all forms of vice may be inaugurated by feminist leaders, but the tolerance and perhaps the wisdom of the mass of women, makes them follow slowly, except as intelligence guides along the path of social hygiene. It is questionable indeed, whether their attitude is much different from that of the mass of men upon most of the questions upon which there is more emotional preaching than sound practice.

In my experience women have shown the keenest interest in the problems of schools, recreation, health, city waste, housing, the protection of women and children, the care of the immigrant, and in general in all measures for the protection of the weak and the helpless. Questions of finance, engineering, most public works, industrial controversies, and public utility problems, have been of less interest, although not without capable students. Yet I must not forget that a woman, Helen Culver, gave the funds for the first systematic survey of municipal finances in Chicago; and that another woman, Mary McDowell, the "Angel of the Stock Yards," started the campaign for the City Waste Commission subsequently appointed; and that Margaret Haley has been a stalwart champion of municipal ownership and fair taxation. One might almost say that I must beat a retreat and recall the statement, but broadly speaking it is still true that these subjects have been of less general interest to womankind.

As pointed out by Plato, hundreds of years ago, the truth is that generalizations as to the characteristic qualities of men and women are highly dangerous, and most of the dogmatic conclusions of a generation ago are rapidly being overturned, as women enter the fields of education, of business and the professions. The fact is that most of the differences supposed to be fundamental turn out to be the product of custom and habit, and are readily overturned in a relatively short time. The tradition of woman's ineptitude for political and economic life may easily be found among these shattered traditions in another generation.

The effect of women's entrance into active political life upon the party organizations has thus far not been pronounced in the national field. As a leading Chicago journal once said, women are wanted in the gallery but not on the floor of national conventions except for the decorative purpose they may serve. And thus far they have not been able to function effectively in the national field. They have been called in for purposes of ratification rather than of consultation. But in the local field where the party tradition is much weaker, and women's organizations older and stronger, the feminine influence has been more readily exerted. Doubling the number of voters did not double the number of jobs, but it doubled or increased materially the work of the party manager, and by so much their control over the electorate is weakened. The task of reaching all the women voters is a huge one, and the number of skilled women workers is not adequate. Hence, in local questions the counter activity of the women's non-party organizations is correspondingly larger. The local machine does not feel as sure of the women's vote as of the men's, and is often in trepidation as to what this unknown force may do.

Women politicians and women grafters have already appeared and in the long run may affect the women's vote as powerfully as the man's vote at present. But during the interim, if it is such, the old-time bosses are thrown into doubt and confusion. Often their fears are unfounded, as the result shows, but there still remains the lingering doubt. It is demonstrably true that in Chicago, where the men's and women's votes were kept separately, women were less susceptible to the appeals of the machine than men, and on the whole responded somewhat more readily to the appeal of intelligence. It has been charged that women are responsible for the injection of the religious issue into the Thompson campaign of 1915, and the consequent career of buncombe in the city hall. An analysis of the primary vote shows, however, that Thompson was defeated by the women's vote in the primaries of that year, and elected by the preponderance of the men's majority; and likewise in the election the Thompson candidacy was less favored by women on the whole, than by men. Further, in the various ward contests where the Thompson administration was the issue, the women were less influenced by the confusing cries of the occasion than were the more experienced and presumably less easily stampeded males of longer experience.

Those who predicted that the entrance of women into politics would usher in the millennium, and there were such, waiting on the housetops, were, of course, disappointed when this result did not follow; but those who have observed the progress of self-government in democratic communities entertained no such illusions, and are satisfied to find even a margin of advance.

Specific organizations such as the Woman's City Club, the Illinois League of Women Voters, the Chicago Women's Club, and others, with their ward branches, have done notable work in the field of political education, and in the advocacy of particular causes. In general women's city clubs have shown more vigor and enterprise in the last few years than those of men, although why they should remain separated is a matter for tradition to answer, rather than modern intelligence. In general these organizations have suffered, however, from the same difficulties that men's reform organizations have encountered, namely the lack of adequate representation from the labor groups and from the various nationalistic groups. They have struggled hard to overcome these known weaknesses, but thus far have not been able to overcome them, notwithstanding the fact that some of the most useful work in these groups is that of women. Consequently a spot map of the city, either geographical or class, shows many points where there is relatively little participation in their work, and little disposition to follow their leadership.

On the other hand, selfish interests have not been able to organize groups of women and exploit them in the name of womanhood, for their own advantage, as was done in the case of the opposition to Judge Lindsey in Denver (who was attacked by a woman's committee using a perjured witness, who afterwards confessed). If the industrial class struggle increases in severity, presumably women may divide into groups with opposing opinions upon capital and labor, but thus far they have been able to coöperate closely. In municipal affairs these divergencies are as a rule less sharply presented than in the case of state and national legislation, where class contests are vividly marked. A strike or a public utility question may cause a division, but on many other problems there is relatively little dispute, and large possibilities of united action. The forces that commonly rend men's action, such as the professional politician interest, the business and the labor organization, the professional nationality leader, are far less powerful among women, and are not able to function as disruptively in their case; and there is likely to be found a desire to agree upon a program, sometimes vague and even sentimental, but different from the program of the men's groups in its lack of definite group demarcations.[1] Women, it is true, may represent these interests just as effectively as men, and in time probably will, but for the present they do not. In their conferences there is no woman sitting around the table with thousands of office-holders at her command, or owning a powerful newspaper, or representing directly some powerful utility corporation with an immediate interest of millions in the city government, or some other special privilege watching with eagerness the political drift, and eager for political control that can be cashed. To be sure, women are not in a social vacuum, but these interests are only vicariously represented, and their influence is less direct and effective. Of course they are there—the rich no less than the poor are always with us.

As political workers, women are likely to be somewhat naïve and amateurish as compared with the experienced male party canvasser, but on the other hand they are often more conscientious and faithful in the performance of their duties, than the seasoned veteran who often falls into a way of talking about what he does more than doing it. He loves to gossip and swap stories when he ought to be out mending his fences. Many women are also past masters in the fine art of political persuasion, and need no handicap from any man in that race. I have often listened to their telephone canvass of voters with great admiration for their ingenuity and adroitness. Sometimes I learned things that were not true, but the intentions were always good. The housewifely busyness and bustling about of women, even when futile in immediate result, has a deep effect in producing that psychological atmosphere so favorable to victory and so influ-

[1] These may be traced in the Bulletins of the Woman's City Club, and the Illinois League of Women Voters.

ential in determining the attitude of the bandwagon voter who often determines the issue. "When we saw those women 'manning' the polls with their baby carriages, we threw up our hands," said a veteran, in one campaign. All my fellow husbands are fully appreciative of that swift determination of women which often sweeps the boards without much regard to logic or facts—a triumph of righteous indignation and deferred protest, bursting forth. Honesty, determination, fresh enthusiasm accomplish more in this world than they are generally credited with, and in politics this is equally true, perhaps more than in most circumstances indeed. Women have many of these qualities and often employ them with marked success, as organizers, workers, lobbyists and propagandists in municipal affairs.

Only the most unusual type of tyro could overlook the patent influence in local affairs of a woman like Jane Addams, a statesman without a portfolio and a professor without a chair. Or of organizers like Janet Fairbanks and Louise de Koven Bowen. And it would be easy to enumerate a long array of others equally competent and successful in special lines of municipal activity.

PRESS

No analysis of the working forces in urban politics would be complete without an examination of the function of the press. Perhaps less powerful here than in national and state affairs, the newspapers are still widely influential in cities like Chicago. They advocate and oppose persons and policies. Their newsgathering forces accumulate masses of information available to no one else; their daily pages broadcast such facts as they care to publish, their editorial writers express their convictions upon all large questions of local importance. Day in and day out, year in and year out, they furnish much of the data upon which political judgments and conclusions of large numbers of persons are based.

But beyond this they may undertake the rôle of leaders of opinion in respect to important public policies; or they may become the Warwicks or the Nemesis of officials.[1]

They may employ their columns to promote the political advantage of themselves, of their friends and allies. They may attack, ignore, or treat by glancing innuendo, in primary, in election or in the great between-times. The sessions of their consulting committees may be full of meaning and their conclusions as important as ordinances and decisions. Their editors and proprietors command the attention and interest of all politicians and reformers alike, and they hold a unique position in a world where publicity is so important a consideration in the making and unmaking of the reputations of the chief performers.

The newspapers of Chicago have not lacked in color and in power and they have at all times been an influential element in the control of the local political situation. Two powerful journals command the morning field and four divide the attention of the population in the evening.

Broadly speaking, the *News* has been the consistent champion of reform, the Hearst papers of Hearst politics, the *Tribune* "consistently inconsistent," progressive and reactionary in alternation.

The *Tribune* is not merely a local organ but holds a wide circle of readers throughout the middle west, and is perhaps more influential in Illinois politics than in Chicago. The Hearst papers also have wide circulation outside the City, and in this respect are a part of the national policy of Mr. Hearst.

[1] Fremont Older's *My Own Story* is a fascinating account of the political experiences of a San Francisco editor in one of the most thrilling periods of the city's municipal history.

The *Journal* is the only regular Democratic organ. The *Post* reflects a liberal conservative attitude consistently.

There is, however, widespread distrust of the papers, resting on a lack of faith in their sincerity of purpose and in other cases on a belief that they represent a class attitude. Newspapers are owned by men of great wealth with fundamentally conservative attachments, and even when liberal in their tendencies it is easy to arouse against them the suspicion of the many. As in Boston and New York it has even been possible in Chicago to use the fact of newspaper opposition as a means of obtaining support for the persons attached. Both the elder and the younger Carter Harrisons, and later Thompson capitalized successfully the opposition of the press. In the last seven municipal campaigns, the *Tribune* and the *News* were successful in only two, and in the earlier period the score was much the same. But in battles for the Council and for other local offices they have been much more influential. The long ballot with its extended series of offices, many of them unimportant, induces the newspaper reader to follow the recommendation of some journal.

All of the newspapers offer recommendations to the voter both in the primaries and in the elections. Generally speaking, but with some exceptions, the recommendations of the Municipal Voters' League, the Legislative Voters' League and the Bar Association are followed. The *News* prepares an elaborate account of all the opposing candidates and makes specific recommendations in each case.

In many instances notable campaigns have been begun and carried through single-handed by a journal. Conspicuous among these are the *Tribune's* year long campaign for the unseating of Senator Lorimer, a costly but successful undertaking. Likewise the *Tribune's* suit to recover funds wasted on real estate experts, ending in a judgment for $2,000,000 against Mayor Thompson, Comptroller Harding and Michael Faherty, head of the Board of Local Improvements; the long crusade against Governor Small in both civil and criminal proceedings. Less spectacular has been the steady and unrelenting attack of the *News* upon all forms of municipal graft and crookedness. Of another type was the crusade of the Hearst papers in behalf of public ownership and the referendum, parts of the Hearst program.

Analysis shows that much of the constructive and destructive initiative is supplied by the press, who in many cases take on the functions ordinarily vested in political leaders. The journalists become in effect political leaders of the most important type, and great decisions in political affairs cannot be safely made without them. They form a superpolitical committee, which may either initiate or ratify appointments and policies. Were they a unit their authority would be almost irresistible, but competition for position and the natural differences between men usually prevent concentration of authority in this field.

The foreign language press, often a neglected factor, has a circulation of wide proportions.[1] It includes a dozen dailies with more than 20,000 subscribers each, with some in the forties. The daily circulation of these journals is over 400,000, and of the weeklies over 600,000, to say nothing of other widely-read periodicals. The foreign language journals are consulted by thousands of persons who read no English paper. Their influence is far-reaching in the circle of their readers and together they constitute a factor of material importance in the working forces of Chicago politics. They are usually neglected altogether by reform agencies who fail to realize their large significance and power in the very

[1] See Robert E. Park, *The Immigrant Press.*

communities where reform is weakest because its purposes and methods are least perfectly understood.

Unfortunately many of these papers are in a precarious condition financially, and sometimes their columns are for sale, although by no means in all cases; or in other instances they may be influenced by the attitude of local chiefs whose interest may or may not be an unselfish one. On the other hand, many of these journals are well disposed toward the advancement of community interests, and often display extraordinary interest in the problems of the city.

Local and neighborhood papers also have a considerable circulation, and interest themselves to a very considerable extent in local improvements of immediate value to their readers. Many of these journals are ephemeral, however, and the group is never united upon questions of personnel or policy.

In recent years group organs of various descriptions tend to increase the range and intensity of their influence. To list these would be to catalog almost all of the lines of industry and activity in Chicago, and would serve no purpose except confusion. Journals like *Commerce* influence many readers; so the *Bulletin* the Labor group; Margaret Haley's *Bulletin* the teachers; the *Bulletin* the Illinois Manufacturers' Association. Special political weeklies have also been able to wield some power in the local field during campaigns.

All in all, however, it is the great metropolitan dailies, with their continuous and well-directed attack upon the attention of the public that shape or interpret most commonly the opinions of the average man. And in these journals the common denominator of politics still occupies the front page and is the center of interest. In an intensive study of these journals and their relation to the mental and social attitudes of the average voter would be found many of the secrets of political control in Chicago as in many another American city.

And behind all is the gossip of the great city which buzzes as incessantly as in the tiniest village. Rumor has a thousand tongues and they are not all echoed in the daily press. It is an old saying that the best stories are never printed, and surely some of them are not. They may not be true or they may be too true; or skirt the bounds of libel; or touch too closely some of the sacred cows of the city; and some are withheld by common consent of the press in a spirit of kindliness. The daily gossip of Chicago would make an interesting sheet.

My own attitude toward the press is not colored by personal prejudice, as I have been consigned to heaven, hell, purgatory and oblivion by every one of them from time to time, but in each case came to earth again after a while. Both the *News* and the *Tribune* opposed me for the Council on extremely critical occasions, and on others supported me. In 1911 the Hearst papers sent out a carload of experts to scarify me, but on many other occasions were friendly and helpful. The *Journal* undertook to destroy me, but thought better of it.

My observation is that one who tried to steer a course indicated by any one paper or by all of them would encounter stormy political seas about as soon as one who did not make this effort. Generally speaking I found that newspapers could be counted upon in any graft or efficiency campaign, where their personal or immediate political interests were not involved; or in campaigns for public improvements. But I found them often lukewarm as the public utility or labor zone was approached by any project. Persons of liberal tendencies like Jane Addams, Walter Fisher, at one time called "King Fisher," Raymond Robins (Twittering Robin),

Governor Dunne and others, were adroitly assailed by powerful press influences and in general radicalism was more feared than reaction. But many exceptions must be entered here.

The situation was not as bad as might be, however. If the combined newspapers assailed an individual or a project, they might be fought back with the powerful support of the anti-newspaper sentiment. If only one or two are opposed, the others may be favorable. All that any public man can ask is fairness of treatment, especially with reference to a statement of his position, and most newspapers are not disposed to kill a good story or real news, except where it cuts across class lines or the special interest of the particular journal. Then the rule of queer and smear may be invoked.

In Chicago a generation ago the situation was very favorable to progressive measures. At that time the press led a strenuous campaign against the Yerkes-Lorimer utility domination of public life. They helped to blaze the trail and to win the battle for an honest Council, and for the supremacy of the public over the private interest in utility concerns. Later they led a like battle on Lorimerism. But as the public moved forward to demand new measures, such as municipal ownership, the initiative and referendum, repeatedly voted by the electors, they would not advance or give their support to those who would. The liberal leadership fell into the hands of scheming demagogues and plain rogues with no motive except that of personal plunder and loot.

In the pineapple primary of 1928 the press again centered the battle as in the Lorimer days upon the utility—machine combination in the persons of Insull, Small and Thompson, and pressed the issue to a successful close. In general journalism has been strongest politically when it has assumed a liberal attitude, and driven against the combination of privilege and politics, so frequently a factor in American municipal life. After all, the press is not the creator of a city but chiefly its representative, and will reflect the underlying conditions in the life of the community; and the hour has not struck for labor or radical press of power and influence, as it probably will when the solidarity of the labor movement is more fully achieved than at present.

The newspaper, then, is one of the effective working forces in urban political life, often tearing down and setting up persons and policies, continuously acting upon public opinion. It should not be concluded, however, that the press is omnipotent. There still remains the formal speech to vast crowds of people, the informal man-to-man communication that may run like wildfire through the group, the weekly journal or periodical likely to be much more thoughtfully read, the trade or occupational organ of increasing influence, the wide circulation of books. The modern newspaper tends toward the billboard and pictorial effect, and to influence by suggestion and proportionate emphasis rather than by the old-time moral or political leadership of the trusted personal journalist, and in the end its political editorials may disappear altogether.

The use of the radio as an instrument of political propaganda has become a part of modern politics, and tends to overshadow all the established agencies. It upsets many established traditions and methods even in aldermanic campaigns.

These then are some of the working forces in the political life of a metropolitan community. In the foreground and continuously active are the party organizations and their factional organizations, the press, the civic organizations, the public utilities. The civic committees of innumerable social groupings are usually inactive, except as they may be aroused to energy from time to time. Classes, races, religions, regions are the background against which the whole play is built. Occasionally a committee is formed upon which all of these elements are represented, as in time of some great disaster, the death of some outstanding personality, the initiation of some great public improvement, the reception of some distinguished guest. Then on some widespread representative committee are assembled the titular representatives of these groups, and in concord they express the unity of civic action.

But usually the government of the municipality is in the hands of some combination of these forces, or more properly speaking, some of the numerous governments are controlled by one combination and some by others. Coöperation and coördination are watchwords of accomplishment in common affairs. Almost any large interest has a veto power upon new municipal enterprises and can block them if it will. Business has a veto, labor has a veto, the middle class has a veto, and the parties have vetoes where united action is required.

The possible combinations are very many, when we consider that there are at least ten nationalities, three religions, two national parties without reckoning the factions within the parties, three economic classes with many subdivisions within them, three large regions within the city and as many more outside. So there may be German, Republican, Lutheran, business, North Side; or there may be Bohemian, Democratic, Catholic, labor, West Side; or there may be Jewish, Republican, middle class, South Side; and so on through a great line of possibilities within which feasible combinations may be calculated. Not all these would be winning combinations with votes and force behind them, sufficient for the political control of the city. But there are many possibilities; and the shifting nature of the groups makes the problems all the more complex for the political combiners. One may of course say, this is the commonplace of social organization and of politics as of urban politics. It is in the wide variety of interests and in their mobility that Chicago differs from European cities, but many of its political problems are much the same as those of other American cities.

Underneath all, there is a form of civic patriotism, akin to that of the nation. All groups make a nominal appeal to this spirit as their guiding principle and follow it, even if remotely at times. There is a Chicago spirit which runs through the diverse groups and upon which they all agree in temper at least. In the main each group regards itself as the most competent interpreter of the general welfare of Chicago, even if unwilling to assume the responsibility for its government. There are a few individuals who are entirely irresponsible, assuming that others will supply the necessary framework of authority and coöperation. A much larger number will not face the situation but proceed upon the tacit assumption that their plans would be safely generalized for the community. Smaller groups are quite willing to undertake the responsibility for common management, believing that their policies and personnel can adequately control the situation in the general interest.

A major phenomenon in the government of a community is the emergence of this group loyalty rising above the local and special loyalties when dealing with questions of common organization and policy. One of the most fascinating studies in modern history is that of the rise of nationalism to a dominant position over the numerous racial, religious, regional, and class factors of which the state is made up. Switzerland is a striking example of the success of the central organization, and Austria-Hungary an equally impressive instance of the failure of civic unity and solidarity. The United States itself is a great example of the rise of the national spirit over many discordant and conflicting elements, in the end, however, triumphant over the others.

Although the city is not a self-governing community and must exist as a part of a larger unity, the problem of the organization of group loyalty is not essentially different from that found in the larger national field. Races, religions, regions, classes, compete for the first place in the affections of the inhabitants, and tend to push the city into a secondary position at the price of their own advance and recognition. These groups have already been described in the consideration of the working forces in Chicago politics, and they reappear now in order to indicate the relation of these group attitudes and loyalties and allegiances to the larger city attitude, loyalty and allegiance.

It is clear that if every Catholic, Protestant or Jew votes only for those of his own religious belief, if every American, Pole, German, Italian, Scandinavian, Czech, does likewise, if every representative of business and of labor follows the same course, or if they support only those who are pledged to a policy narrowly favorable to any one of these races, religions, classes, that the chances of the city as a whole must be materially reduced, in any case seriously prejudiced. If racial, religious and regional groups coincide for a long period of time and if at the same time economic class interests are found in connection with them, the city or the state has a difficult situation to meet.

In any cosmopolitan city this problem is likely to be found, and it exists in Chicago. The group called Chicago is likely to suffer in comparison with the other and competing groups, presumably incorporated in the City and employing the city government as a common medium for the realization of common purposes. Police and health are clearly not matters for any religion, or race or class to handle, for they require a different point of view and a system of common control. But to these various groups, their own special leaders or special needs may and often do seem more human, more real, more vivid than the more abstract considerations of municipal policy. Powerful and colorful is the symbol of group recognition, especially among those who crave it because they may occupy a difficult position in a society of which they do not yet feel themselves a genuine part. The colored man may prefer a crooked alderman who exploits him, to clean streets and better housing; the Pole may prefer a Pole in office to lower taxes on his little home; the German may prefer an empty gesture of friendship in war to better schools and parks; the native American may refuse to vote for any "foreigner," preferring a crooked "Yankee."

The City is in constant struggle with these group symbols, not to destroy them, but to make them a part of a common group, to integrate them in the life of the community, to induce men to think in terms of the common enterprise of which they are a part; to develop personalities, policies, symbols that cut across the lines of other loyalties and raise the flag of the City itself, supreme for local purposes over all others. The mobility of the population and the assimilative capacity of America makes this a relatively easy process, but in the meantime there are many opportunities for combinations in terms other than those of urban interest and advantage to be made by casual adventurers in the political world. In the long run, the surprising thing is the speed with which new groups are made parts of the city itself new, and with which they enter into the common life of the municipality, and with which shams and frauds are detected by them.

Modern politicians have adroitly seized upon the clannishness of newcomers and upon their economic weakness, their desire for recognition and participation and built political power and prestige around it. The precinct committeeman is in many cases something of a social worker, not recognized by the profession. Employment, information, economic aid, friendliness and petty favors, often form a part of his stock in trade, the capital upon which he realizes when election day comes around, and without which those who appeal for votes upon larger considerations of civic advantage may find themselves at a serious disadvantage in a struggle for control.

Here again clannishness and personal friendship may enter in to upset the development of the broader city spirit, upon which the successful operation of the government is conditioned. This is particularly true if the larger Good is championed chiefly by the richer, the American and perhaps by the drys;—a circumstance which astute local representatives of the political organization will not fail to bring home or maintain even if it is not true or wholly true.

Running at right angles to these social groupings are important political trends that pass through many groups. These are attitudes or tendencies to act politically, aversions and attractions, that break through the groups in the face of local political loyalty, and set up new bases of combination themselves. Indeed almost everyone in a number of many groups, racial, religious, regional, class and party, finds himself constantly in conflict with himself on questions of public concern. He must reconcile the conflict. He must make an adjustment. In a sense this is the heart of politics, for as interests, experience, personalities, inventions, shift the scenes, large groups of persons must likewise make a shift, silently perhaps; but often with much discussion, conference, wavering and oscillation, until the old and the new are reconciled or by revolutionary process one has overthrown the other.

It is through these attitudes, which may be called drifts or grooves or runs that the political groups, politicians, inventors, leaders can find room for play. Some of these grooves run almost straight through. Thus city planning is such a groove; city zoning is another; traffic regulation is another. Either all groups are affected and agree, or some one group is so vigorous in assertion of a claim that the others recognize its justice and agree. Some of these are general human trends, and others are American, or urban or peculiar to Chicago.

Some lines find overwhelming support but not unanimity, and others are the open roads to conflict. Thus the merit system, fair taxation, reasonable economy in expenditure, liberality in liquor regulations, enforcement of the ordinary criminal law, are lines in which the opposition may be vigorous, but in which the overwhelming combination of interests makes the outcome inevitable. Open roads to conflict are such situations as municipal ownership of traction lines, control of public schools, Loop District and outlying territory, birth-control clinics and the health department, use of the police force in industrial disturbances. These are broad roads to sharp conflict between powerful groups.

Whether the town shall be wide open, or merely wet, or wholly dry is in Chicago one of the sharpest dividing lines in local political affiliation, coloring attitudes toward policies and personalities; whether the city is radical or reactionary or middle of the road is another, for radicals are strong as well as the extremists on the right wing; and the fact that these antagonisms are relatively unorganized makes the possibility of conflict all the greater, for the personality of the candidate and the shading of the policy may be decisive here. The metes and bounds between the honest, the dishonest and the friendly dispenser of favors is another point at which attitudes are strongly developed and may prove to be decisive. The line between "highbrows" and "high-hatters" on the one side and "regular fellows" on the other, with all that lies between, is also another test of affiliation to candidates and policies. Combinations of groups, attitudes and personalities, are of course infinite in their possibilities, and make the politics of a new city a kaleidoscope of colors never to be anticipated, except as a set or type may for the moment hold the pattern.

Thompson's propaganda against the British, following a similar campaign in New York under the auspices of Hirshfeld, was not seriously directed against the English, but was a gesture for the benefit of the Irish and the Germans, intended to attract them to his standard for the moment, an appeal which it was hoped would be especially attractive when coupled with a liberal attitude toward the liquor law. That he was "wetter than the Atlantic Ocean" was undoubtedly much more effective, but the other was thrown in for good measure. A slogan like "America First," widely employed in his campaign of 1927, was calculated to cover his own record in two previous administrations. He could not well discuss administrations and compare his own eight years with those of Dever, his opponent. He could not well deal in promises after eight years of performance of a type he could not defend. And America First might serve as a subject of discussion during a campaign when it was useful to say little of the real purposes of the candidate and this group. It also served as a screen for an attack upon Superintendent of Schools McAndrew, to whose removal he was pledged and in return for which he received substantial but by no means unanimous support from the teaching force of the City.

To be sure an attack upon England would not appeal to the Italian voters with their traditional friendship for Britain, or to the Scandinavians, or to the Czechs or to the Poles, with all of whom the British have cultivated friendly relations. But Czechs and Poles were strongly Democratic in any case, and if reached at all, through the emphasis on the liquor problem. The Scandinavians, Republican in disposition, were likely to go along with the ticket, and were inflamed by attacks upon Dever as a Catholic and a tool of the Church.

Demagogues may organize racial and religious and other prejudices with ease in unorganized conditions, playing lightly upon blind hatreds and desires, unmindful of consistency and relevance, satisfied with momentary combinations which will produce power and prestige, and more solid financial benefits for those who want them. When mobile groups have found their level and their leaders, this is not so easy a task as in the transition state of disorganization, through which we pass now on the way to a closer integration. In a period either of group organization and group responsibility or of group assimilation, the process of community political action will be simpler, although complex at its simplest.

It would not be far wrong to say that in Chicago, as in other large American cities, the typical difficulty is that arising from disorganization. The city government itself is not organized, but divided hopelessly among eight large and 1500 smaller governments, with part of its population inside and part of it outside the city walls; the social groups are not organized, but eight or ten large nationalistic groups remain, neither wholly assimilated nor themselves organized;

the economic classes are unorganized, and business and labor just now approach a type of politically useful concentration; the middle class of consumers and renters is not organized and has no recognized and responsible sponsors.

And above all the whole situation is new as fresh paint, and in a state of constant flux. Mobility is a characteristic feature of urban life in an American city, a physical and class mobility unknown anywhere else, and possible only under our exceptional conditions. Mobility has its advantages. It prevents the crystallization of prejudices and hatreds of long standing, and the obstruction that comes from the conduct of a living government on the basis of events of centuries ago, as in many European cities, where economic, nationalistic and religious considerations make all government difficult.

But mobility also makes difficult the genesis of these common understandings upon which government rests, and makes easy the spread of misunderstandings and prejudices of an ephemeral but powerful nature. Veteran warriors learn to know and respect each other and delimit somewhat the field of conflict; but in a battle royal every man is for himself and no one can predict the dubious outcome of impulsive combinations. Anything may happen, and does.

CHAPTER VI

SOME CHICAGO LEADERS

A MORE intimate view of urban politics requires a closer acquaintance with the personalities who are active in the public affairs of Chicago, for politics without personalities is not at all.[1] We speak of a government of law, but laws are our human ways of looking at things, made and applied by humans. Limitations both of time and space forbid discussing all of the important figures and the significant types of leaders, and judgments will differ as to which are more useful for an understanding of the situation, but I have chosen half a dozen important figures for the purpose of illustrating the actual process of political events.

Four of these leaders are "in politics"; two are in business and incidentally interested in political events; and one is a philanthropist who would disclaim political influence. One is a lawyer who at the age of seventy-six became Chicago's chief crusader against crime and fraud.

United States Senator Deneen, "Cousin" or "Uncle" Charley, Mayor Thompson, "Big Bill" and "your Mayor," George Brennan, "Old George," Chairman of the Democratic Committee of Chicago and Cook County, Carter H. Harrison, five times Mayor of the City and son of a five-time Mayor, represent diverse points of view and varying tactics in the political world. Two of these men, Deneen and Harrison, came from Illinois, one from New York, Brennan,

[1] An analysis of the qualities of leadership and an appraisal of some leaders is given in my *Four American Party Leaders*.

and one from Massachusetts, Thompson. Brennan was the son of a coal miner and worked in the mines until he lost a leg. Deneen was the son of a professor in McKendree College, Illinois. Thompson was born with a silver spoon in his mouth, son of a valiant soldier in the Civil War, a wealthy real estate owner in Chicago, inheritor and trustee of a good name and a substantial fortune.

Deneen and Brennan in their earlier days were school teachers and might have been called to their embarrassment, professor; Thompson never finished school beyond the grades, but ran away and went West for a while where he acquired a cowboy hat, and in lieu of an education took on a dislike and distrust of the intellectual. Politically Brennan was the rightful heir of Roger Sullivan whose position and power he took over on the death of the former leader of the unterrified Democracy; Thompson was the legitimate successor of Lorimer, whose following and methods he took over, and who still holds the well-known ex-Senator as his familiar adviser; Deneen, once under Lorimer, early broke away and established a position and following of his own, in which patronage, the independent press and the reform element played an important rôle. Harrison was to the manor born, son of a popular mayor.

Samuel Insull and Julius Rosenwald are both men of business successful beyond the dreams of avarice, with fortunes rising far into the millions. Neither followed the traveled road in business affairs, for one sought adventures in the organization and development of electrical power and later of other public utilities; and Rosenwald found the way to wealth through the organization of the mail order business which does not bear his name but the impress of his ability. Insull was born in England, but left his native land for adventures in America with Edison and electricity. Rosenwald was born in the city of Lincoln (Springfield) and carved out his fortune in Chicago. These two, an Englishman and a Jew, have loomed large in the government of Chicago affairs, diverse as their points of view and tactics are. Appropriate this is for a cosmopolitan city, and not without its unique interest. Neither of them has held or desires to hold public office, but both of them have been deeply concerned in the standards and attitudes of public men.

Let us look also at Frank J. Loesch, gray-haired, seventy-six years old, militant in the battle with organized crime and fraud, attorney by profession, and attorney for the Pennsylvania Railway at that. Never in politics, never a holder or seeker of office, most of his life unconcerned with the more active aspects of political life and yet in his declining years summoning the hosts to battle and leading them in determined charges and countercharges! He is also a part of Chicago's political life, not in the same sense that are Brennan and Thompson and Deneen, heads of far-flung political organizations, but as the leader of volunteer forces in desperate encounters not sought by many others.

There are likewise impressive figures like those of Raymond Robins, Jane Addams and Clarence Darrow, whose interest is not primarily local, but assumes a more general nature. Yet none the less compelling personalities in the city, and from time to time heard in the counsels and battles of the town. Who are they in Chicago and what part do they play in the organization of its affairs? And what manner of persons are they since we are dealing now with personalities?

The longest political career in this group is that of Deneen, who since 1892 when he became a member of the Illinois Legislature has been continuously in public life, eight years as state's attorney, eight years as governor of the state, and now four years as senator. Son of a professor and grandson of a Methodist minister, he has preserved the traditions of the family, and while creating and continuing an organization on the basis of patronage has maintained standards of integrity and competence, quite superior to those of the competing factional and party organizations. Left-handed alliances at times with Sullivan, Lorimer, Small and Thompson have not in the long run turned him aside from the generally high standard of political life which he set out to hold.

A statesmanlike figure in appearance, Senator Deneen has never understood the art of political dramatics, nor has he relied upon a magnetic personality for his position in his group. Given these qualities or either of them, and he would have been irresistible. He is not without courage, but caution is a quality more characteristic of him, a caution that has often been the despair of friends and foes; at times bringing him to the edge of indecisiveness and fatal delay, but on other occasions saving irretrievable ruin or heavy loss. His strongest points have been organizing power and many-sided group contacts, in both of which he was ably seconded by the astute West. No Chicago leader has been in more constant touch with the many social elements of the community; business, labor, the press, the reformers, the nationalities, the religions and the regions were all within reach of his antennæ, and his knowledge both of personalities and of group trends enables him to avoid obstacles and to build up strength in diverse directions.

But Deneen throws little light on the municipal situation, except that his powerful organization was chiefly interested in the government of the state and nation, and in local affairs concerned itself with the County chiefly. In a sense Chicago has been sacrificed to Illinois and this is important. Had Deneen continued his eight-year term as State's Attorney, certainly the criminal history of Chicago would have read differently during the last twenty years. Had he interested himself primarily in city affairs, instead of in state and county and later national concerns, it is possible that a different story of Chicago might have been written during the last quarter of a century. Or again Deneen might have gone down in the whirlpool of the local currents, for his type was clearly better adapted to state than to local combinations and attitudes. It is not probable that either he or his intimate political companion, Roy O. West, could have been elected Mayor of the City, or maintained their authority as minority figures in the political contests of the City. Indeed one of his organization once declared, "We do not want the mayoralty. It is a political liability rather than an asset, and always ruins whoever gets it."

Presiding over the destinies of the Democratic organization, until the summer of 1928, was George Brennan, white-haired, concealing the fact that he was once a professor, suave and forceful, full of chuckling humor and equally full of guile and intrigue, leading as difficult a group of men as falls to the lot of any human being. Tony Cermak, the powerful leader of the Czechs, Michael Igoe, Pat Nash and Tim Crowe and Denny Egan with their following, Stanley Kunz, irreconcilable Pole, Hinky Dink and the Bathhouse, Johnny Powers, and all the others who might fall upon him and rend him to pieces, if he faltered. Inheriting the mantle of Roger Sullivan, Brennan carried on and maintained control of the old organization. By the choice of Dever for Mayor in 1923 he reconciled to some extent, although not wholly, the old anti-Sullivan group and consolidated the power of the central organization. As did the old régime, he maintained the policy of jobs and spoils as the joker of the system, with friendly relations with the utility companies as the right bower and some of the reformers as the left. Bipartisan alliances might be called the center of the combination. As did Roger Sullivan of yore, he tried his hand at a futile struggle for the senatorship of the state in the triangular contest with Smith and Magill, independent.

Strong in personal contacts was Brennan with his infectious chuckle and his apparently universal benevolence, an attitude difficult to hold when there are so many hungry mouths to feed, and so many who must be somewhat hungry, but all the more useful if this is one's habitual disposition. He met and dealt with them all, man to man, genially except when it was necessary to growl a little and fight, else the smile became of little value. Even the rigid Davis of the Anti-Saloon League was captivated by his smile for a time and a distance. And Insull likewise was his intimate friend and "Janet," the leader of Chicago's 400.

But in group contacts, Brennan was not so strong as, say, Deneen. True, into all the heterogeneous groups that make up a cosmopolitan city he reached, but not with such inspiring confidence as the more sedate and conventionally statesmanlike Deneen. He experienced more difficulty in dealing with the press and with the independents. But his range with the nationalities and the religions was wide and deep.

He did not know how to deal with women, a puzzling factor in political affairs, new to his political life as to all of us. He feared and did not understand them. He might delegate his power to a woman, but this way lies discord and difficulty, as he discovered. Nor did he so readily speak the language of those who do not seek either jobs or favors. He understood and could be understood, but not so well.

The cause which Mr. Brennan championed when he became a candidate for the Senate and also steadily championed since, was that of the wets. The Volstead Act is anathema to the Democratic organization and its head. Why then his alliance with the dry Dever and subsequent overthrow by the wet Thompson? Here we come upon one of the deeper mysteries of politics which will not be uncovered until the day of final revelation, and which will make that final day one of compelling interest to many in Chicago.

A Democratic leader of a local spoils machine is never happy with a Republican spoils mayor in control, especially if of the predatory type; for the enemy will eat his men away and undermine his authority and his organization. This was the unhappy lot of Brennan during most of the days of his Democratic premiership. Thompson was Mayor from 1915 to 1923, and again from 1927 on. With thirty-two Democrats in the City Council of a total of fifty Brennan could find no alternative except that of trading across the lines and withdrawing for the time his opposition to Thompson. And in 1919 the situation was not dissimilar. But the effect is demoralizing upon one's army, and the general public, unmindful of the embarrassments of political authority and not caring if they did understand, lose confidence in the sincerity of subsequent attacks upon the putative enemy. But here again is illustrated in striking fashion the weakness of the local leader and the essentially disintegrated character of the national political party in local affairs.

A likable person, this genial Irishman and ex-professor, whose cordial humor covered his cunning and his steel. But without knowing him, who could have an intimate view of urban politics in recent years? Suddenly smitten in the summer of 1928, just as he was laying the plans for the fall campaign, he fell at the threshold of what might perhaps have been his greatest triumph in the field of political strategy. Upon whom his mantle will fall is a problem still to be determined by the group he had led.

Alongside the statesmanlike Senator with his powerful organization and the white-haired Brennan, one might see the present Mayor Thompson now in his sixtieth year. A shorter career his than some others. Two years an alderman (1900-'02), two years a county commissioner (1902-'04), then Mayor of Chicago (1915-'23 and 1927-?). Child of the wealthy and the well born, he escaped the Yale for which his father planned and an education other than that of the grades, and fled to the West, and for some fifteen years lived a drifting life, into which his paternal inheritance conveniently fell. Allied with the faction headed by Senator Lorimer, he was a candidate on the Lorimer-Lincoln League for Board of Review, and presided over the famous meeting in the Auditorium, where Lorimer after his "vindication" in the Senate was compared by an enthusiastic orator to Jesus Christ. With the final dismissal of Lorimer from the Senate in 1912 his organization was taken up by Thompson and with it he rode to the Republican nomination for Mayor in 1915 by a margin of a thousand votes. Mayor Harrison, crushed in the Democratic primaries, turned the City Hall strength to Thompson and he found himself Mayor of Chicago by a majority of 150,000, and the good will of the community in his hand. Retiring in 1923, he was reëlected against Dever in 1927 by a margin of over 80,000.

Unaccustomed to organization and uninterested in it, he turned the management of the machine over to Fred Lundin, a former Lorimer lieutenant who called himself the "poor Swede." Later after breaking with Lundin, he turned to Lorimer himself, now returned from South America, and a group of his allies. In general the political tactics of this group have been similar to those of the traditional Lorimer type, made familiar by the Senator in his long and varied political career. The basis is organization resting upon patronage and spoils, and flanked by the support of predatory business interests, with open defiance of the press and the independents. "Attack and smear them all," was the cry of Lorimer and it has been reëchoed by Thompson. As the chief allies of the Lorimer faction were certain packers and the lumber group in the early days, so the utility interests centering around Mr. Insull became the chief bulwark of the later flowering of the Thompson group.

Heavy and not unhandsome in earlier days, with an engaging smile and the air of a *bon vivant,* Thompson made himself an interesting political figure, with many attractions and aversions centering around him. Endowed with a gift for personal contacts he has gathered around him a large group of followers and admirers, and to his attractiveness he has been able to add profits and emoluments of a still more princely type. Winning manners have often enabled him to overcome opposition and smooth the path once more, and fat bankable perquisites have helped.

But if Lorimer was chiefly an organizer, Thompson has more of a flare for showmanship. He soon learned to value political dramatics and to like them. A very indifferent speaker at the outset, he acquired the arts of the stumper, and became an effective haranguer of audiences, who flocked to hear his unbridled attacks upon his foes. Carefully trained at first by Dynamite Jim Pugh, Fred Lundin and Dr. Robertson, he rapidly acquired facility and even bettered their instruction, and finally turned his teachers out to grass.

In the 1926 campaign in a Cort Theater speech, he brought on the stage two rats which he exhibited to the audience as "Doc" and "Fred," his old managers and pals. "Doc," he said, "you have not had a bath for a month"; "Fred, you rat, you do not look well."

In the America First campaigns, his entrance on the stage

was preceded by two buglers in American uniform and by the singing of patriotic songs. "The League of Nations is a scheme to compel us all to give up our national anthem and sing 'God Save the King.' To hell with them all." In the 1927 campaign, the song of Big Bill the Builder was substituted for the "Star Spangled Banner," perhaps as an evidence of local patriotism. Followed damning of his opponents, the *Tribune*, the *News*, the Municipal Voters' League, Dever, Brennan, crooks and traitors to the city which is to be rescued from their iniquitous hands.

He will make King George keep his snoot out of Chicago; he will drive out McAndrew, the Superintendent of Schools; he will put the policemen on their beats and prevent their snooping around in hip pockets and refrigerators (this is the real point of the campaign); if he kissed a negro baby, which he did not, Dever did some kissing too (the ring of the Cardinal).

From time to time, he will send Victor Lawson, venerable editor of the *News,* to jail; he will drive the M.V.L. out of town; he will chastise the whisky barons (this in earlier times); thrash the traction lords; drive the grafters out of the City Hall; make the city too hot for criminals; twice he will drive them out, once in 6 months and years later in 30 days. Whatever he does will be vivid, colorful, exaggerated and difficult if desirable, but it will be entertaining and will relieve the tedium of the time. And the absurdity and irrelevance of one slogan will melt into another without the change attracting attention. He is not interested in statesmanship, but in showmanship; not in logic but in votes.

From such materials as this is made the picture of his followers, who saw him as a regular fellow, a fearless fighter denouncing the rich and the powerful (except Insull), a liberal against restrictions and restraints variously interpreted by those who want a drink and by those who want to pick a pocket. It is on this world of the stage that the Mayor lives. All else is subordinated to this hour when he plays the rôle of orator and mob master, as his own followers say, without perhaps realizing the implications of the term. The cowboy hat, the buglers, the claque, the crowd, the applause that echoes his tirades, in this there is vast satisfaction and recognition. The details of city government are dry and uninteresting but they may be turned over to willing hands, relieving the Master, until another hour of showmanship comes—and it will not be long.[1]

In many-sided group contacts, he has been less successful. Business has been distrustful, labor unconvinced, the press hostile and the independents unreconciled. In the business group, however, he could count consistently upon the powerful aid of the Insull order, accompanied by the choice of the city's law officer from Insull's firm. One faction of the labor forces was attached, and the friendship of Hearst has brought the support of his papers during recent years—although not at the outset.

Among the racial groups he had greater success. Strong support has come from the Black Belt with its increasing population flowing North since the gates were closed upon immigration. With Fred Lundin at the helm support was found among the Scandinavian voters. The Germans have given aid since the War, and alliances have been made among the Irish. Energetic attempts have been made to obtain the favor of the Czechs, the Poles and the Italians, with little success in the first instance, and more in the last two.

[1] See W. A. White's vivid description of Thompson in *Colliers* of June 18th, 1927.

Broadly speaking an advocate of a wide open town, he has played gingerly between the lines of religious associations. Now he has utilized the Guardians of Liberty or the Ku-Klux prejudices as a means of support, and again has played into the hands of the orthodox by Sunday closing of saloons in one instance and in another shift by the appointment of a Catholic as School Superintendent.

It is difficult to discover in the Thompson policies any central thread except the perpetuation of power. The first campaign was anti-machine and wide open town in the primaries, but in the election became anti-Catholic and anti-German and anti-Gas Company against Sweitzer. After the election he proceeded to the organization of a powerful machine, and appointed the Gas Company's attorney as law officer of the City. Having signed promises both to the wets and drys, under threat of indictment by Charley Deneen he said, he closed the front door of saloons and opened the back door. In his next campaign he urged municipal ownership under the Thompson plan, declared for the nickel fare and belabored the traction barons (the surface lines), but with the quiet support of Insull and the Elevated lines. In a much divided field, he won by a narrow margin.[1] The election passed, this issue faded, after futile gestures against the iniquitous lords of transportation, on the surface, and against the newspaper trust. In the meantime the tide of corruption mounted ever higher culminating in the indictment of the School Board and Fred Lundin the boss and many others. After a vain effort to persuade the Democrats to nominate a weak candidate as a prelude to his running as an independent, he withdrew from the field, and remained

[1] Thompson, 259,828; Hoyne (Ind.), 110,851; Collins (Soc.), 24,079; Sweitzer, 238,206; Fitzpatrick (Labor), 55,900.

completely submerged so far as local affairs were concerned for nearly four years.

Mayor Dever's unexpected enforcement of the dry law gave Thompson his opportunity, and he returned in 1927 to advocate the wide open town, "wetter than the Atlantic Ocean," and coupled with this engaging program the advocacy of "America First," a sheer irrelevancy with little effect upon the outcome of the election.

It is obvious that no line of continuity runs through these policies except that of an opportunism, availing itself of whatever comes, with a keen eye to observing what will probably go. Patronage and spoils are floated by the use of such slogans as will reënforce the combinations of interests in prospect or in process. To Thompson himself these slogans may seem rational, but his more astute advisers, of the more sophisticated type, entertain no such illusions regarding the intellectual content of these crusades.

It is now 14 years since either of the Harrisons sat in the impressive office of the Mayor of Chicago, and the activity of the younger Harrison in local affairs is now very slight. But the Harrison dynasty ruled Chicago for ten terms, five for the father and five for the son; and their rule illustrates a type of political leadership long possible and a type which may come again. The Harrisons are still a part of the political life of the city, even if in tradition rather than in living fact.[1]

The Harrisons, elder and younger, were college trained, in real estate and journalism, gentlemen, and above all consummate politicians riding the stormy waves of a metropolitan community with unparalleled success. Their personalities were strikingly different, but their policies were much alike

[1] *Carter H. Harrison, Sr., as a Political Leader,* by C. O. Johnson, gives an interesting analysis of the political traits and tactics of the elder Harrison, against the social and economic background of the municipality.

and their tactics similar. The elder Harrison was a picturesque figure, with his white horse and his broad-brimmed hat, and his fetching ways; one of the characters of the town. On the West Side men are voting yet for Carter or would if they had the chance. A skillful and powerful orator, although he never made a political speech until he was 45, he had no equal on the municipal stump of his day. The younger Harrison was less magnetic in personality, yet likable and with long enduring friends, master of newspaper style from his training, and capable in political tactics and combination and organization.

Father and son built their political strength upon much the same base. Both cultivated the nationalities, both adopted a liberal policy, and both refused to yield to the dictates of the public utilities; both were personally honest and did not encourage organized dishonesty among their followers, however negligent they may have been in ferreting it out and punishing it. Johnson tells the story of the elder Harrison accepting some $15,000 from the gamblers, a sum which he deposited in his private safe. But during the campaign he called in an intimate friend, and said, "Please return this money if anything happens to me before the election. I will return it afterward." "Why did you take it then?" "Well," he replied, "if I did not take their money they would not trust me, and would go against me."

In both, the liberal policy adapted to a cosmopolitan community was extended to democratic liberalism with reference to public utilities, freedom of speech and other aspects of a liberal attitude. The elder Harrison carried on vigorous encounters with the press and the clergy, but the younger Harrison in general received nominal if not always cordial support from the journals and made terms with the Municipal Voters' League in the effort to build up an honest

Council; and did not run foul of other organizations when he could readily avoid it. Both received a large measure of support from business men, on the Republican side nationally.

The nationalistic support of the Harrisons was widely distributed, but was especially strong among the Germans, the Irish, the Poles and the Bohemians, who had been won by the elder Harrison. A strong Jewish following remained faithful to both of them, especially on the West Side.

Both the Harrisons built a city hall machine partly on patronage, and partly on personal prestige. The younger Harrison at first openly attacked and ridiculed the merit system, but later made public apology and defended the system thereafter. Some of the most notable steps in the development of civil service were subsequently made in his last administration.

Here then are other types of technique familiar to and effective in Chicago:—the use of a patronage organization, but deference to the merit system; amenability to journalistic suggestion, but not servility; willingness to heed civic suggestion, but liberality with reference to cosmopolitan customs; touch with business, but independence of public utility concerns; a shrewd holding at arm's length of all forces, while dealing with them, and the retention of decisions in the Harrison hands. Much in common there is between Harrison and Deneen, except the cosmopolitan adaptability of the Harrisons.

The Harrison dynasty has passed, but its tradition is still a part of Chicago's political mores, and ten terms of it illustrate possibilities in the Chicago situation, never to be ignored, illuminating a phase of Chicago political life in which urban liberalism and democracy loom large.

Let us compare with these professionals two leaders from

the world of business, two moneymakers, incidentally but not primarily interested in the control of the political world. Their interest in politics is serious but not exclusive in its claims upon their time and energy. But their points of view and their methods are at opposite poles.

Born in the city of Abraham Lincoln, Rosenwald spent six years in New York and turned westward again to Chicago (1885), where he developed the industrial contrivance known as the mail order business, and a fortune so large that estimates have little certainty. Merchant prince primarily, his secondary interest, his chief interest indeed for many years has been philanthropy, and his political interests have always occupied a subordinate place in his scheme of life. He has not held or sought office; he maintains no organization of a political nature, and supports none; but of the unofficial government, which is so large a part of the city's initiative both in politics and administration, he has been a notable figure.

In local charities and education, his rôle has been very active; but beyond this he has interested himself in the promotion of civic causes closely related to the purposes of government. A list of the civic undertakings of Chicago would doubtless find him a backer of practically all of them at one point or another; and a rehearsal of them would be a useless enumeration. His most direct contact at this point has been the chairmanship of the Chicago Bureau of Public Efficiency since its foundation in 1910 and he has given specific attention to its detailed recommendations for the improvement of municipal finances, standing by it through thick and thin, for both times come to all such organizations.

But in a more direct fashion, he has given aid and comfort, both in the form of financial help and of counsel, to specific political campaigns, leaders and movements, in which civic standards and improvement of a liberal conservative nature seemed to be at stake. Conspicuous among these in later years was his championship of the independent candidacy of Magill for the United States Senate against Frank L. Smith, after the Senatorial exposure of the latter's campaign funds. Yet this is only one among many excursions into the domain of the political, for his activities have not been limited to the city, but have reached into the state and nation. How many spots have been watered by his political beneficence, I do not know; nor is this so important as the general trend of his interest, a curve regarding which there need be no conjecture, since it follows a steady line of honesty, intelligence and merit in public affairs, and wears away from crookedness, spoils, prejudice and ignorance.

The personality of Rosenwald is not that of the political leader nor are his ways those of the politician. He does not possess the magnetism of manner or the skill in dramatics of voice or pen that is so much a part of the equipment of one type, nor the interest in political organization and intrigue of another; nor the sharp and sensitive political intuitions of either. His intuitions and inventions are those of the industrial world in which he is a master, and not those of the world of political affairs, and his organizing power is an economic rather than a governmental one. In the social sense a statesman, he is not in the political meaning and application of the term. Perhaps the use of the word statesman is not the term needed, but his policies involve the field of the state and government in their range and development.

What rôle then does such a personality play in the government of Chicago? How does he figure in the councils of the City, if neither a member of the government or of a party organization? How can he measure forces with

Thompson, with what weapons and on what field and to what conclusion?

The power and prestige of great wealth have a magic all their own especially in an industrial American community, and the voice of their individual representative is always heard when decisions of moment are to be made, heard but not perhaps followed. And it is the voice of an ambassador of business as well as an individual voice, not indeed an accredited ambassador, but an interpreter of the responsible business group. To this the factions and the parties and the leaders are not indifferent. The Rosenwald denunciation of Smith was not without its effect even though the immediate effect of the campaign following was not achieved. Other and more successful efforts followed. A deep pocketbook and a retentive memory are not to the liking of any politician, if on the other side of the road.

Spoils, graft, demagogy, find in such a man a steady and sturdy foe, easily driven from the field in one encounter, but constantly returning to the field with new resources and unshaken determination. Scattered and hard driven independent groups are encouraged and reorganized. Research and education in the field of civic affairs are given additional strength in the slow process by which they must inevitably attain their ends. All this assumes that selfish ends are not sought, or seem to be sought, and that sufficient courage exists to resist the inevitable counter-attacks from which the wealthy and respectable so often shrink.

This philanthropic citizen has no selfish purposes in City affairs either in the direction of personal ambition for office or in political recognition of an honorary nature, and no special economic interest apart from that of the community itself, with whose general prosperity of course his own industrial interests will be united.

Rosenwald has met the attacks of those who sought to entangle him. Once he was indicted for failure to file a personal property tax schedule, under a law which taxed an honest schedule upon a confiscatory basis, but stood the gaff and was vindicated. And once his company was investigated by a State Senate Vice Committee seeking to find the relation between low wages and prostitution, but the storm died away; and nothing was left but a memory of a spiteful assault.

In a more specific sense, the Rosenwald gifts to public or semi-public undertakings are the measure of his vision of civic progress on its constructive side. The education and later the housing of the negro, the industrial museum now under way, the Chicago School of Civics and Philanthropy, and latterly the establishment of the Rosenwald Foundation with its wide scope of activities; these are significant contributions to community welfare, far-reaching in their effect upon the development of the new Chicago which constantly emerges from the ashes of the old.

In a single campaign the Rosenwalds are not a match for the Thompsons, but in a series of them the outcome is different. The demagogues and spoilsmen win battles but they lose the war.

But another representative of the business world in Chicago politics is found in the person of the redoubtable Samuel Insull, center of a radiating web of politico-industrial influences of great moment in determining political decisions in the city by the Lake. An Englishman this with English accent and manner, combined with the aggressiveness and decisiveness sometimes attributed to an American promoter. But he did not bring with him English political standards or methods; adapting himself he would say to the new environment. Now in the seventieth year of his life he wields vast industrial and notable political power. Born in London, he came to America at the age of twenty-two, to become the private secretary of Thomas Edison, and so began his notable business career.

Since 1892 a resident of Chicago, he has been president of the Chicago Edison Company and of the Commonwealth Electric Company. In 1907 the Commonwealth-Edison was consolidated, later acquired the control of the People's Gas Light and Coke Company, and later the underlying bonds of the Chicago elevated railways. Among electrical organizers and developers the name of Insull is cited with respect, and in banks the bonds of the Insull properties are good. For his organization is not local in character but widespread and far flung; northern Illinois, northern Indiana; Middle West, and on the Pacific and the Atlantic coasts his properties and interests are found. Unquestionably an organizer and promoter of competence in the electrical world, and a figure in the development of the electrified America ahead of us.

Manager of many properties, quasi-public properties, public utilities they are called, and thereby hangs a tale, for these properties are "affected with a public interest" to use the judicial language. Their rates may be fixed and their service may be regulated by governmental bodies. Sometimes franchises must be obtained or averted in the case of rivals. Issues of stock and bonds may be authorized or refused by governing commissions. They may under certain circumstances be taken over and operated by governmental agencies. And this has brought the Insull interests into contact with the politicians and into the picture of the political control of Chicago, squarely in the center. For many years Insull has taken a benevolent interest in the election of aldermen, of legislators, of mayors, of senators, of all the complicated apparatus of the elaborate political machine that is found in our great political parties. In earlier years his most intimate ally was Roger Sullivan, viceroy of the Democratic organization, and later a heavy stockholder in the Insull company in his own right. But on the death of Roger he continued his friendship with Brennan. He backed the rising Thompson when he came to power. Thompson when elected held some 1000 shares of Insull stock, and Insull contributed generously to his campaign fund in the first battle. He did not neglect contact with Deneen through his relationships with the astute West. His personal enterprise and his corporate relations brought him in touch with a wide range of industrial, labor, journalistic and civic connections, more even than common to a man of affairs in the business world.

In the outcome of primaries and elections he has manifested a wide and impartial interest, including all parties and all factions in the scope of his observation and often of his generosity. While he made specific alliances with particular individuals and factions, he contributed liberally to many and even conflicting causes, recognizing realistically that political control is not a matter of parties but of combinations often without much reference to party affiliation, and that friends in all camps may at some moment or other be found useful. Thus he contributed $150,000 to the campaign fund of Frank L. Smith, chairman of the Commerce Commission, in charge of the regulation of the rates and service of utility companies; but he also contributed to the campaign funds of Brennan and Deneen on a more modest scale yet still with generosity. Indeed, he called up Brennan and asked if funds were needed and in a way thrust the gold into his hands. While not improvident in the use of funds, having a canny sense of the value of a dollar, yet almost any promising group or individual might look to his office in an emergency for financial support. The "Insull Foundation" established by a political philanthropist, was in possession of large sums of ready cash, available for substantial political causes and individuals, trusting to political gratitude and more than that to continuing financial appetite for a friendly feeling in return. Thus while the Insull moneybags became a center of political expectancy, his office became a center also of political intrigue and deals of far-reaching importance to the municipality, of quiet conversations from which impressive words went out as quietly through the community. He could call in his friend Brennan, or his friend Thompson, or his friend West, or consult through them or his attorneys with other forces in the political world. Dunne and Harrison were a different story, representatives of a more radical or at least independent grouping.

Nor did he neglect the arts of publicity while concerned with more private conferences. His publicity bureau was efficiently organized under the leadership of skilled and experienced journalists, whose eyes missed nothing; Mullaney, Wheeler, Culver, a formidable trio. Insull himself made many public addresses carefully prepared and well displayed in the press. In these speeches he dwelt on fundamental trends and problems in his special field of electrical power, but also incidentally pointed out the dangers of over-regulation by meddlesome governmental officials, and the folly of municipal ownership of any utilities. There was much sound wisdom in his talks, and always a little adroit propaganda for the electrical interests.

A man of high intelligence, he was not unmindful of cultural values and obligations. Married to a charming woman of high histrionic ability, he became a patron of the theater and head of the civic opera company of Chicago. Likewise a supporter of many charities and causes and trustee of a university.

But all this general interest and benevolence in the political world was not left in the air without some valid consideration in return, to bind the contract, so to speak. Thompson as Mayor chose as Corporation Counsel, a partner of Insull's attorney. The partnership was dissolved but historic bonds of interest were only imperfectly broken, and the firm went on and waxed greater as a center of political interest and power, close to the Thompson throne; and the high law officer of the City was not harsh with the Elevated and the other Insull interests, so that none could say the company's interests were menaced by his sword. Smith was chairman of the State Commerce Commission and likewise dealt at least considerately with the Insull gas and electric lighting interests.

But what of the plan of his ally Thompson for municipal ownership and the nickel fare? How does this fit into the picture? The "plan" was a dud for dupes, and useful only to ensnare the unwary, and to threaten the surface lines. The nickel fare was for his opponents, the surface lines, not the "L." Control of the traction situation in Chicago with millions of profits in consolidation and in construction and operation was the goal, and the legislation proposed might have given him a strangle hold upon his opponents and compelled them to cry Kamerad to their new conqueror. Mastery of electricity, gas, and traction in an imperial city, capital of the Middle West, is a stake worth struggling for, and many have fought for the prize, not yet held by any. Thompson was Insull's tool ready to hand for this purpose, but tragically ineffective, faltering even when the goal seemed at hand during the legislative session of 1927, through some unexplained break between the Governor, the Mayor and the Magnate.

Intelligent, dynamic, realistic, this powerful figure stands astride the political straits of Chicago, entering into the reckoning and the plans of all who come that way. Cynical of politicians, public, reform, of parties and factions and political promises, he nevertheless becomes a center of political influence and power, cutting across the lines of party and faction, and focusing in the central electric point of control, control sometimes for advantage and sometimes for immunity, sometimes positive and sometimes negative, yet in any case control.

If Insull could have turned his organizing ability, his dynamic power, his genius for publicity, his interest in political combination, into other and broader channels, how differently the history of Chicago might have read. He might have made the political credit of Chicago as good as the faith and credit of an Insull bond.

But no. Insull is not merely an individual, but a symbol of a situation, a Chicago situation and also wider in its sweep. And this situation and this attitude stand in the way of other developments in Chicago and elsewhere as well. Given a corrupt and incompetent government, and a somewhat listless public, what shall the attitude of business be where intimate relations must exist and where public corruption, incompetence and mediocrity may interrupt the development of a great industry, and perhaps stand in the way of the community itself? Some may say, let us as realists recognize the situation as it is, undesirable as it is, and deal with it accordingly. Let us protect ourselves as best we may, and if it is necessary to buy our way with purchasable politicians or labor crooks, then let us pay the tribute, and be on our way. We find these conditions, we cannot alter them; well, let us act accordingly. With this too there may be a touch, unconsciously, of the Nietzschean ethics, which makes the world belong to the superman, and the ethics of power the ethics of mankind. We shall be better off, and in the end perhaps the city will be better off, if our plans and purposes prevail. What the community wants to save through a little fussiness, we shall more than repay them, when our plans are carried through.

Insull is then a Chicago attitude, not perhaps without its few but powerful supporters, who may find political contributions a means of business grace and abandon responsibility for the maintenance of governmental standards, and their progressive improvement through the unceasing struggle by which alone this can be achieved. In the long run honesty must find a realistic basis. The margin between the responsible and the irresponsible attitude is not a wide one. It is a jagged zigzag line, and sometimes not a margin at all, but in the long run it is also realistic and the lines lead to different political levels and heights and depths.

An American outside Chicago or a European might ask, and what part do Jane Addams and Clarence Darrow have in the political process of Chicago? Have they no rôle to play in these interesting scenes? Or are they always saving the world outside Chicago?

Enter then Jane Addams, Saint Jane, national and international representative and interpreter of womankind, and her part in the new world into which we come.[1] Hull House founded by Miss Addams and of which she has been the head for now thirty years is a symbol of her interests and

[1] A study of Jane Addams as a political leader is in preparation by Marion W. Lewis.

Twenty Years at Hull House presents the picture of Miss Addams' most active years in Chicago; in the period since then she has been less active locally than in national and wider causes.

her influence in the community. Her earlier years saw many close relations with the city government, as inspector of streets and alleys, member of the board of education, battling against the control of the ward by Johnny Powers, as protagonist of the Progressive Party in its national and local contests. Not so happy she was in these relations, or perhaps so successful as in other phases of her activity, yet not avoiding them.

Without the wealth or the organizing ability of a Rosenwald or an Insull, Jane Addams is rich in human sympathy and in intuitive intelligence, rich in the ability to express and interpret human situations vital in their nature. In a sense a statesman without a portfolio, a professor without a chair, a preacher without a pulpit, her activities have been essentially non-political in one sense of the term, in the sense of office-holding, parties and party organization, but essentially political in another and a deeper sense, in the sense of sympathetic interest in community problems, and in intelligent leadership in the organization of plans for their betterment. The cause of the immigrant, the interests of the weak and the dependent, the life of children, the development of recreation, sympathy with municipal art and beauty in all their forms; all these are a part of her program, if such it may be called, a program escaping, however, the boundaries of party or factional platforms, or even platforms at all, since it continues a form of living sympathy, difficult to define and delimit. In *Twenty Years at Hull House*, in the *Spirit of Youth and the City Streets*, and in *Democracy and Social Ethics* she has given many illuminating views of the cosmopolitan city and its special types of problems, neglected in the novelty of urban growth, under American conditions, and indicative of her own interests and plans.

For a quarter of a century she was in the very center of the unique settlement movement, which in many ways vague and intangible in its purposes, was effective in stimulating emotional and intellectual movements touching the heart and conscience of the city, and radiating beneficent influences in myriad directions. Care for the working and living conditions of the people, sympathy for the organization of labor, tolerant regard for the cultural values of the cosmopolitan elements in the city, efforts to appreciate them and place them in their new setting, care for children, recreation, schools, mental hygiene, minimum of human living standards, art and beauty in the grimness of urban life; all these were parts of the general program or spirit of the settlement group in which Jane Addams played so important a rôle.

Are these part of politics? In the genuine sense of the term, there can be no politics without them. What these groups, innocent of direct political power and influence did was to supply the initiative which the nominal and responsible leaders lacked, and to direct attention to these unrealized possibilities in urban development; possibilities of a type which so-called reform was overlooking in its zeal for the merit system, for structural changes in local government, for economy and efficiency and for sounder electoral methods.

Sentimentalism and radicalism were the first bombs thrown at these disturbers of the common political peace. It is not easy to ask a fair trial for an anarchist; or a hearing for strikers; or to protest against an hysterical campaign against the Reds such as swept Chicago. Still more difficult, as Jane Addams discovered to her pained surprise, to ask for peace in time of a great war struggle when nationalistic passions are stirred to their depths. The larger toleration emerges slowly in communities hastily built and without traditions upon which to rest in support of the unwelcome plea. Yet here the Settlement leader often appeared in her most beneficent rôle. Friend of John Dewey, friend of Tolstoi, friend of many great spirits of the earth, she radiated breadth of view and toleration in many a situation stained by ugly and harsh conduct on the part of those who sat in the seats of industrial and political power. Is not this as important politically as being ward committeeman or even chairman of the whole organization, in the political life of a great city? Nor did she stand forever alone in these trying moments, but gathered to her aid prominent men and women from all walks of life, and helped to build not merely a bridge for a crisis but a broader way of life.

And again like Rosenwald and Insull, Jane Addams must be taken not merely as a vital personality, but as a symbol of a situation in which the makers of the great city found themselves, and from which emerged new attitudes and new interpretations of persons and policies. She may be taken as the voice of womankind in Chicago, speaking for the helpless, expressing the brooding care of the mother element in the race for its weaker ones, and yearning over them with infinite and ingenious pains; taken as the vision of the city, vision of beauty as well as power, of grace and art as well as of strength and command, financial or political. Not a mother herself, she represented the mother spirit of the city, awkwardly expressed in the forms of traditional politics, of ward and city battles for votes and the trappings of ancient authority, but gracefully and vitally expressed in attention to the deepest needs of the community and in incessant pleas for their satisfaction. Alone, hers would have been a voice in the wilderness, but one of a group of noble women, she was able to arrest the attention of the city and arouse its legislators and administrators.

But of course we deal here with an individual symbol

of a larger group of companion influences. Here should come Graham Taylor, founder of Chicago Commons, Nestor of settlement and civic activities; Mary McDowell, the Angel of the Stockyards and Head of the University of Chicago Settlement;[1] Margaret Robins, organizer and leader of women; and many others with them, building in the same fashion the structure of their common city.

Another striking type of personality in Chicago political life is that of Clarence Darrow, Clarence the Magnificent, magnificent of presence, voice, intellectual equipment, understanding of human nature, as it really is. An Ohioan is Darrow, and a lawyer, a lawyer for many causes.[2] Sometime attorney for the Northwestern Railway, sometime for the City of Chicago, sometime counsel for Debs, for the McNamaras in Los Angeles, for Bill Haywood in Colorado, for Leopold and Loeb, for Scopes in the Dayton case. A philosopher is Darrow, and partner of one of the literati, the melancholy Masters. An anarchist by philosophy, as seen in his *Resist Not Evil,* but not disposed either to throw bombs, to non-resistance, or non-intercourse as a means of making his philosophy. Rather, a realist in a real world.

During the recent War, I came to a meeting of a committee organized for national defense. Next to me sat Darrow, and I remarked: "Is this the place for an anarchist?" "Well," he replied, "I am an anarchist but until there seems to be an appropriate moment for putting my principles in effect, I am going to take a hand in things as they are."

I was reminded of a similar comment by De Ambris, a radical member of the Italian Parliament, who was vigorously pro-war. The Germans, he said, would so regiment the world that there would be no chance for ever putting

[1] See Howard E. Wilson, *Mary McDowell.*
[2] See his *Farmington.*

our principles into effect, and he was for the Allies in order to prevent a sealed-up world in which all revolutionary movements would be impossible.

At one time a political career seemed to open up before Darrow. Elected to the Legislature in 1902, he might have continued there. He was active in the municipal ownership campaigns of Dunne and legal counsel for Mayor Dunne in 1906. But in the last twenty years, he has been less concerned about political campaigns. I believe his last great political speech was made in my behalf in the mayoralty campaign of 1911. Then his eloquence almost convinced me of my availability. And if he had not been called to California, who knows what might have happened? In later times he has been a free knight, most of the time absorbed in his practice, but occasionally breaking a lance in the fray, as the spirit moved him. But often his practice has made it difficult for him to act except in his professional capacity. He was the attorney for the shale rock defendants under Mayor Busse, and for Lundin and the School Board defendants under Thompson, and for many others charged with wrongdoing. What he must have learned there would make it difficult for him to discuss these administrations judicially, or is it judiciously?

His contribution to the local situation has thus been in the main a part of his general philosophy, and the striking factors in this have been the great vigor of his attacks upon the inconsistencies and prejudices of the criminal system and his championship of the cause of the wets. Probably political Chicago does not know that he champions a mechanistic interpretation of the universe, but they know that he defends men accused of crime, and this philosophy would transform prisons into hospitals and punishment into treatment. They know that he hates shams and frauds, and that intolerance is to him a capital crime, perhaps punishable if nothing else is by capital methods. They know that liberal causes find in him a powerful champion, not a tender-minded, but a tough-minded person, with rough strength and with matchless subtlety of reasoning. Uninterested in office-holding or in party organizations or in the technical "reform" of independents, Darrow stands apart, a powerful figure, only occasionally raising his battle cry and dashing into the arena.

Of these types on the edge of organization politics, it will be observed that the patterns differ widely. Rosenwald and Darrow would agree on many points, but not upon attitudes toward labor and the radicals. Jane Addams and Clarence Darrow would agree upon many questions of broad humanitarianism, but not upon the problem of intoxicants and the control of vice and gambling. Rosenwald and Jane Addams would agree upon many points, but not with respect to labor and to militarism. Three types of liberals, with varying interpretations of what constitutes a liberal or progressive movement. Rosenwald thought Taft a progressive; Jane Addams thought the label belonged to Roosevelt; and Darrow looked to Wilson as his representative. Rosenwald is concerned with efficiency and economy in the administration of government, but neither Darrow nor Jane Addams is much perturbed over municipal waste of this type, and Darrow is not interested in the pursuit of those responsible, concerned rather with the larger environmental influences shaping the situation from afar, and minimizing the rôle of individual evildoers, or benefactors either for that matter. Rosenwald would be doubtful of municipal ownership of the traction lines, standing perhaps with Insull on this point, while Darrow and Jane Addams would not regard this as a panacea nor yet be alarmed at its imminence.

SOME CHICAGO LEADERS

A powerful and picturesque figure in Chicago is that of Raymond Robins, for a quarter of a century in the storm center of the City's most tempestuous moments. Coal miner in Kentucky, seeker (and finder) of pure gold in the Klondike, both lawyer and minister by profession, settlement worker, married to Margaret Dreier, of the Dreiers in Brooklyn, a wise and forceful leader of women. But above all a flaming orator of marvelous power, commander of humor, satire, tenderness, emotional appeal in their finest forms, he has been a flaming sword in many a Chicago battle. With broad democratic sympathies, incorruptible honesty and indomitable courage, his blade has been a ring of fire, and his voice a trumpet call in many a fray.

Champion of labor, he was once cruelly beaten by labor crooks, denounced by the press as twittering Robin, he faced them down and won their commendation, advocate of municipal ownership of traction lines he clashed with the powerful influences in this important world, and advocate of democracy in the schools battled with intrenched influences; but always an advocate of democracy and justice, and a brilliant and forceful one, never to be despised in any contest by wise and prudent battlers.

Not a seeker or holder of office, Robins was once a member of the Board of Education and reluctantly became a candidate for Senator on the Progressive ticket in 1914 against Sullivan and Sherman. But in the field of official position, he has been a Warwick rather than a responsible incumbent, both by choice and situation. For this dramatic figure is essentially an orator of magnetic power, with rare gifts of persuasion and inspiration, not easily to be held to the bounds of a local office, but better adapted to wider ranging movements.

In recent years he has turned to the nation-wide championship of the outlawry of war, with his friend Levinson, to the promotion of the enforcement of the XVIII Amendment, earlier to the "Men and Religion Forward" movement, and to participation in national political campaigns, where his oratorical talents may have full swing. This has limited his local activities in extent because of his preoccupation with larger movements, and to some extent also because of his break with the liberal elements of the population on the problem of liquor.

But he still stands a formidable figure in the political arena, vigorous and effective, whenever he chooses to unsheath his sword and begin to fight. His advocacy of Mayor Dunne, his championship of the Progressive cause and his eulogies of Roosevelt, his pleas for religious toleration in 1923,[1] and his excoriation of Thompson in 1927, his brilliant contrast of the origins and life of Dever and Thompson, the two Bills, are a part of the traditions of the community.

A political crusader, a practical political evangelist, a statesman of broad democratic sympathies, Robins has been a unique figure in the life of the town, a man without whom Chicago would have been much duller and much worse. He has evoked the sparks of political idealism which lie within the hard life of the city, waiting for some force to strike them forth.

A stalwart figure in the field of local affairs is that of Victor Olander, seaman by trade, secretary of the State Federation of Labor by occupation now. Statesmanlike in figure, voice and manner, Olander might pass for a Senator, an attorney, an executive of important affairs. In truth he is an industrial statesman of the highest order of ability

[1] "You will never nail the sign of the Klan upon the City Hall of Chicago," was always the signal for frenzied demonstration.

both in human contacts and in organization and advocacy of causes. For many months with eyesight gone, his massive and pathetic figure was still seen in the places of discussion and decision of weighty matters.

A native of Chicago, an orphan at an early age, a sailor for fourteen years, educated chiefly in the school of experience, his rare abilities were early recognized in the Seaman's Union and in the labor movement.

Olander has been the faithful and effective champion of the measures of the organized toilers, especially in the legislative halls of the Capitol, but also the foe of corruption and betrayal in the ranks of labor. Broad visioned, he has seen the importance of labor as one of the responsible governing groups of the community and has steadily assumed an attitude of responsiveness to civic demands and urban situations where counsel and coöperation are important. Olander "sits in," and his voice is heard where city policies are determined. It may not always be followed, but it is listened to with respect, in civic conferences as well as in the stormy sessions of Labor, where both power and finesse are necessary to give a man weight. Undeceived by demagogues or crooks, either in the ranks of labor or elsewhere, and not over-impressed with the prestige of wealth and social position, he maintains the even tenor of his way under the most difficult circumstances, a genuine diplomat in a world of struggling social groups. Without abating one whit from his stanch advocacy of labor's chosen measures, limitation of the use of the injunction in industrial disputes, or the limitation of hours of labor for women, he nevertheless is willing to join with other civic groups in hammering out such municipal policies as taxation, education, structural organization, election of officials, where the common judgment of a wide variety of groups is indispensable.

For he believes that the interest of labor will best be served by the assumption of joint responsibility for joint affairs, and not by exclusiveness, or irresponsibility or aloofness. Massive, powerful, astute, this half-blind seaman might have fared better financially and socially if he had chosen law or industrial management, but would not have served his community so well as in the more difficult place he now fills with unrecognized distinction. There are elements in Labor who fear and fight this man, because he may interfere with their plans for personal aggrandizement by sale and delivery of labor; and there are business men who prefer to deal with labor crooks and others who fear the rise of able champions of the labor cause, for they rightly see in the Olanders the symbols of a rising power one day to be more fully recognized both in political and in industrial councils.

Now Olander is not much concerned about economy and efficiency in municipal management, or with the dry law and its struggles with practical administration, and in these special movements he does not share; but in the broad problems of democracy in government and in democratic personalities and policies he is vitally interested, and for the working and living conditions of mankind his care is grave; and in the broader social justice, which he ranks as one of the supreme ends of human life lies his deepest hope.

Not a lone star is the blind Seaman, but one of a constellation. John Fitzpatrick, one-time blacksmith, honest and courageous head of the Chicago Federation of Labor, bluff Ed Nockels, downright and forthright in speech and action, the gentle Agnes Nestor, indefatigable in industrial and civic action. And others of whom these are only types.

A picturesque figure in the political struggles of the day in Chicago is Loesch, gray-haired, 76 years of age, militant leader against the organized forces of crime entrenched in the officialdom of the municipality, smiting them whether in high places or in low, on the bench or elsewhere. Born in Buffalo, graduate of a Chicago law school, and practitioner for more than 50 years, attorney for the Pennsylvania Railway for over 40 years, trustee of the Chicago Historical Society and member of the Literary Club, Loesch has been a peace-loving citizen quietly pursuing the practice of the law. How does he happen at a time when he might claim the privilege of his age, how does he happen to be mingling in the center of the bloody and dusty arena?

Slumbering in him there have been latent political interests, perhaps. Thirty years ago he was a member of the Board of Education, and twenty years ago a special state's attorney for the prosecution of election frauds. Undoubtedly his connection with the great railway system of which he was the Chicago representative made a continuing interest in public affairs and a political career difficult, and thus was delayed what might have been a brilliant political life. Always maintaining an active but quiet interest in political events, and bearing the part of the load that seemed his share, he was called into action in a critical moment, and on a fundamental issue.

Not a man of magnetism, or of wide group contacts, nor an organizer of political forces, he has the qualities of high intelligence, courage and an unconscious sense of the dramatic in public performance. There is a simplicity and directness in his courage and in his behavior that reflect a widespread general attitude toward a perfectly obvious situation. The masses speak frankly of crooks and thieves and so does he; have their opinion of feeble prosecutors and spineless judges and so does he, and thus Loesch is their voice—a voice their ears have been waiting to hear for many years. The speaker must be an attorney of distinction and he must have an appropriate occasion, and there must be no question of his motives or his personal ambitions. And this is the situation into which Loesch stepped, all unconscious perhaps of what awaited him, either in vicious attack or in public acclaim.

Made chairman of a somnolent Crime Commission which for mysterious reasons failed to register the will of those who made it, he transformed that extremely dignified office from a figurehead into a fighting head of the forces rallied against organized crime and politics. He led a battle against a state's attorney in the primaries and routed him by a quarter of a million in what seemed a few weeks before a hopeless contest; he boldly charged three judges of the Circuit Court with negligence in the handling of criminal cases and appeared before the special committee of these judges, colleagues to speak in plain terms of the situation; he accepted appointment as special assistant of the Attorney-General of the State for the prosecution of election frauds; he procured the indictment of a judge of the Criminal Court, and he went out to speak to citizens, addressing them in plain terms regarding the political and criminal situation. When the new state's attorney triumphed he became the chief of his staff.

Here then is a Cincinnatus type called from the plow to save the state, and returning to his occupation. It is a type found in all communities, and the environment of Chicago produces it as well. In the gray background these types are the nemesis of astute politicians who believe that the field is clear, and advance to meet an enfilading fire that withers and wilts them. "Let him that standeth take heed lest he fall," applies to the modern situation. Just when the boss becomes strongest he becomes most exposed and weakest, for the very tyranny of the situation, its greed, ruthlessness, mockery, will produce the inevitable opposition, and the necessary leaders of the uprising against the throne of Power. Loesch is one of these avenging figures, rising to smite oppression.

A painter of political portraits would take pleasure in drawing the likeness of many of the business men of Chicago, who have power and weight in civic counsels; the diplomatic Dawes, brother of General Charley, Cyrus McCormick and the McCormick group, Wrigley, Wheeler, Swift. In the labor world, Fitzpatrick and Nockels, Levine of the Amalgamated, Agnes Nestor, and a host of others. Among the regulars it would be necessary to depict shrewd and cunning organizers such as Fred Lundin, for eight years Thompson's boss, the only and plausible "Doc" Robertson, George Harding, boss of the Black Belt, Robert Crowe, one-time state's attorney, Roy O. West, *alter ego* of Senator Deneen; Brundage, Attorney-General and foe of Small; Tim Crowe, silent but powerful figure in the Democratic organization. Powerful journalists must be seen, the towering figure of the departed Lawson and his successor Strong, the McCormicks with their aggressive *Tribune,* Schaeffer and his *Post,* Hearst, a Chicago figure as well as a national one, would be a part of the picture, and in a larger picture many of the editors of the foreign-language press.

We could not omit the striking portrait of Judge John Swanson, newly elected state's attorney; of Judge Jarecki, head of the election machinery of the city; or Antony Cermak, Czech leader of the wets and President of the County Board, or Judge Harry Olson, organizer and chief of the Municipal Courts; and certainly not the picturesque figure of Senator Lewis, "J. Ham," as he is known to Chicago, Chesterfieldian and urbane, capable of addressing the First Ward in evening clothes, and "getting away with it," but overthrown by the downstate waitress who said she had been "kidded by experts before"; Congressman Ruth McCormick and Assemblyman Cheney, organizer of Voters' Leagues and community centers; former mayors Dunne and Dever, wise in the ways of politics.

Many professional figures should appear. Prominent among them are Margaret Haley of the Teachers' Federation, "Maggie" to many, Anathema to others, skilled organizer and master of political tactics, courageous and practical head of the Battalion of Death, whose flag has waved on so many sanguinary fields; Harry E. Kelly, fighting member of the Chicago Bar Association; Silas Strawn, sophisticated and indirect, but likely to be present when local councils are in session.

A notable gallery is that of the independents. Harold Ickes, most experienced and astute of organizers and managers, courageous and democratic leader; Graham Taylor, the Nestor of reform, as full of wisdom as he is of years; Allen Pond, whom nature meant for a lawyer but who became an architect, but also an architect of political structure; the incomparably astute and austere Fisher and his offspring; George Hooker, inventor and enthusiast of unrecognized value to his city; George Sikes (now departed) whose alarm broke up many a raid and whose constructive influence radiated far; the radiantly optimistic Chandler, steady friend of all good causes; General Davis and Congressman Hull, quietly in the background; "Si" Watkins, the oracle of the M. V. L.; Singleton, Sutherland and Keeler, executives of powerful civic groups; "Old King Cole," now resting on his hard-won laurels as maker of aldermen; Brunker, enthusiastic leader of the citizens' committee in the recent revolution; Louise Dekoven Bowen, magnificent organizer and leader of women; Janet Fairbank, leader of society and of politics and an accomplished author in her own right; and a long line of others without whose persistent and unrewarded efforts there would be a different Chicago.

One would find it important to include the reformers, and chief among them the stalwart Davis, the champion of the Drys, and his unterrified companion, Yarrow, with many others equally devoted to their cause. Competent women are also arrayed here, types of whom are Amelia Sears of the United Charities, Jessie Binford of the Juvenile Protective League, and Mrs. Mathes of the Christian Citizenship Council.

Nor would the gallery be complete without some of the striking figures among the aldermen euphoniously termed by the Municipal Voters' League the "Gray Wolves," and some of the later weasels. The squat figure of Bathhouse John and his diminutive colleague, Hinky Dink, who says little but does much in his imperial domain of the First Ward; the now fading Johnny Powers, long master of the Hull House territory; or we might look at Morry Eller of the Ghetto and the bloody 20th, or Congressman Kunz of the 26th. The dramatis personæ of the bootleggers' world is a swiftly changing one, and subject to constant revision by the morticians, but the traits of Al Capone are interesting, and other members of this furtive but apparently useful gang would also serve a purpose. In a working manual of politics, many names would be included, perforce.

Now in truth, these sketches are not designed as fundamental studies of political traits, but to illustrate the political life of Chicago. Many features are found in the blended likeness, and the composite picture is the town. There is something of Thompson in Chicago, love of a show, distrust of the responsible powers that be, appetite for spoils and graft, drifting irresponsibility susceptible to demagogic appeals, a dangerous mood in every man and in every group, with which we must always reckon. It has its low level lure, which when written large alarms us. There is something to be said for a spree, but not when it is repeated to the point of delirium tremens, and the nerves begin to shake.

There is something of Deneen in Chicago, survival of rural environment in different surroundings, but more of Illinois; something of the Puritan appreciation of honesty, and regard for economy and for progress, but where self-interest is involved not too many scruples as to how results come. There is an American tendency not to regard too closely the ways of the newcomers, and to sacrifice the new urban development to the older state, and this has its place in the life of Chicago, if we look at it as a whole.

But there is more of Harrison, with his willingness to adjust the urban government to the needs of the cosmopolitan community, with its broader tolerance of individual ways. Yet without sacrifice of the standards of honesty and democracy in the political world.

There is something of Insull in Chicago, in its powerful and dominating business world, some willingness to sacrifice the interests of government for those of the expansion of industry, and particularly of larger industries which government may wish to check or curb, or seems to; an impatience with the forms of traditional control and haste in brushing them aside for the shorter cut of direct action. This, too, is a cross section of Chicago, and a section not only in the world of business but also of realistic labor, where too great nicety in observance of law that impedes the cause is also not uncommon. Corruption and violence are twin methods, impelled by the same basic motive. Of such moods the Thompsons and the gray wolves and the underworld are the unwelcome but indispensable tools, the evidence of things as they are, the mitigating circumstances, extenuating the deed.

There is likewise something of Rosenwald in Chicago, a responsible attitude of the industrial world, a reluctant recourse to political activity, and a reliance upon indirect methods of securing political results through education, housing, research, patient tilling of the soil and watering and weeding of the plants. This is the responsible attitude of those who have and hold, but benevolently contrive the betterment of the community, and encourage projects that point the way, assuming in the main a conservative political world and the existing status quo in the economic order.

There is in Chicago something of the social idealism presented by Jane Addams, a sympathy with the needs of an urban industrial civilization with its urgent clamor for adjustments, with its hunger for more vivid beauty and richer life, an urban pragmatism and liberalism unsatisfied with things as they are, looking and straining forward toward a finer day and a new order of life. In a sense this is a respectable and conservative proprietary view even, but in another it is a revolutionary attitude, indifferent to the claims of any traditional order or symbols, as revolutionary as the Galilean ethics in a Roman world of power and order. Chicago, or some groups in Chicago or in some moods, has sensed and feared this, and others have sensed and welcomed it. Her attitude is not authoritarian, nor proprietary, nor formal nor legalistic, nor reformist in the structural, financial or narrowly moralistic sense, but in one way realistic and in another idealistic, seeing things just as they are, the life situations that really matter, and dealing with them as they might be or become.

There is something of Chicago in the militant figure of the valiant Loesch, holding his six and seventy years as nothing, and hurling himself into the forefront of the savage battle against organized crime entrenched in the places of authority, and defiant of law and order. This is the spirit of the crusader gone to rescue the tomb of the Holy One from the grasp of the heathen. Or it is the spirit of the vigilante of the West stung to madness and desperation by the audacity and success of the outlaws, and throwing personal and property safety to one side, in the determination to set up again the altar of justice polluted by the black mass of Satan.

There is no radicalism in this, no social idealism of the constructive sort for the moment, but a type of outraged determination to be rid of those who make a mockery of justice, and substitute defiance and lawlessness for the reign of order. An attitude of Chicago this is, echoing the days of Old King Cole, when the citizens rose in their wrath, and dangled ropes from the gallery over the heads of the aldermen about to give away the streets of the people; reminiscent this of the later day when Chicago representatives in the General Assembly of Illinois drove the offending Speaker from his chair, demanded justice in the halls of legislation, and brought the Speaker back a suppliant and a penitent. If there are relics of frontier days in the composition of Chicago, when, with bombs now, cowboys shoot up the town, well, then, there are also vigilantes who know how to face and fight and beat down the impossible organization of disorganization; and Loesch is the symbol of their mood, and the measure of their power when once aroused. Against this spirit when it wakes, the combination of mayor and governor and the state's attorney and sheriff and police, and judges even, and patronage and spoils and slush funds unlimited, and all these reënforced by the technicalities of an outworn law and outgrown system cannot prevail. Down they go like a house of cards, and, shamefaced, the culprits shrink back to their proper stations. This too is a mood of Chicago, and for a moment Loesch embodied it, and made it human.

This is not a constructive spirit, but there are times for righteous indignation in the economy of things, and this is one of the occasions when a little unreasonable wrath may sweep the boards clean, unreasoning perhaps in minor things but looking toward the goal of reasonable standards of order.

There are other moods and tenses in Chicago, not all typified in these few leaders, for a great city has as many moods as humans have, and more than most. But these illustrate some of the phases of civic life and help perhaps to give a more intimate view of urban politics in Chicago.

CHAPTER VII

ACTUAL GOVERNMENT

WHAT does a cross section of the government show in actual practice? How does the machinery really work? In the following paragraphs, an effort will be made to illustrate some of the phases of the urban governing process in the city by the Lake, not with any description of formal structure and legal powers, but from the point of view of an observer of daily behavior. The charters and the laws of a city reveal something of its life, but on the whole fall far short of conveying an adequate idea of what really transpires. Students sometimes study charters, but the personalities who rule are often ignorant of their detail and sometimes of their general principles. You will not find Tammany Hall in the statutes or ordinances of New York, nor will you find Chicago in the lengthy laws of the state, or ordinances, revised or otherwise, of Chicago, or in the learned decisions of the erudite judges who interpret them. As I have been a part of this process for some twenty years, it is possible that I may be disqualified as an impartial observer, but if not impartial, although endeavoring to be, I am at least informed, although not omniscient.

The City Council of Chicago has long been a body of great influence in the city. Its legal powers under the state law are broad, and its character and standing at one time well established. The powers of the mayor are large, but the Council is also strong, and is in reality a coördinate branch of the government. The Council has power to make the city budget, to create new departments and distribute city powers among them, to pass a wide variety of local ordinances. The powers of the City as a whole are inadequate to its needs, but within the circle of authority possessed by the municipality, the position of the Council is strong both legally and morally.

As a member of the department of political science, and in charge of the subject of municipal government, I was familiar, on entering my six years' service in the Council, with certain phases of the municipal problem and was continually studying the urban question. My first practical contact with the city government was in the collection of materials for a study of the municipal revenues of Chicago, which I had undertaken for the City Club (1905-6), with the aid of Dr. Fairlie and others. Subsequently I had been appointed by the Governor a member of the Chicago Charter Convention of 1906, and was a member of the Steering Committee of that body, as well as chairman of the Committee on Revenue and Taxation. In this capacity I had come into intimate contact with many of the inner problems of the city's management and control. In 1907 I had been made secretary of the city's harbor commission organized for the purpose of studying the local water shipping facilities. I had also been an active member of the City Club, and been obliged to examine closely many phases of the city's development.

The Chicago Council contained a group of aldermen who have been denominated "Gray Wolves." Alderman John Coughlin, known as the "Bathhouse," was one who regarded me closely. On better acquaintance with him, however, his curious attitude wore off, and in fact I had many interesting experiences with him. Upon one occasion he obtained an opinion from the Corporation Counsel's office, upon my pronunciation of the word "apparatus." I had always pronounced this word "apparātus," and he stated that if my pronunciation was correct it would upset some of his best poetry. Alderman Coughlin had obtained considerable local fame as a poet, his best known production being "Dear Midnight of Love," which I attach hereto.

DEAR MIDNIGHT OF LOVE

When silence reigns supreme and midnight love foretells,
If heart's love could be seen, there kindest thoughts do dwell.
In darkness fancies gleam, true loving hearts do swell
So far beyond a dream, true friendship never sell.

Chorus

Dear Midnight of Love, why did we meet?
Dear Midnight of Love, your face is so sweet.
Pure as the angels above, surely again we shall speak;
Loving only as doves, Dear Midnight of Love!

When lone hearts are serene, can wakening be their knell?
Were midnight but between, sleep night, say not farewell.
Stars! O, what do they mean? Do you to wake 'tis well;
Look, mother, on the scene, for you my love will tell.

Your promise, love, redeem; your gentle words do thrill;
Live as the rippling stream, always your friend I will.
Now I must bid adieu; so cruel, why did we meet?
List! What shall we do? Good-by, when shall we greet?

As a matter of fact he did not write these poems himself. They were written for him by a newspaper reporter, and he simply allowed his name to be used.

His quiet little colleague, Michael Kenna, commonly known as "Hinky Dink," has much more judgment and brains than his well-known partner. Alderman Kenna had been a member of the City Council for at least ten years, but it has been said that in all this time he had never been on his feet to say a word, and during my time I never heard his voice in the Council Chamber, except on roll call. Aldermen Kunz, Brennan, Powers, most notorious of the old gang, were always very friendly and courteous to me. Alderman Cullerton, the patriarch of the Council, commonly known as "Foxy Ed," seemed to have an instinctive feeling that I would "make trouble" some day.

There are many lines of cleavage in the Council. There is first the old line division between Republican and Democrats, with an occasional sprinkling of Socialists; and each party is divided into two or more factions, often more hostile to each other than the parties themselves. Then there is a group made up of those, on the whole favorable to the claims of the public utility corporations, and those more disposed to protect the public interest. There is a division between the wets and the drys. Sometimes geographical lines are drawn between the North Side, the South Side, and the West Side. Occasionally lines were drawn between the Catholics and the Protestants. There was a division between the purchasable and the non-purchasable vote. We calculated that one-third of the members were on the market; one-third were not for sale; and one-third were watching the press and the public, with wavering impulses. But these are not warranted as up to date statistics. These various lines crossed and recrossed in various ways. At first I had a chart of them, but later did not need one.

Personal contact with the aldermen quickly dissipates any idea that one race, religion, class, section or party possesses a monopoly of honesty or ability. There are reliable and unreliable Republicans and Democrats as well; there are counterfeit rich, and respectable and sterling poor; there are honest Catholics, Protestants, and Jews, and also dubious representatives of all these faiths. Likewise the races were represented by different types. Men like Aldermen Herrman and Pretzel were fine representatives of the German stock; Dever and Kearns of the Irish; Kjellander of the Swedish, Kerner of the Bohemian, and so on through the list. When serious issues were at stake, it never occurred to any one to consider the party, race or class label of an alderman. Class marks were significant, but by no means conclusive. The wealthy might be liberal and the poor might be in effect the purchased friend of privilege.

The organization of the Chicago Council differs from that of most parliamentary bodies in that the Mayor presides over its sessions. If the Mayor acted as the Czar type of speaker, arbitrarily granting or withholding recognition, refusing or allowing roll-calls, declaring *viva voce* votes carried or lost under gavel rule, the situation would be serious for the independence of the Council. As a rule, however, and with some exceptions, the presiding officer has been moderate and fair in his parliamentary position, and sometimes his explanations of disputed points helped to expedite the transaction of business. It must have been embarrassing to give the floor to a member certain to launch an attack on a pet measure, or raise a perplexing point; but on the other hand there was the advantage of making an immediate reply. Mayor Harrison was able to do this very effectively at times, but the others were less adroit.

In later years Mayor Thompson became more arbitrary as he became more powerful, and broke the early traditions of fair play. On one occasion he declared the Council adjourned in order to block action he did not desire, and hastily left the Council Chamber to break up the meeting. An alderman, however, hurled a bulky volume at the departing executive, and the Council continued in session, organizing by the election of a chairman and continuing the conduct of legislative business.

Discussion is restricted to five minutes according to the rules, but leave is usually given indefinitely in case the speaker has anything important to say. The practice of reading speeches or delivering addresses solely for the benefit of constituents is likely to be rudely broken up by the loud banging of copies of the Council *Proceedings* on the desks of members. One alderman who had overtaxed the patience of his fellows by much idle speaking was refused the floor for many weeks by this impromptu, but crudely effective method.

Much of the Council work, as is the case with our American legislative bodies generally, is done in committee. These committees were selected in an unusual way, abandoned since the non-partisan method of choosing aldermen has gone into effect. Committees are made up largely although not wholly on a non-partisan basis, and are usually, although not always, controlled by reliable men. In any event, Republicans are continued at the head of important committees while the Democrats control the council, and vice versa, in a manner unknown to most legislative bodies. Hearings before these committees are often of great interest and value, and on other occasions of little merit or use. Most of the active committees employ capable experts to advise them in any matters of importance. This is in addition to the services of the regular administrative staff of the City Hall. Engineers like John F. Wallace, Bion J. Arnold; experts of the type of Walter Fisher, Professor Bemis, Judge Foster, Fletcher Dobyns, and others were selected in this way by the several committees. Council records of committee attendance are kept and published as the "batting average" of the aldermen, and roll calls are also preserved and made matters of public record.

Committee recommendations are by no means sure of adoption by the Council, however, and are often roughly handled on the floor of the House; and of course even if passed are subject to the veto of the Mayor. In financial affairs this veto extends to specific items in appropriation bills. In Chicago, furthermore, the practice of submitting certain important ordinances to a referendum of the people has been developed. This is required by law in the case of bond issues and of amendments to the charter of the city; and has been established by custom in the case of street railway franchises. There is also a public policy law under which any question of public policy may be submitted on petition of 25% of the voters—a rigorous requirement which has seldom been met. In a few instances the County Judge in charge of election machinery has placed questions upon the ballot without any specific warrant of law, and in the absence of any opposition.

The City Council differs from most aldermanic bodies in the extent of its power. The Council can create new departments of government, in its discretion; it can reject the appointments presented by the Mayor; it can grant franchises and regulate the rates of public utility companies; it can make appropriations for all municipal purposes; it can challenge the Mayor's projects. It is certain of public attention and interest to a greater extent than other local bodies, or even the Legislature, or Congress. At one time it possessed men of courage and ability with the qualities of leadership. It took the initiative in very many constructive measures, and coöperated in others, and often effectively blocked raids upon municipal finances and the merit system.

The Mayor may influence the Council through various

methods:—by the appeal to the public, by patronage, permits, favors of various kinds; by active opposition in the alderman's ward; but on the other hand the Council need not respond to his requests for money or for legal power; they might obstruct his appointments; they might investigate and criticize; they might present constructive plans which he must either accept or reject, with the odium of rejection; finally and not least, they might be very influential in his renomination and reëlection when the inevitable end came to his term. So that, given a group of honest, courageous and competent men, the powers of the Council are very wide, and may be, and have been, effectively exercised on many occasions.

Local legislation differs in many respects from state or national legislation. The problems are nearer at hand and more familiar in the city. The state legislator serves on many committees and passes on a wide variety of problems, so wide in their scope that he is often bewildered by their multitude and complexity. Furthermore, the Legislature ordinarily meets only once in two years, and the time for deliberation is short. Most laws are passed in the last few days of the session, and the confusion is great, so great as to make much legislation a travesty on deliberation. In national lawmaking the wide sweep of national powers makes the difficulty of following the legislative movements all the greater. The congressman is often as worried as the state legislator, when confronted by the series of bills upon which he must register a verdict.

In the city, however, there are fewer types of measures, and there is more time for their consideration, as the Council sits the year round. Not only is this true, but the legislator may see the situation for himself, and may obtain his information at first hand. Misstatements may be more easily corrected, and misrepresentations are far more difficult to support. And the currents of public opinion flow freely through the local legislative process. The alderman is more accessible to his constituents or to the citizens of the community than is the legislator of the state or of the nation, and he receives many more expressions of popular opinion or will than does the lawmaker in the other and larger fields. A milk ordinance, or a street railway franchise, or a traffic rule regulating automobiles, touches immediately the life of thousands who have their facts and opinions on the propriety of the proposals. There is therefore a realism about city lawmaking that is not found in many other legislative bodies.

If one asks where do the ordinances come from, he raises an interesting question, never closely studied in legislative bodies thus far. Some originate with the administrative departments as a result of contact with some practical problem; some come from the Mayor as a part of his program; some come from local organizations either directly or through the Mayor or aldermen; the Association of Commerce, the real estate boards, the civic clubs, the Federation of Labor, or any one of a hundred organizations may work out some plan and submit it to the Council. Public utilities may suggest grants they desire to have; the aldermen themselves may discover some weak spot in the city's affairs and endeavor to fill the gap; newspapers frequently start crusades for specific measures and put on all steam to carry them through in a hurry; shrewd contrivers may plant an ordinance with an innocent alderman and obtain support for a measure which in reality, however disguised, spells some personal profit. Analysis of these measures would show the complex forces playing upon the legislative body of the city, and would illustrate the psychology of the lawmaking process much more clearly than is usually possible.

The time of most aldermen is not occupied with affairs of general interest, but with work of strictly local concern. Street improvements, street cleaning, lighting, policing, the schools and all local community concerns are constantly claiming their attention. In many wards unemployment is a constant source of anxiety and activity, and constant search is made for positions in the public service, with utility corporations and contractors or with anyone else who might be able to place a man. In many cases a great mass of local services is rendered in such ways as securing free permits, taking out licenses, looking after building permits, adjusting disputes with the health department and the police, tax adjustments, disputes with gas, electric and telephone companies.

Another section of duties in some wards is social, consisting in attendance upon many weddings, christenings, funerals, dances, and other social events. Another set of duties consists in the relief of the needy and distressed, those who cannot pay their rent, or perhaps their gas bill, or the doctor's bill. Sometimes relief is given by direct payment, and often by intercession with the creditor.[1]

The enterprising alderman is always at hand, only a few minutes away, and always on call. His diary, if he kept one —which he does not—would be a little world in miniature in which the political desires and emotions and ideals of the community appear—their fears, their distresses, their greeds. On graver questions men may speak with some reluctance, but on personal questions they express themselves promptly and urgently, without reservations. The household where the sewer has backed up in the basement, the woman "held

[1] See J. H. Curran's interesting study, *John Citizen.*

up" at the corner, the "strap hanger" on the street car, the irate parent of the half-time pupil, the people in the block where the lights have gone out, the shame-faced speeder or the wet-brained drunk, the family whose neighbor's roosters crow too early in the morning, or whose neighbor's cats are too much of a nuisance, those who are out of luck, out of a job, down and out—all these are a part of the daily routine of the City Father. Much depends of course upon the character of the community he represents, but after all the problems are much alike underneath the superficial differences of race or class. In the poorer wards and those more fortunate financially the demands differ somewhat, but after all men really are seeking favors and adjustments through their government differing more in degree than in kind.

Of course this mass of favors and adjustments readily shades over into complicity with violations of the law and into collusion with organized lawbreakers. The line is easy to cross, and it is not merely the poor and needy who press their claims. The peddler who wants a free permit and the contractor with a claim for extras; the little delicatessen store and the big department store in the grip of the health or building department; the automobile speeder and the truckman—all show the same general characteristics.

There is, however, a wide difference in the prestige of aldermen in different districts. In the wealthier districts the alderman is likely to be looked upon as an actual or probable boodler, whose office confers suspicion rather than distinction upon him; but in the poorer districts he may be a Great Man, a Big Friend, a Little Father or a Big Shot. If he takes money, it is from the rich, and it is redistributed among the poor. He is at worst a sort of Robin Hood whose banditry is for the common benefit. Whatever his abstract principles may be, his relationships are purely personal and loyalty to him is personal. In wards where the needs are less personal, there is less of the human bond which plays so large a part in determining human attitudes.

Yet on the whole it is safe to say that too great gratitude and loyalty are more likely to be characteristic of electorates, than too little or too light. The influence of personality is far-reaching and long-enduring as every careful observer must discover. The greater leaders are enshrined in the affectionate memory of the people, while the lesser ones are given more humble places in the smaller communities where they have faithfully served.

My office became a center for persons from all over the city, and from the outside in many cases. With touching confidence those with a personal or general cause to plead came in to talk it over. My files were so burdened with cases that it became impossible to attend to them, and doubtless many felt that their complaint or their suggestion was buried or forgotten. Some came with immensely valuable information or plans, and others were of the lunatic fringe.

One enthusiast brought me a device for checking speeders. When the legal rate of speed was exceeded, his device would throw out colored slips of paper bearing the number of the machine, and the rate of speed at the time the slip was thrown out. All that would then be necessary would be that the officer pick up the slip and summon the offender into court with his own slip as evidence against him.

Another visitor merely wanted to show his device for transforming breweries or distilleries into factories for the production of other goods. I did not take him very seriously at the time, but if he held on a few years he must have stepped into a prosperous business.

An occasional ray of light was shed by Carl Sandburg, then reporter for the *Daybook.* Just what he found in the prosaic office of an alderman in the city of Smoke and Steel I do not know. Perhaps it formed an effective and striking contrast to the poetical images that were gathering in his active brain. If he ever writes the ode of the alderman or the epic of the city hall, I may be able to identify some of the material.

In earlier times there were exciting Council episodes. In 1897, when the proposal to extend the franchises of the traction companies was pending, and it seemed probable that such an ordinance would pass, notwithstanding the general opposition to it, extraordinary measures were taken by the aroused citizens. A number of patriots attended the Council and sat in the gallery in silent protest. Their indignation was emphasized by ropes that were dangled from the gallery over the heads of the aldermen in a menacing fashion. The ropes proved to be influential lobbyists, although pursuing tactics contrary perhaps to the principles of the Fathers. In later years the citizens expressed their approval or disapproval of traction ordinances by the more orderly process of voting them up or down in a referendum.

One evening, in our time, the Council was startled by an explosion in the ante-chamber, and the members rushed out, only to discover that one of our colleagues had been shot. His assailant was a young woman who was settling her account with him in this unlawful and summary manner. Some years after in recalling this event the alderman's colleague said to me: "Yes, but you never knew the whole story. Did you notice how often I left my seat and went over to the other side of the Chamber? Well, the reason was that she had threatened to shoot him from the gallery, and I did not enjoy sitting beside him, when I saw her looking down from the gallery as she often did."

Encounters between aldermen, however, were confined to

verbal duels with hostile epithets and gestures as the chief weapons. The favorite missile thrown at me in extremes was the term of opprobrium, "Professor." I always knew at once what the attitude of the speaker was by noticing whether he said "Alderman" or "Professor," but in time even this crushing epithet was worn out and relatively little used, reserved, as it were, for great occasions. For one thing, among many of the foreign-born groups a professor is a person of some importance, and it turned out to be an unfortunate choice of an epithet. For my part I kept strictly within the sure boundaries of parliamentary usage, and on the whole was treated by my colleagues with fine personal consideration and courtesy, which I shall always recall with pleasure.

I remained in the Council until 1911 when I became a candidate for Mayor. I was offered a place on President Taft's Economy and Efficiency Commission, but declined, and in 1913 was reëlected as an independent after a three-cornered fight, carrying the load of opposition of the leading newspapers of Chicago. In 1915 I was nominated in the Republican primaries without opposition of any character, and elected. In 1917 I was asked to take a position in President Wilson's administration, but felt it desirable to remain in the Council where I was bearing the brunt of the Thompson attempt to break down the Council and exploit the administrative services of the City. After a bitter primary campaign in which the City Hall, the *Tribune*, and certain business interests joined hands, I was by the decision (from which there was no appeal) of a judge formerly characterized as a gray wolf by the Municipal Voters' League, held to have lost by 5 votes—a decision arrived at by throwing out enough votes to make the result. An independent petition was circulated at once by my friends and some 3000 signatures obtained. In the same week this was thrown out on thin technical grounds. My friends rallied again, and with the opposition or silence of all the papers except the *News*, some 10,000 voters wrote in my name on the ballot, and found to their surprise that, although intending a protest, they had fallen short of actually winning by about 1500.

Then came the Great War and a year later I was in Rome, Italy, at the head of a desperate campaign to restore the fighting morale of the Italian people.

Although the parliamentary process is one of the great institutions of democracy, it has never been made the subject of thoroughgoing analysis. Aside from the interplay of the social, economic, and political forces represented, there are many factors of fascinating interest and of fundamental importance. Among these are the rôle of facts in discussion, of reputation for public interest, the place of personal prestige, the significance of powerful presentation and defense, the technical knowledge of parliamentary rules, the ability to sense the temper of the group, the facility in compromise at critical moments, the place of personal likes and dislikes, the function of organization within the body, the temper of the group at given moments, the relative importance of action at the beginning and the close of long sessions, the factor of surprise and its opposite, tenacity and persistence; the influence of sheer fatigue; all these are significant phases of parliamentary processes which might profitably be studied, either by sharp observational analysis or in many cases by the methods of the psychologist and the statistician.

The motivation of the groups outside and the motivation of the groups inside are of equal interest and importance, while the interaction of one upon the other is even more interesting as well as more complicated. Observations and experiences in these fields are numerous, but few of them have been set down by participants or observers and none of them have been adequately analyzed. They constitute a rich field of inquiry in the domain of political control. Let us take a specific case.

When one speaks to the City Council he does not merely address fifty other individuals. He speaks to a composite group of interests represented by a complex set of individuals. I look them over as they are ranged about the Council Chamber, wondering what is going on in their minds, and how the pending proposal will affect them. One-third of them I can count upon. They will be hostile. One other third I can count upon. They will be friendly. But the other third hold the key to the situation, and if they are unfriendly, the favorable third will melt away. If they are friendly, the unfriendly third will tend to melt away. Their own minds are running swiftly through the possibilities. How will it affect them? What will their boss say? What will the newspapers say? What will their constituents say, or the element of their constituency they represent? What will the administration, potent factor in city affairs, have to say? What will the Municipal Voters' League say? What will the gang say? It is an ordinance establishing a Department of Public Welfare. It provides for a Bureau of Employment and for a Bureau of Social Surveys, to study the fundamental causes of poverty, unemployment and crime. It is endorsed by many organizations. It is designed to help the weak and the poor and incidentally the whole city.

They whisper and confer. The administration gives no sign. The leaders remain silent. It seems to be a high-brow measure but ostensibly in behalf of our constituents. Very well, but there is no opposition, and "Omnibus" carries it through without a dissenting vote.

But here is a measure to place the Deputy Commissioner of Public Works under the merit system. This position has been the backbone of the spoils system in that department. Now there is less doubt. The administration voices its disapproval. The spoilsmen and those who deal in favors see a loss to them:—an encroachment upon their prerogatives. And so voices arise. We must not carry the principle of the merit system too far. The Mayor must be trusted with the important executive positions. The hard-boiled third begins to make inroads upon the tender-minded third. There is doubt as to the legality of this measure. It has not been sufficiently considered. There should be no hasty action in so important a matter. Why was this not done when the other party was in power? Reënforcements from the reliable third arrive, hoping to show the bosses that they are not unmindful of the uses of patronage, even if in the hands of the other party. And so the storm goes, until "the band of hope" is thrown into rout and defeat. The spoilsmen have won the day by detaching some of our own allies and hurling them against us. We foresaw this but could not find a way to stem the tide.

A few illustrations may show this more clearly. I introduced an ordinance creating a commission on city expenditures to investigate and report on the efficiency of such expenditures. I asked to have it deferred and published. It falls like a bomb. Shall it be denounced and destroyed? Or referred to a committee? Or shall we demand a bill of particulars? Or would he give one? I hold my breath, listen to the ominous murmurs and whisperings, but the gate opens and the measure goes through without a vote. A week later it comes up for passage, and again the same procedure, with the same outcome. A single voice might have raised an outcry that would have shaken the walls. There is already such a commission. There is the finance committee. This is a reflection upon the administration. This is the foolish notion of a new member who is totally uninformed. Why not? The answer is that the resolution followed the passage of a state law providing for a referendum upon certain pending bond issues, and in my explanation of the resolution I had said that if we found the expenditures were efficiently conducted it would help the bond issue, and that if they were not efficiently conducted, we could report that also to the people. The administration took a chance upon what we would find—and guessed wrong.

But when once we came upon the direct trail of wholesale extravagance trouble arose. Alderman Kunz throws this bomb. He has examined the detailed expense statement of one of our investigators, Mr. Tom Welton of New York, and he finds there an item of $1 for "valet." After various whereases he concludes his resolution with instructions to the City Comptroller to equip all of the employees of the Merriam Commission with valets. A shrewd thrust, coming without warning to me. If not answered, it throws our work into disrepute and worse than that—into ridicule, all of a petty sort, but yet effective. The eyes of the room are fixed upon me, exulting or pitying as their sympathies lead. I hastily run over a half dozen expedients, for the Alderman speaks well and long, not realizing that his length of discourse helps me gather my forces and arrange them. I congratulate my colleague on his laudable interest in the subject of municipal economy—a little belated perhaps—even to a single dollar. I explain that Mr. Welton was called here to study shale rock, which was paid for as solid stone, but turned out to be soft clay—one of the greatest frauds in the history of the city. He slipped on the clay and paid a dollar to clean his pants. The whole affair is dirty business, and I appreciate the keen interest my colleague takes in it. Will he support the whole investigation of grafters and thieves and crooks as heartily? I move the reference of the resolution to my own Commission and the motion prevails amid great amusement. And to my very great relief, for this is a trying moment. Not because of the amount of money involved, but because of the peculiarly satanic reflection upon the work of the efficiency committee.

On another occasion we were discussing the budget, and particularly an item for expenditure on street cleaning under the auspices of the Citizens' Street Cleaning Association. The city's appropriation for the first ward, the business section of the city, was turned over to this association of business men who added much more and themselves took charge of the cleaning in the central district, giving extra and special service. This was always fought by the aldermen of the ward, because it deprived them of patronage otherwise at their disposal. Alderman Cullerton, "Foxy Ed," denounced the transfer of city money to a group of unknown men, and growing bolder as nobody contradicted him declared that not a single alderman knew the name of one of the members or directors of this "fake" association. And no one did. It was a very bold raid and almost succeeded. I managed to eulogize the association, however, until my secretary had time to go to the telephone, and return—to my very intense relief—with a list of the directors, including the leading business men of the city. But what if he should not return in time, I was thinking, as I rambled along through my explanation of the work of the association and the high character of its members and managers. Or what if Cullerton should break through and insist upon his original point, demanding forthwith the name of some one member.

On other occasions I was less fortunate, and often fell

heavily. For example, I introduced an amendment to the Council rules forbidding aldermen to solicit jobs for themselves or their constituents from public utility companies holding franchises from the city. This was a common practice which was a great source of strength to some of the aldermen, and a great nuisance to others. I showed the difficulties in the situation, cited some instances in which aldermen had been punished by the removal of their constituents as a result of a vote adverse to the company, and urged the need of protecting both the city and the aldermen from this influence. The majority of my colleagues were really in favor of the rule, but the minority adroitly succeeded in making it appear that we were indifferent to unemployment in the city, that in some wards we were not troubled as in the poorer wards with large numbers of men out of work, and that as representatives of a highbrow territory we could not be expected to understand their situation. Aldermen who had little to gain from the custom began to fear that they might be looked upon by their constituents as heedless of the urgent need for more jobs, and hence they voted, "No." I knew very well what was happening, but I could think of no formula by which to stop the stampede. Ability to demonstrate the relations between the utility companies and some of the loudest declaimers in behalf of the unemployed, would have clinched the case, but we could not prove all that we suspected, and I was not at liberty or did not feel it wise to make public all that I actually did know.

A year later the struggle was renewed with somewhat better results, but still was unsuccessful. I was swept over again in the same way. The third time I was able to secure the passage of the rule, but chiefly because some representatives of labor wards, socialists, it happened, came to my rescue, and declared that the working class was not benefited by the custom, but in reality the aldermen used the situation to improve their own personal prospects at the expense of the workers. With this support the rule finally prevailed, and lived to be followed by some and defied by others. About the same time I introduced an ordinance for the establishment of a bureau of unemployment, which for some time served a useful purpose in relieving both the unemployed and the aldermen.

Luck plays a part on the Council floor. On one occasion we were considering the budget and making strenuous pleas for economy in order to prevent the overloading of the appropriation bill. At this juncture a shrewd move was made to eliminate the appropriation for the prosecution of a pending suit against the Gas Company, on the plea of economy, of course. Many of those whose pet projects had been nipped in the bud were in the mood to punish the "economizers," and seemed likely to do so, all the more perhaps because a friend of mine was in charge of the litigation. While the debate was raging, I happened to see one of the aldermen writing a letter which was taken by a page to one of the lobbyists for the Gas Company. I arose and remarked that the coming roll call would give a clear line on those who were representing the public and those who were representing the Gas Company, and charged that the company was communicating with members and directing their tactics. A loud demand was made for an explanation, but I declined to go into details, maintaining an air of mystery; in fact, I begged them not to force my hand. In the meantime I received a frantic note from the writer of the letter, protesting his innocence of anything more than sending to the Gas Company a bill which a constituent believed to be excessive. This was actually true, as he showed me later.

But there were no votes for striking out the item containing the appropriation for the prosecution of the litigation.

In committee the process is still more complicated, largely because the tempo is faster, although it can be slowed down, like the movies. We are face to face now, around the table. There is room for personal courtesy and for bitter personal recrimination, not much of the latter usually as we try to maintain the dignity of the committee. On this point they always go with me, I must say, and externally maintain the best traditions of councilmanic decorum. Those who offend must apologize or retract or both. Personally I am always treated with great courtesy, as I treat the others, even when I may call attention to the fact that they are allowing themselves to be made the tools of crafty interests.

What goes on in the committee? The interplay of administration, of expert authority, of personal prestige, of foxy self-interest, of practical judgment on community situations. There are endless references to sub-committees, a matter to be carefully watched for here is room for blackmail, even in the case of worthy measures unless the sandbaggers are offset by those of an opposite persuasion. Here are endless hearings where all interests have their say and day, and are elaborately if awkwardly examined by the members of the committee. The amateurs and the experts jostle each other, literally and figuratively. Committees are often dilatory, but they are democratic, in that everyone is given his day in court and fully heard upon his cause, whatever it may be.

Here is a pure milk ordinance on which the committee sits in session after session. It comes from the Health Department and is defended by the official experts. It is reënforced by many civic organizations. But the attack comes from other alleged experts who are summoned by one of the aldermen and given every opportunity to offset the testimony of the city's physicians. Many of their objections are cunningly made, couched in technical terms as imposing as any, accompanied by specific cases apparently genuine, all plausibly presented. And finally it is argued that the pure milk ordinance is the clever plan of the larger dealers, the "big fellows," to put out of business the "little fellows" who cannot afford the plant necessary for pure milk. This is the final blow, relied upon to frighten the aldermen away from the ordinance. Here we have the administration with its technical experts, supported by the press and by civic organizations arrayed against certain milk dealers with their experts. The weight of opinion in the committee and outside with the public falls toward the ordinance and after a prolonged struggle it finally passes.

Here is my billboard ordinance, forbidding roof and restricting other boards. The committee looks askance at it. The opposition is formidable, for it includes the billboard interests, with their national counsel, skilled in "handling" recalcitrant aldermen, and always busy. The ordinance is unconstitutional; and the Corporation Counsel's office agrees with the Billboard Counsel's office upon this point. It is unreasonable, in that it tends to restrict business upon which the whole life of the city is built. It is the work of the Municipal Art League, and a set of such folks. Who made the City of Chicago, gentlemen of the Committee, its business men who advertise on billboards, or the Municipal Art League with its bewhiskered president who leads the organization? I make a mental note that he does look the part of the artists I roomed with in the Quartier Latin, and am almost convinced myself. The battle goes against me, as law and practical business seem joined against any such restrictions. But the day is not lost yet. Has any one a list of the members of the League? Yes, here is one. Read the names, and we hear a list of Chicago's leading business men, including, as fate would have it, the chief billboard man of the city, Mr. Cusack himself. These are all leaguers and the Committee is amused.

Is the measure unlawful? So says the City's law officer, but here is opinion to the contrary signed by a number of the City's leading attorneys who have given their time to studying the question. Perhaps they are right and in any event the Supreme Court will have the last guess. Here is a set of briefs presented by the billboard companies through their eminent counsel for use in many cities, and it is interesting to see that he finds the ordinance illegal in one city for one reason and in another for another reason, and sometimes for diametrically opposite reasons. He is hanging on the ropes now. Let us hear the testimony against the billboards, how they serve as lurking places for footpads, how rubbish accumulates behind them, how firemen must fight their way over them at times, how they sometimes fall and injure the passers-by as in the cases of Smith and of Brown. And here they have ruined a neighborhood by their intrusion. So the discussion goes back and forth for many days, the result hanging in the balance.

Finally, the scale turns toward the recommendation of the ordinance and it issues from the committee triumphant. The civic organizations and the press were too strong for the billboard men, who after all were just as well off with the space that was left them. And to my great dismay, a few months later, I saw high on the roof of a building a new, freshly painted, huge billboard, with the legend, "Vote for Merriam." So thoughtless are one's friends.

Here is a telephone regulation ordinance, involving both rates and service. The company insists that its rates must be raised $900,000 a year, or else money will be lost. Its claims are apparently supported by competent engineers and accountants. The press loudly calls upon the Council to show as great enterprise and courage in raising rates where necessary as in lowering them where found necessary. Will the Council demonstrate the possession of high moral courage?

No, we will lower the rates $900,000 and the company will accept the ordinance. But not without a long contest. My own expert finds the joker in the plan and it is abandoned. Then begins a battle royal with both sides fully equipped for the contest, with experts galore from all parts of the country and more to come if necessary. The room is ringed around with high-priced skillful telephone experts, the flower of the land in full bloom, fragrant with the aroma of telephony. Long days of testimony by the experts (metered service), and counter testimony by other experts, and then testimony again by those who came first. In between, the comments of the weary but determined aldermen, bent on overlooking no point, whether private or public. And there are hearings of various bodies of citizens. The Federation of Labor, the City Club and all the rest of them advise us. Being weary, we prefer not to be advised any more, but *noblesse oblige*, and they must have their day, or night. The stout and plausible Professor Bemis valiantly defends the city's case, and does not waver under the fire of the opposition or the heat of midsummer, equally oppressive. Finally comes the conclusion. What has determined it? The pressure of public opinion for lower rates, the solid stand of the city's experts, the persistence of a small group of aldermen. The press has not helped us much, but the telephone subscribers, and they are many, have followed the struggle and have supported us. The business group has not come to the rescue of the Company; and after all, the bargain with the city is not an unfair one.

But at the last moment the Committee is suddenly convened again. A motion is made for further concessions to the City, and it is carried with the support of those who had been company men hitherto. The President of the company is furious and will abandon the ordinance. Very well, he is told, that is just what has been planned. How will you be any better off? So he finally withdraws his opposition and the ordinance passes the Council with the solid opposition of the gray wolves.

What actually goes on in the committee is the clash of contending forces and sometimes of contending principles and sometimes of contending personalities. The decision is not determined by the argument alone, but by the argument plus expert opinion, personal prestige, or the lack of it, administration influence, pressure of particular group interests, campaigns for or against by the press, aldermanic interpretations of public opinion in their localities where no special groups are in evidence. It is out of these influences that a line of conduct finally emerges. The aldermen are not merely jurymen, they are jurymen, leaders, and tools, all in one. The adverse influences working upon them are stronger than the positive influences. The press has a veto upon most ordinances; the opinion of experts has a veto; the mayor has a veto; business and labor have a veto; the nationalities have a veto; the religions have a veto in most cases; the party organizations have a veto; liquor has a veto; and this does not exhaust the list of the interests that may intervene to prevent the passage of a law. But if no powerful interest blocks the way, then almost anything may pass, and "slipping by" is one of the great legislative arts. The public often dozes until it is too late.

There are many other interesting and important but almost wholly untouched phases of the parliamentary process. One of these, by way of illustration, is the factor of fatigue in the control of committees and of legislative bodies. To what extent does sheer physical or nervous strength triumph over weakness and inability to sustain a prolonged physical or mental strain? At times it seems as if the stronger were literally so in the physical sense of the term, and were able to wear down the opposition by exhausting them to a point where they yielded. This is a familiar fact in a jury where agreement must be reached, and it is also seen in legislative halls. Especially is this true where there are no sharply drawn party lines upon which the weary may stubbornly fall back and refuse to yield.

Important measures are not infrequently passed in the early hours of morning when weariness seizes everyone, and especially those on the margin of physical strength. The strenuous effort to follow with intense concentration the progress of an involved measure is exhausting, and the invention and construction of arguments calls for a high type of activity, not the highest, but still difficult. Many are worn out and offer only feeble resistance to proposals that at other times would arouse the most spirited opposition.

In the Finance Committee of the Council, we had usually a long docket to consider. The chairman continually shuffled the papers, and I became curious to know his system. He protested that he had none, but finally said: "Well, I put at the top a lot of little items that will stir up talk. After a lot of talk they get tired and then I take up the big ones." In this there was evident a certain soundness of observation. Anyone who has watched the discussion of a measure in a legislative body, may see the same process.

There are not many knockouts in the legislative struggles, but many are worn out by jabbing and thrusting, until their resistance is reduced and the way is cleared. Precisely what happens in the making of laws is a subject which the political psychologists will some day understand better than now.

The element of humor is another factor of importance in the making of laws, as well as in the conduct of government more generally considered. Smiles and laughter smooth the way for the advocate, and they may rout the adversary on occasion. In public bodies, often made up of men who dearly love a joke, the occasion is opportune for humor.

A sense of humor may be a dangerous thing for a political leader, especially if he acquired too great a reputation as a jokesmith, but a ready wit is always useful in the touch and go of all relations and especially in political relations. In a negative sense a lack of it may be fatal, especially in urban situations, where statesmen-like traditions are constantly changing, and new types arising, such as the Harrisons in Chicago, or Walker or Smith in New York.

Amid what most people undoubtedly regard as the dry bones of municipal finance, many amusing incidents occurred. Every year in the Finance Committee we "initiated" the new aldermen into the inner mysteries of the craft. This was staged when we were considering the ward appropriations for street-cleaning, garbage and ash removal. The novitiates were informed that their wards were being considered and that it would be well to ask for a hearing on their ward needs. Alderman Brown of the 'steenth Ward is informed that the appropriation for his ward will be $75,000. Has he anything to say on the adequacy of this amount? He demands more, of course. Who ever admitted that the streets were too clean in his neighborhood, or the ash and garbage service more than it should be? We show a sympathetic interest in him, and ask about new paving, about new buildings, about the cost of collection and cost of haul. Either sober-faced Alderman Jim Kearns or I then state that, although in general we are against overloaded budgets and all municipal extravagance, yet in this particular case, realizing the alderman's good cause so strongly presented by him, we believe exception should be made, and move that an additional appropriation of $15,000 be granted. Others protest, but we overbear them, and all opposition gradually ceases. The Chairman puts the question: "As many as favor the motion for the increased appropriation of $15,000 will say aye." Dead silence and, quickly, "Opposed no," with a great and unanimous chorus of no's. The effect was always good, dramatically speaking, although sometimes it would be several moments before the novitiate could catch his breath. On one occasion even the seasoned Alderman Johnny Powers was caught in this way, with his colleague Alderman Jimmy Bowler. As the moment of the vote approached he was heard to whisper to his colleague, "My God, Jimmy, we should have asked for more. I didn't know they were so easy."

Whether aldermen are better or worse, more or less efficient than the community as a whole, is unusually answered to the advantage of the community; but this is not always true. Sometimes the aldermen are better than the community and sometimes they are worse. If the general tone of the representative body is good, the members may rise to a relatively high standard, and if it is bad, they may fall below the standard they brought with them. There is such a thing as education of the members by contact and experience, and this may be a good education or a bad education, depending upon the general atmosphere surrounding their deliberations. I have seen aldermanic bodies resist vigorous popular crusades pushed with great skill and strength, when the community itself wavered and would have yielded. Examples of this are the crusade for one thousand extra policemen, demanded by certain newspapers, but resisted by the aldermen who saw through the plan. Another case was the settlement reached between the Illinois Central Railroad and the South Park Board. This came to the Council for ratification with very general popular support and frenzied newspaper advocacy. The aldermen stood firm and obtained modifications and betterments for which posterity will bless them, if they ever know what was done. Another case was the demand of the Pennsylvania Railroad for an immediate permit for its terminal location. The aldermen would not be stampeded and by their firm attitude obtained something like $7,000,000 for the City and saved the City Plan from serious mutilation. The tone or temper of the City Council was for many years determined by the Municipal Voters' League and the sentiment it represented. When this weakened, the Council spirit began to break, and a deluge followed.

The bewildered alderman is often sorely puzzled as to how to vote in a critical case, where his constituents have given no clear sign, or where they have given opposing signs. I have seen the majority of the aldermen change their votes after the roll call, when it appeared that they were going the wrong way. Those whose names came early in the roll were often vexed at their position. Of course, there were as there always are bellwethers of various sorts—administration, wet, public utility, party, factional and otherwise. And when the bellwethers move in opposite directions, the aldermen who are disposed to follow any of them are left in a sorry plight.

Whether or not a policy prevails depends upon the equilibrium of the working forces already described, and of course upon the interpretation or calculation of them by the group in immediate authority. If the Council is willing and if the mayor agrees, and if the press is not hostile, and if no "civic" organizations intervene, and if no special groups or regions or religions protest, the measure will prevail. But of course the Council and the mayor will hold back a little to see what are the pros and cons of the case, before they make the leap. The press will have a freer initiative, and also the independent organizations. Back of all there is the intangible yet powerful influence of the man in the street, which may sometimes find expression outside of the regular organizations.

Is there no small group of inner forces whose agreement makes a policy possible? no combination of Big Fellows whose word would carry the weight of law? True, if the mayor, the council leader, the Big Fellows in industry, labor, press and reform came together, opposition would probably disappear, but in few such cases could they come together. And there are notable cases in which these combined forces have not been able to ride the waves. In 1912 all these forces agreed upon a settlement between the Illinois Central and the South Park Board, but it was stopped and materially modified by the action of an outside group of citizens who rallied public opinion against it. The proposed Constitution of 1920 was endorsed by all these forces, but was overthrown by a vote of 20 to 1. Potential rulers are always on the edge of the scene, awaiting their turn, and they may upset the established calculations of the best sages.

In 1911 the Busse Administration was well intrenched in the groups of the type discussed, but in a few short months the revelations of my commission destroyed that complete confidence, yet in this case with the active support of the ruling agencies as soon as the facts were known. Again in 1928 the Thompson regime seemed in perfect control, but within six months was on the scrap heap. Almost any one powerful factor in any one of these groups can break up the *entente cordiale,* and upset authority if care is not taken to interpret public sentiment in a variety of groups and in a more general fashion.

Which way the great ball will roll, when all the interests press against it, not even the most experienced and observant can safely predict in many instances. And the municipal situation is much more complex than that of pushball.

Nor can anyone who wishes to understand the government of Chicago forget that there are many city halls, and many governments. The eight large governments and the four hundred in Cook County and the sixteen hundred in the Metropolitan Region are independent jurisdictions and they must all be consulted from time to time. Health and Police and Parks are not the affair of one sovereign but of many, and the rivalry and power of these magnates enter into all practical calculations for local action. Across the lines of the party and social groupings run these other threads of competing governmental jurisdictions, which make the structure of Chicago a crazy quilt of political colors.

While one group centers on the City Hall, another is busy with the County, and another lays siege to the Drainage Board, while others bring their pleas before the three great park districts and demand action. It requires indeed the services of another group to coördinate the governments themselves, as a special and important function. And the judges have little ways of their own in interpreting and applying the will of the lawmaker of state or city or other municipality.

It is true that the City Hall looms largest and overshadows all the others, may furnish leadership to them if it is disposed, but influence from without and centralized authority from within are not equivalents, and many a well-laid plan has died wandering in this maze of governors.

This is not the time to describe and discuss the whole government of Chicago. Its administration and its judicial organization, important as they are in the scheme of things, must be passed by,[1] in a volume that aims only to make clear the workings of the political machinery of the community. These must wait upon some other day, some more convenient day that may never come to me.

A glance must be taken at the office of mayor, however, in order to illuminate the whole process of government. The American mayor is an unusual specimen in city government, and an experiment of a most unusual kind, as the cities of the world go. There are Lord Mayors and Burgomasters, a-plenty of them, but the American mayor and the Chicago mayor must be something of both, and more than that; and he must be chosen as neither of these by the electorate in a swirling political flood. What are the tasks of the office and what manner of men survive?

The impressive office on the fifth floor of the City Hall is the clearing house for a wide variety of community activities, the range, speed and importance of which demand the attention of the Chief Executive. If John Kelly, who has survived many administrations in the outer office, were to write his observations of the inner office, he would illuminate the social and political history of his city. The fact that he has lasted for years is proof positive that he will not do so, however.

[1] Interesting light on the public service is thrown by L. D. White's *Morale in the City Hall,* 1926.

The Mayor of Chicago is the City's most impressive showpiece; he is its chief personnel agent; he is its city manager; he is its chief lawmaker, its chief financier, its diplomat, its leader; all in one; or he should be, if he did all that is expected of him. Which of these rôles he will play and which the city will best enjoy, depends upon the man and the occasion.

It would be a man's job to welcome distinguished guests, the queens and princes and potentates and adventurers and heroes of earth and air and water. If he accepted all the pressing invitations to dine and speak with important groups he would never need food at home; nor would his voice ever be at rest. The convention bureau of the Association of Commerce alone could utilize his full time and make him weary at the end of the day.

He must select men for the most important administrative responsibilities in the city's service—health, fire, police, public works, finance, law, and on him rests the choice of members of the Board of Education and the Public Library Board; and more than all this he must choose the personnel board of the whole municipal service, the Civil Service Commission, to say nothing of many important boards and commissions for special purposes. City manager, he is also; for he must supervise these heads of departments and through them direct the general course of the administration, and create a type of public service.

Lawmaker also, for he may veto acts of the Council, and through his patronage and his prestige control them. He may initiate laws and will do so many times. Diplomat he must be, representing the City in unending conferences between social groups, and between governmental groups also. More than this, he must be in a sense a leader to fulfill the high trust reposed in him by his community.

Interpreter of the city he must be, but also an interpreter who will point the way at times, who will initiate and suggest at times, subject to the approval of those he represents. More than this, he must be in a certain sense a symbol of the City. Vague this may seem, but tangible in that it connotes the kind of man or type of man the City wants to think of as its spokesman.

His power is not limited by his authority, but by his prestige; and his duties are not limited by the law, but as broad as the occasion. More than any other of its citizens he may become an industrial and cultural liability or asset of the community at home and abroad. If he is chosen, his aptitude for all these duties may be considered, and his performance of them will be qualified by the thought of another campaign in which these problems will again be raised.

A formidable task is this, and there are few who pass all the tests in Chicago or outside, of the experts and the public alike. But the same observation may be made of governors of states and presidents of the nation itself; for the elective executive is an experiment, and for cities a dubious one, which many have abandoned for the experiment of the city manager, also not an American fixture,[1] although not unlike the well-known burgomaster of German fame.

All too great is the danger that he may turn out to be some gallant figure of a man, whose amiability is a cover for futility or worse; or some more austere and narrowly efficient one-termer, inefficient in the larger things the dollar sign does not so readily measure; some mediocrity aspiring to position and willing to purchase it at the price Faust paid to Mephistopheles, his soul harrowed by the struggle to

[1] See L. D. White, *The City Manager*, 1927.

serve both God and Mammon in the same term. But now and then emerges a figure in whom nobility and power are combined, and whose leadership adorns the city. No one should be harsh with mayors, for their task is an impossible one, and we have made it so, not they.

Of Chicago's mayors in recent years, a number have been admirable Lord Mayors. The elder Harrison was a captivating and impressive figure of a man and adorned the World's Fair with grace and dignity. Dever was also born to the part, in appearance a majestic, dignified figure, courteous in manner, and pleasant in his public relations. To see him on a public occasion was to think well of one's municipality. Dunne and the younger Harrison were excellent figures, but Busse would never appear, and Thompson was too obviously a showman. The elder Harrison was an orator of parts, and Thompson was successful in crowd harangues but not impressive on other occasions.

Harrison the younger had many of the qualities of a good administrator in the political field and had he been free of political entanglements might have made a brilliant record in this direction. His intimate knowledge of city personnel, his wide acquaintance with the details of administration, and his feel of the whole situation gave him great advantages over any other incumbent, although he did not possess the energy and drive desirable in the circumstances. Busse had drive in an unusual degree and knowledge of men when he chose to utilize it, but did not live up to his personal possibilities. On one occasion he found it necessary to release one of his important heads on the basis of an investigation by my commission. "I knew he was a counterfeit the first time I set eyes on him," said the Mayor. The obvious question would have been, Why then the appointment? Like Harrison, I believe he knew when he made a bad appointment. A story is told of some of Busse's boon companions, and some of them were very boon, finding him at the Red Star Inn, his favorite resort, and urging some appointments to the Board of Education. "Say," said the unlettered mayor, "you've got to give me a guy of some class for that Board. We ain't appointing no stiffs here."

When Harrison and I were rival candidates a committee from the Chicago Medical Society came to me and asked that the Society be given the right to name the Health Commissioner. To this I could not agree although willing to consult and confer and give grave consideration. "But Harrison has made you a promise, and you have it in your pocket. Yes, you guessed it." After Harrison's election the Society presented a name which Harrison found unsatisfactory, asking another; the second likewise; and so on to the end of the list. Harrison finally consulted one of my backers and made the appointment suggested, a very good one it appeared in the end. In another case a mayor or his friends promised two men the same office, and each held the position for two years as a compromise, a wise and Solomon-like decision.

Party considerations and pre-election promises determine many positions, and very greatly narrow the range of the executive's choice when he has come into power. Harrison was accustomed to take the blank resignation of his appointees at the time of their formal appointment, so that the date could be filled in and the office made vacant. In the famous School Board case, however, this form of resignation was held invalid, as it was made before the individual had any office to resign from. Generally speaking a mayor may have the resignation of any of his cabinet, but political alliances may make this inexpedient.

An amusing case was that of the School Board Trustees

who under Thompson had tendered their resignations. They were not accepted and Dever found them in the files when he came. He promptly wrote an acceptance of the resignations and the members were out, the police aiding in the execution of the verdict of the mayor.

Dever had many of the qualities of an excellent administrator, especially in dealing with situations requiring quick wit and righteous indignation. Having an appointment to meet a committee of the Firemen he returned to find the office and the outer office filled with firemen in uniform. They addressed him on an increase in pay, and the spokesman waxed warm on the injustice with which they were treated and on the charge that no one cared for them, shaking his fist in his enthusiasm close to the mayor's face. "Who do you think you are talking to?" said the chief executive. "The mayor of Chicago, I suppose." "Oh, I thought perhaps you had forgotten. Get out of here, all of you, and go back to work." Exit all meekly but returning to apologize with no ill humor, for they realized that the speaker had gone a little too far.

Thompson's first troubles came when he promised the Republican Committee that he would recognize them after the election in the making of appointments. When the chairman of the committee called upon him, he could not be seen, but the caller was asked to consult with Mr. Lundin, and he was found to be very busy. And no "recognitions" were made for the faithful, who perhaps had not been very faithful after all, but might have been pacified pro rata to their delivery of votes.

In Chicago the mayor's appointments are subject to ratification by the Council. At times this has been found a useful check, but on the whole is a useless provision, for appointment becomes perfunctory and criticism of an appointment equivalent to a serious challenge to the administration when it might be intended only as a disavowal of responsibility. On the other hand the mayor may hold excellent aldermen responsible for appointments in which they did not really concur.

When appointments are once made the spell of the Fifth Floor still pervades the administration, and is its animating spirit. What the mayor wants goes, as the phrase is, which must be qualified by the condition that he asks for it and knows what is going on. Otherwise it may be yes, yes and once or twice, and nothing more. It is just at this point that detailed knowledge of administration, interest in its course and capacity for its supervision comes into play. Otherwise, there is a vast amount of sabotage in every administration; perhaps this is too strong a term but resistance is true enough of that quiet opposition which a permanent administration may use against a policy they do not approve. And this is as true of private corporations as of public. But if the man on the Fifth Floor, magic word, chooses to order action, it will follow for a time beyond question, for none will defy him openly.

A police department, for example, may wreck an order in its execution and escape blame. In one administration public criticism was made of the extent of gambling. The mayor blamed the police by inference and issued a strict order on the enforcement of the anti-gambling laws. That night many places were raided, and two of his cabinet officers were taken, to their embarrassment and that of the Great Chief as well.

Dever's orders for the enforcement of the dry law were likewise deliberately crippled in their application. Innocent men were raided and sometimes liquor planted, private citizens were searched roughly, and private houses entered without much excuse. The same thing may happen in any department, for it is very difficult to administer unfamiliar material, in any walk of life, political, business, academic.

The course of things administrative is honeycombed in Chicago and elsewhere as high up as Washington by the members of the legislative body, in this case the aldermen. Holding office for many years beyond the term of the mayor, with many local acquaintanceships and connections, the aldermen swarm over the departments seeking favors and adjustments, ranging from the entirely legitimate and necessary to the vicious interpretation of ordinances and collusion with graft and corruption. So far has this gone at times, that ordinary courtesies are refused citizens who are told to see their alderman, and he obtains a favor for them, justice perhaps to which they were fully entitled. A vigorous administrator at the top might resent this practice, but as he often bargains for votes for the support of his policies he may tolerate or even encourage it. It was Lundin who once said that an alderman could be bought for a garbage wagon, meaning the right to rent one to the City.

A movie of a city hall on a typical day would show the offices besieged by many citizens, asking for information, for interpretations of rules and ordinances, for reasonable and unreasonable adjustments of requirements, for services of various descriptions of the most miscellaneous character. Some of these are accompanied by aldermen but most are not. Aldermen also are bustling about seeking to satisfy their constituents by fair means or by foul, and often their constituents are highly unreasonable in their demands. Perhaps they have not all profited by the kind of instruction given me by my predecessor in office, who advised me, "Never tell them you won't do anything. Tell them you will, and then don't do it, unless they ask again.

Make them put it in writing and they won't take the trouble."

Some of these administrative requests may be handled readily, but others require the sanction of the precinct committeeman, of the ward committeemen, of some big fellow qualified to command, or even of the Fifth Floor itself in emergencies. To the ingenious there is always a way. Every employee in the Hall lives somewhere in some ward and precinct, and has some friends. This is the way, however circuitous it may be, and the persistent follow it.

When the administration becomes local, it enters the zone of greatest danger. The local politician likes to have a friendly police captain and officers, a friendly building inspector and a friendly ward superintendent of streets especially, for these men may make him much trouble, helping him either to favors or to graft. Indispensable this control is for the organization and protection of bootlegging, gambling, or other devices under the ban of the law, and many a bitter struggle goes on for this form of local control. To many this looms larger than the general policies of the mayor, or what he is or will do in a general way. America First may mean gambling and vice control in the territory of the loudest shouter, or any other irrelevancy will be as readily accepted if it gives promise of practical results. The grafter follows the dollar sign rather than the lights of principle or policy.

Vexed with favoritism and flexibility in administration since it has led to fraud and graft, the next alternative may be that of rigid enforcement of all provisions, reasonable or otherwise, an attitude which some identify with that of "reform"; yet indeed one of the handicaps of reform. But in rapidly changing urban situations the law is likely to be out of date, and serious inconvenience and damage may be wrought by insistence upon literal compliance with requirements obviously unreasonable. Everyone who administers anything knows that no one but a fool will attempt precise compliance with every provision of every rule. There is an equity in administration as there is in law, which must be invoked, if substantial justice is done.

It is the law that a city is not liable for its torts. If a child is run over by a fire truck, the city cannot be sued. But in the Council Finance Committee we always paid something at least for funeral expenses. This was not the law, but was it not justice? It is the law that a building may not occupy the street without permission and compensation, but if a building is fifteen inches in the street, what is to be done? Sometimes we let it stay. The law may be changed, but in the meantime grave injustice must be done. It is the law that personal property upon which taxes amount to five per cent be taxed at its full value. The widow's estate brings in a return of four and one-half. What is justice in this case? In these difficult cases, either blackmail may come in or reasonable adjustment within the spirit of the law.

Administration is an organ with many keys, and many tempos and varying volumes of sound; and skill lies in the combinations that produce harmonious music. It is not enough to strike some of the keys and to be loud and strong. It is easy to be firm alone, or amiable alone, or efficient alone in the narrower sense, or inventive alone. These are all important but they must be played together or discord will be the result. Particularly is it difficult to play a duet with the party organization whose ideas of harmony and time may be found confusing.

The theory of the elective mayor system is that it will provide an element of leadership for the city, a form of leadership in which will be fused the elements of political organization, legislative dominance and administrative supremacy. But few there are who can combine all these qualities in one person, and produce the necessary pattern of political behavior, in Chicago or elsewhere. The City Hall is too small to build a political organization as all those who have tried it have discovered, and too big to be bossed from the outside. The consideration of large policies for the City is an engrossing task, requiring special aptitudes, experience and leisure for mature reflection; and few can find this formula. The administrative service is large and complicated and its problems incessant in their demands for attention, and few know the material with which they deal or have the qualities requisite for success in this slippery field. The combination of all these abilities is extraordinarily difficult, and thus far Chicago has not found a Roosevelt or a Wilson, or a Hoover or a Smith, or a Tom Johnson or a Mitchell, or a Couzens or a Hoan, or a Brand Whitlock or a Golden Rule Jones. After all the mayoralty is not a career for which one may prepare with some promise of achievement if aptitudes and experience are favorable. And if one were to focus his vision upon such a place through long years, it would narrow his view and distort his perspective. The mayoralty comes in an accidental way, so to speak, and the city is lucky if it finds some person who can fairly deal with the vast responsibilities of the task.

Above all else, a continuously elective mayor must catch and interpret that subtle and intangible but solid and irresistible thing vaguely known as the spirit of the town. This is something more than the details of administration, or appointments or ordinances or consistent and statesmanlike qualities. Peculiarly difficult to catch this is, for there is something much like it which is poisonous, the momentary fancy of the community which a showman may seize but a statesman will avoid. The spirit of a city is made of traditions and aspirations, of interests and experiences, to which symbols and attitudes and types of behavior are adapted and incarnated in personalities.

This lies deeper than the negatives, which the politicians often understand very well, the things to avoid in conduct, or the positive amiabilities to be cultivated. It lies in an intuitive or if you like synthetic sense of the course indicated by the equilibrium of social forces and traditions and hopes, but it is not reasoned out that way. It is not something that can be learned by rote, but must be felt and reasoned as well. Carl Sandburg, for example, might catch the spirit of the city, and interpret it poetically but not politically, as he has done in a way in *Smoke and Steel;* although Carl might do as well as Brand Whitlock in Toledo.

Well, then, must a mayor be a poet? Nonsense, he must not have long hair or dreamy eyes. He must be hard-boiled and practical, dealing with grim stark realities of daily life. He must know what the people themselves do not know, namely what they want, expressed in personality and conduct, in human form. Bad luck to him if he guesses wrong, but if he knows the city and is not deflected too far by personal or special group advantage, and if he has this special faculty of political divination, he will most of the time guess right, or perhaps more accurately a batting average of .300 is considered excellent. And he cannot escape responsibility by never guessing, or accepting a chance. During four years there will be many crises, and he must act. Disasters, industrial disturbances, epidemics, tense moments in urban life when great policies are shaped, or when trifling ones cut across the grain of the community. Emotions rooted some of them in 300,000 years of race experience and some of them thirty years and some of them without precedent, must be felt and interpreted in these tension times.

In 1886 the anarchists were holding meetings which many demanded be suppressed. The elder Harrison went out to see and hear for himself, and sat on his horse near by, smoking a cigar. He found nothing that could not be said and rode away. But through an unfortunate confusion in orders a squad of police came up shortly afterward, and a bomb was hurled in the midst of them.

During the War Thompson permitted the meeting of the War Aims group, which the Governor attempted to suppress, a move which made the mayor many friends, not only among Germans but those who believed in freedom of speech. He had interpreted the City. But a short time afterward, when asked whether he intended to receive the Allied Generals, coming to Chicago, Joffre at the head, said he did not know, that there were many Germans in Chicago. He had missed fire, and in fact later received them.

The younger Harrison caught the spirit of the City in opposition to domination by traction interests, and his firmness made him lasting admirers, and for a time the almost unanimous support of the citizens. But Dunne and Dever lost ground in attempting to give this idea concrete form in a traction ordinance.

Dever and decency were a strong combination, but Dever and decency and drink were stronger, and when the last mentioned was removed from the combination, the town fell away quietly, even while special groups were acclaiming the sacredness of the law. Thompson caught the spirit of the City in a pledge for a wet town, but lost it in a wide-open city. Deceived by some applause for America First, he became ridiculous instead of patriotic in popular esteem.

The channels are full of the reefs and shoals of hatreds and aversions with which men's minds are filled, and navigation is difficult enough at any time. But when the storm comes, still more perilous. But this is just the time when the Pilot is needed and he cannot leave the vessel, and if he is a brave leader will not want to.

But who knows in the years that are to come what noble figures may arise to lift and swing the great sword of the City, too heavy for ordinary hands; or what prophet may come to win men's hearts in other and milder ways; or Solon richly endowed with political wisdom; figures to brighten and adorn the City, to polish its granite, to release its untold possibilities for finer forms of beauty and of power?

CHAPTER VIII

THE PINEAPPLE PRIMARY AND OTHERS

THE struggles for political control center in the political campaigns which often assume the appearance of a spectacular battle. In reality what happens between campaigns is often more important, but this is less exciting and less appealing to the imagination and the emotions. A mayoralty campaign in a metropolitan community is always vivid and sometimes reaches the stage of the lurid. The pineapple primary of 1928 is an example of what may happen when the contest reaches the most acute stage, and bombs and murder take a hand in the encounter.

It has been my lot to observe political campaigns in Chicago for the last twenty-five years, and to participate in some of them. What follows now is some snapshots of these contests as they appear to one who is in the thick of the fray or views the battle from a favored spot of the military observer. These pictures are not intended as scientific accounts, but as glimpses of a scene of conflict for the use of those who are always asking what really goes on.[1]

My first direct and personal contact with practical politics in Chicago came in 1909. An aldermanic vacancy occurred in our ward, and it was suggested that I become a candidate for the position. The Council was a body of ability and energy, and it seemed that it would be possible to continue

[1] An interesting portrayal of the 1926 campaign is given by C. H. Wooddy in *The Chicago Primary of 1926.*

within the official Council the work I had been carrying on unofficially for some time. I remembered also that my old German professors had been members of official bodies and had also carried on their scientific work. The combination of theory and practice seemed to me eminently desirable, and in fact essential to the full development of either. The experience of a number of years has only served to deepen this conviction.

The campaign for the nomination was held under the direct primary law,[1] the first trial of the new system. My candidacy was endorsed by the Republican organization, not very enthusiastically, however. At the last moment another nomination was filed by a part of the organization, and a vigorous fight was made by my opponent, a well-known attorney of attractive appearance and manner.

Now I had been named for my father, and to distinguish us I was called by the middle name. My campaign had barely begun before I received a rude shock. The party manager in charge of getting the place on the ballot called up to get my exact name. I told him "C. E. Merriam."

"You cannot use initials," he said, "how do you sign your name?"

"C. Edward," I said.

"That will never do," he said, "it is bad enough to have a university professor on the ticket without having his name parted in the middle. What is your first name?" So he put

[1] In the early days nominations were often made under remarkable circumstances. In one case in a North Side district divided by the Chicago River there were two hotly contesting factions of about equal strength. The members of one faction arrived promptly at the appointed hour for the convention, but the other faction from across the River were held back by the lifting of the Bridge to permit the passage of a vessel. The first faction with exemplary promptness organized the convention, seating enough delegates to constitute a quorum and completed the nominations, just as their retarded rivals arrived on the scene. This illustrates the value of prompt action, and the advantage of the convention system in the way of economy of time.

my name on the ballot as Charles E., and I have never been able to change it. I remonstrated with the remorseless man of affairs, but received no sympathy, as his own name had been changed in the same way, and also the name of my campaign manager.

There were no particular issues in this campaign and the result turned largely upon the personality of the candidates. Arguments of a certain type were not wanting, however. My opponent constantly asserted that a university professor was not a fit man for alderman. He and his friends argued that a professor, even in a department of political science, must necessarily be theoretical and impractical. My opponent even went so far as to print and circulate lithographs of himself, with the legend on the card "Choose this man or the University Professor."

Not only was I charged with the crime of being a professor, but an additional attempt was made to prejudice the voters by asserting the University of Chicago, with which I was connected, was entirely dominated by John D. Rockefeller. In fact, some of the more enthusiastic of my opponent's supporters went so far as to say that Mr. Rockefeller desired to obtain a representative in the City Council for various reasons which never were specified, and that I had been selected for this purpose.

On the other hand, it was sometimes argued that instead of being unfamiliar with political affairs, I was so familiar with public matters that I would be inattentive to the minor matters of the ward; or as some phrased it, "We want an alderman, not a statesman. We want someone to represent the strictly local interests of the ward, and not the general interests of the city." They reasoned that the Seventh Ward had always had to play through its representatives in the Council a large part in the affairs of the city, and they contended that it was time to choose a man who would occupy a less conspicuous position.

Owing to the novelty of a professorial candidacy, much was made of this argument on both sides. In order to counteract any unfavorable idea, I was advised to circulate as much as possible among the voters. The average man in the Seventh Ward seemed to have an idea that a professor was an elderly gentleman entirely unapproachable and remote from contact with practical affairs. I remember distinctly one of the first neighborhood meetings which I attended. This was held in the basement of a flat building in a room holding perhaps thirty or forty people. As I came in with a friend I overheard one of those present say, "Where is the Professor?" His neighbor said that I had just come in. This did not seem to satisfy the inquirer, however, and he again asked, "Where is this guy from the University of Chicago?" And I was again pointed out to him and this time absolutely identified. His great surprise was shown in his face, and he said to his friend, "Where in hell's his whiskers?"

During the course of the primary campaign, I was urged by many friends to call upon Mayor Busse. They said that although I had been secretary of the Mayor's Harbor Commission for two years I had never met him, and that a social call upon him would help to prevent the appearance of aggressive hostility to him. There was no particular reason for seeing him, but on the other hand, no particular objection to seeing him, and Alderman Bennett volunteering to introduce me, we went to make a call. Upon learning the purpose and errand of these gentlemen, his Honor became greatly excited. Turning sharply upon me he said, "So far as I am concerned, I and all of my friends, we will be against you. I do not favor anyone from the University of Chicago. They are all Socialists out there. There is too damn much Hull House in it for me." My friends were greatly chagrined at the manner of the Mayor and did their best to calm him, and they met with some degree of success. He said to me finally that he had not many friends in the Seventh Ward, anyway, and that he presumed his objection would help me more than it would hurt me. I replied, "I suppose you're really going to help me." Whereupon he and the others laughed, and we went out.

An interesting incident of the campaign occurred on the Saturday before the election. At about ten o'clock that evening I was in conference with some of my friends at the house of a neighbor when two of them said, "We are going to the Algonquin Club. Come along with us." I started to go, but remained, as we had not quite concluded our business there. The Algonquin Club, it appeared, was conducting a boxing exhibition. In some way or other the police discovered this, and raided the place immediately after my friends arrived. Some two hundred men were bundled into the patrol wagons and taken to the Harrison Street Police Station. Among others present was my rival for the aldermanic nomination and although he was not carried away in the patrol wagon, the Sunday morning papers announced that he had been arrested at the ringside. He escaped by taking up the drum and marching out with the band as a drummer boy. This raid was a very damaging thing to his prospects, and he promptly retaliated by accusing me of having instigated this action by the police department. As a matter of fact I knew nothing about it until I saw the Sunday morning papers and might easily have been taken in the net myself had I gone down with my friends. If he had known that I talked with the editor of the *Tribune* and the police captain in the district that afternoon, he would have made a stronger case against me, although his inferences would have been false. Men have been hung on less conclusive circumstantial evidence than that.

As it turned out the primary was a rather one-sided affair. I carried all but two of the precincts of my ward, and received a very large majority. The vote was 4300 to 1500. The campaign for election was devoid of interest.

Aldermanic contests are full of rich humor and racy life, coming more nearly to the real political earth than any other political contests. They are full of savour for those who have the stomach for rough food, and the appetite for the humanly political, but not so good for the more dainty, and for those who live in an unreal world.

For example, one of my colleagues in the Council was elected by this incident. His much older opponent in a joint meeting had twitted the "kid," and hoped he might become a man some day. This in a large ward where large families were the rule. "I am a man," said the young challenger, "I have two children already, and he has none. Who is the best man here?" The Kid won the applause and the election.

In the mayoralty elections the real thunders and lightnings are let loose, and the city wakes up politically. Chicago mayors are nominated in national party primaries and elected on the old style national party ballot. The aldermen are chosen in a non-partisan primary, in which a majority constitutes an election and if no majority there is a second election between the highest two. The non-partisan and the partisan elections are held simultaneously. But in effect the mayoralty election is non-partisan. There is a core of Republican or Democratic voters who stand by the national ticket, but in the main party lines are ignored and the electors redistribute themselves upon other lines.

Other things being equal the party voters stand by, but they seldom are; and in every election important factions go over bodily to the other side, without flourish of trumpets perhaps, but just about as openly.

The difference between the regular party leader and the independents is that the regulars profess regularity but do not practice it, while the independent voter professes independence but often is hoodwinked into not practicing his profession. He would vote for the Democrat except for his red hair, but in reality he must be a Republican; or he would vote for the Republican except for his black hair, but in reality he wants to be a Democrat. The wealthy and the well born are as much slaves of the party label in local elections as are the weak and helpless. If one really desires to be a party man he can always find a pretext, at the last moment perhaps. Only in local affairs he is more likely to find a good one later, since local government is more realistic than any other. What the city does or does not do is before his eyes, and he has a basis for judgment, even if he does not always use it.

Of the various factors in campaigns, such as social interests, party organization, personality, tradition and policies, the element of tradition plays a far less conspicuous rôle in local than in national campaigns. Social interests of various groups, personalities, issues even, play a considerable part in the determination of local struggles.

In the absence of party tradition as in the national field the working forces already described are very active and powerful. While these groups are never or rarely completely crystallized in any candidacy, they are frequently powerful in their action, and their pluralism perhaps foreshadows the coming industrial-social world, not achieved nationally as early as in the higher pressure urban centers.

What we call the "unofficial government" is in effect the rise to power of the effective social agencies asserting themselves in new forms, and taking authority as they may. For the time, these are largely middle-class agencies, but the trend is toward labor and business agencies, as well as professional groups. In some urban centers this circumstance has been interpreted as necessitating proportional representation instead of the older territorial representation, but in Chicago there has thus far been no strong demand for this system.

The personality of campaigners varies widely in urban contests, and differs in many ways from the prevailing qualities of the state or rural or national figure. One type is the good fellow, the mixer, the "joiner," the glad hander, whose chief reliance is the cultivation of the personal friendship of individuals and the acquaintance with all sorts of groups and societies of a non-political nature. Another type is the campaigner whose ability is largely that of the platform, whose reliance is in large measure on his ability to influence masses of voters at critical times by force of oratory, by no means a lost art even in these days. Another type is identified with a cause or policy or program in the defense of which he makes his chief battle and by which he stands or falls. Another may be identified by the possession of forcefulness, executive ability, the native quality of driving leadership which will always command respect and a following. Honesty, courage, forcefulness, intelligence, are always qualities that carry weight, and cannot be denied a hearing even though they may not be adopted.

The pompous type of public servant sometimes encountered in the rural districts, and sometimes presented as the traditional statesman, finds difficulty in surviving in the city. His frock coat, his resonant voice, his patronizing manner, would be likely to meet the destructive ridicule of the street gamin or the inevitable wag of the meeting. Some such figures, to be sure, like Henry Clay Sulzer, continue, but not many, and they must be very good of their type. The old-timer's place is taken sometimes by the fox or perhaps the rat type. The city likes audacity but not the condescending manner. Real ability of some brand for good or evil is required to deal with turbulent masses of moving persons, and power to make a quick if not a lasting impression upon a shifting crowd, more inclined to escape than to remain.

Old-fashioned, impassioned oratory is still accepted, if it is really of a superior type, but it passes, and a more sophisticated form of urban address develops, adapted to the new urban situations. Colonel and Senator Lewis, he of the pink whiskers and engaging smile, is master of this newer form of address. That he could appear and be received with wild acclaim by the denizens of the First Ward in evening dress, and follow with eloquent appeal is a tribute to his peculiar but effective style of oratory. Extremes like the elder Harrison and Jane Addams, Robins and Thompson are well received and effective in their diverse appeals.

Organizers and bosses will of course depend upon another set of qualities, differing widely from those of the campaigner or the candidate. Their ability will lie in keen insight into social forces, shrewd appraisal of personalities, facility for combination and organization, finesse and intrigue, in the executive ability necessary to maintain a going concern built of patronage and spoils. Thus Lorimer understood the art of building a real organization where there had been only paper; likewise Lundin with deeper knowledge of crowd psychology; Brennan knew how to get along with rebellious and incompatible elements; Deneen understood organization and also independent opinion. The feudal system of Chicago has made possible a wide variety of local lords, with more power in their own right and more pronounced individuality than in cities under centralized control, such as New York and Philadelphia; and a wealth of fascinating material lies in the study of these magnates of the political goldfields.

The best working combination is that of the qualities of the organizer and the speaker, for where they are separated the cunning of the organizer is likely to make the emotional skill of the orator a front for his wiles. Or the orator if dominant will lack the wit and the patience to regulate the affairs of the faction and the government both. The Harrisons and Deneen best combined these difficult elements. The orator overtopped the organizer in Harrison, and the organizer the orator in Deneen.

Once the name boss is attached to a personality all sorts of dangerous expectancies spring up around him, those of his followers who scent their prey and those of the public who begin to feel of their pocketbooks. The leader who is his own boss is safest.

Issues in municipal campaigns vary widely, and indeed as in all elections it is not always easy to determine what the issue is. There may have been many, and just what was decided may be obscure, or differently interpreted by different observers or participants. The relative newness of the city and the urgency of its new problems crowd into the background the elaborate references to party history or record which play so large a part in a national campaign, and force to the front other considerations. At times these may be racial, religious or class issues, or they may be essentially practical questions of control over public utilities, relative honesty and efficiency of competing groups, problems of expenditure or of administration. The present and the future are more in evidence than the past.

There is no standard Republican or Democratic platform ready for adoption by the faithful of the group, and the candidates issue their own platforms, often more definite than the pronouncements of the party conventions were or are. The problem is not how to obtain a definite statement from the candidate, but to persuade him to keep his pledges; and to anticipate what he will do about those coming events regarding which no promise can possibly be made. Municipal issues and situations may shift so rapidly that at the end of a four years' term, the public may have forgotten the particular promises made by the incumbent when he was elected. But in a large way, it is of course possible to obtain a broad type of policy or administration in an election. Slogans may of course either conceal or contain a genuine difference of community opinion, and their value will depend upon the responsibility of those who are their sponsors.

In a quarter of a century there has been only one broad question of legislative policy determined by a mayoralty election:—the traction question of 1907. In most instances the issue has been less direct. In 1911 the choice was between the older style politics and the new. In 1915 the chief issue came to be a religious-racial one, in which the Thompson forces were anti-Catholic and anti-German. In 1919 the war issue beclouded the local situation, which turned on Thompsonism, but with the opposition divided among three candidates, Democratic, Labor and Independent. In 1923 the question was between an inexperienced and an experienced municipal public official. In 1927 the issue was partially between the types of government represented by Thompson and his opponent, but in reality the underlying question was that of the drastic or lax enforcement of the liquor law.

Yet in campaigns these factors are not torn apart, but there are intricate complexes of diverse strands of personality, prejudice, policy, interest, woven together in ways that no one can explain. There are very solid forces working perhaps with strong resources in men and money, but there are thousands who do not vote at all,[1] undisturbed by the uproar that goes on around them, and there are thousands who cast their ballot for what Jefferson once called a "light and transient cause." Many are moved by very slender considerations to cast their vote one way or another, and here the pressure of friends and campaigners is likely to be very effective.

Candidates may well be disconcerted when they know for what trivial reasons they may be supported or made anathema. The candidate's voice, his smile, his handshake, his wife, his children, his religion or lack of it, his action in some immaterial case, the fact that some one "knows him"; or a friend knows him, or the friend of a friend, or the place he came from, or the society he belongs to—these are a few in a hundred minor causes by which the candidates stand or fall. It may well be of course that in a million votes these trivialities cancel each other and the more solid forces determine the outcome of the contest.

But it cannot be denied, on the other hand, that there is in every campaign an incalculable fund of intense interest and consuming energy, approaching its climax as the end draws near. If we took our politics as seriously throughout the year as we do on the night of election, we might go farther; but then we should be very different from what we

[1] See Merriam and Gosnell, on *Non-Voting* in Chicago for analysis of these cases, 6000 in number.

actually are. The election is one of the events in democracy that is dramatized, although the actual voting is drab. The election reaches moments of appeal when popular imagination is really touched and moved. It is not an uncommon thing to see strong men crumple when the decision is adverse—sometimes candidates but more often their followers. In national affairs these vigorous enthusiasms may crystallize into lasting feuds and bigotries of a hateful and dangerous character, but in cities they may be short lived and stimulating after a fashion.

Campaigns are complicated phenomena, not so easy to understand as appears at first glance. At first all may seem plain, but on closer examination may become obscure. Underneath is the balance of social interests, of the working forces in politics, which must always be developed, and must be the outcome of skillful and perhaps painful compromise at times. There is the significance of human personality in candidates and of their adaptability in a given situation. The best man is not always the best candidate in the particular situation. There is the problem of the formula or policy or slogan or symbol on which the campaign may eventually turn. There are the traditions of the community, not the party traditions altogether, but the fundamental political mores to be found in any city, and often so powerful in determining a political result. Nowhere it is more important than in a city to be alert and watchful of changes, and swift in the realization that yesterday is gone and to-morrow is at the door.

Even the most astute miscalculate. Adroit as Carter Harrison was, after being mayor four times, he was hopelessly beaten by Dunne in the primaries of 1907; and again slaughtered by Sweitzer in the primaries of 1915. Thompson was overwhelmed in spite of his terrific efforts in the election of June, 1921, by an error of judgment as to the willingness of the people to give him the courts. He wholly misjudged the vote given him in 1927, so that he was routed in 1928. Roger Sullivan staked a fortune on the Senatorial race of 1914, believing he could surely win in a three-cornered fight, and with all his insight and organization never elected a mayor of Chicago. And Brennan again in 1926 was routed.

These cases are instanced in order to show how even the most elaborate calculations may fail, and to indicate how important the careful study of local situations becomes. Campaigns are not blind charges; they must be prepared by long preliminary work of the most detailed character, requiring patience as well as courage and dash. The strong position of the boss is not the result of wizardry, but of hard work, and of the use of trained intelligence in social and political affairs. His psychology may be rule of thumb, but it is experienced; his organization may not be scientific, but it is coherent and its parts well studied and joined.

But the discussion of specific campaigns and particular situations may be more illuminating than that of common practices, and it is now in order perhaps to discuss in more detail the way in which a few battles have been carried on. For this purpose it may be useful to examine the Harrison-Merriam campaign of 1911, the America First Primary of 1927, and the Pineapple Primary of 1928, with incidental comment on other campaigns and on other events between campaigns in which the political process is illustrated vividly. The limits of space and the reader's patience both forbid more than a sketch of a complicated event, the detail of which must be subordinated to the general outline of events.

The campaign of 1911 opened with a direct primary for mayor and a three-cornered contest in both parties. In the

Democratic Party the battle was between Carter Harrison, four-time mayor; Judge Dunne, one-time mayor; and Andrew Graham, choice of the regular Roger Sullivan organization. In the Republican Party, the balloting centered around J. R. Thompson, the Busse-Lorimer candidate; Smulski, the Deneen candidate, and myself as independent.

The Democratic contest proved to be a close battle between Harrison and Dunne, with victory for Harrison by a narrow margin of 1000 votes. Harrison had demanded seventy cent gas and denounced the Sullivan-Gas Company combination. Dunne had denounced the Mayor Busse administration. Graham had stood pat on organization strength and run third.

In the Republican primaries, Thompson and Smulski had made the usual organization campaign. A leading banker-politician had said early in the primary: "There must be an element of humor in every campaign, and Alderman Merriam is the joke of this season." Mr. Thompson assailed me as a professor and a theorist, and Smulski questioned whether I was really a Republican. Our own campaign under the vigorous management of Harold Ickes, was aimed at the political system in vogue, contending that the government was unduly influenced by a combination of political machines, public service corporations and public contractors. From my experience in the City Hall as chairman of an Expenditure Commission it was possible to supply many illustrations of this point.

Although we were unable to find anyone to preside over a public meeting in some wards, public interest was really aroused to a high pitch and the result of the poll was

Merriam	54,000
Thompson	26,000
Smulski	24,000

In a sense the public had already won its battle, for instead of Graham and Busse, who stood for about the same thing, the contest was between Harrison and Merriam, but the election was none the less full of interest, and illustrates some of the typical features of municipal campaigning.

The organizations were turned topsy-turvy. Two of the three Democratic factions supported the Republican nominee; and two and a half of the three Republican organization factions supported the Democratic, not openly of course, for this would be contrary to principle, but in effect. Harrison was really better off, but he was frankly independent of the regular organization and they of him; while part of the regular organization really supported me in good faith and all of them nominally. Our greatest loss was in the lukewarm support or hostility of many of the organization workers, intensified by a misunderstanding with our Speakers' Bureau.

Inevitably an anti-machine campaign will have difficulty in dealing with the machine after the nomination is made. The problem here is a fundamental one, and goes to the roots of the national party system in local elections. In this instance I was obliged to carry the load of an unpopular Republican mayor and an unpopular President, without the support of the City Hall or the organization, while Harrison likewise was obliged to make his way without the aid of the responsible Democratic workers. He had of course the remnants of an organization surviving from the nine Harrison administrations.

A way out would have been the promise of the patronage to one of the factions, in which case support would have been forthcoming; or another more Machiavellian would have been to promise and then forget as did Thompson in

1915. But neither of these commended itself to us as worth while.

My candidacy obtained the support of many business men, but not all, for some packers and many railroads supported Harrison. We had the endorsement of the Chicago Federation of Labor, but by no means all the labor vote. Harrison's traditional strength among the nationalistic groups aided him greatly, although we broke his hold on the Germans and the Bohemians, especially, but lost some of the colored vote, although I had carried the Black Belt in the primaries. An unexpected development of the campaign was that the use of the epithet "professor" in the foreign-born wards was dangerous, because of the high standing of professors among them. It was found more useful to call me a professor in the native American residential wards and an alderman in the others.

During the primary campaign, Harrison's chief issue had been seventy cent gas, as against the Graham candidacy, which was backed by the Sullivan-Gas organization. It happened that I was a member of a Council Committee conducting an inquiry into the cost of gas, and was therefore unable to state a figure in advance of the outcome of the uncompleted investigation. I could promise only a thorough search for the facts and a reasonable return on the fair value of the property. This probably cost me some votes, especially as the Gas crowd supported me, without any agreement on my part, however. This was not, however, an outstanding issue or a decisive one, and probably my simple position was as effective as any.

Inevitably questions of personality are a large part of any campaign, and properly should be in the choice of the American type of elected municipal executive. Harrison was pictured by us as a somewhat slothful drifting executive, refusing to lead a city wanting to advance; while my friends depicted me as youthful, energetic, with a different point of view from that of the traditional politician, likely to carry through a progressive program for the city. On the other hand, the experiment of a professor with two years' Council service as against the tried and experienced wisdom of a four-time mayor, son of a five-time mayor, was the Harrison interpretation of the case. There was much to be said for both points of view, and perhaps honors were even on that score. Not too much could fairly be said against Harrison and not too much fairly for me, and the exaggerations canceled.

A far more interesting and decisive phase of the campaign was the question of personal liberty, the wide-open town. It was charged that the Republican candidate if elected would close the saloons on Sunday, as well as all other places of public amusement, such as theaters, concerts and baseball games. My opponents were dumfounded and for the moment panic-stricken at my declaration that I personally favored a grant of home rule to Chicago, and until this was granted was content to preserve the *status quo*. Great consternation and frenzied cries that this could not be true and I could not be trusted. The German papers supported me. The United Societies, the "personal liberty" organization of the City, preferred Harrison, but only by 11 to 6, and that after a long struggle. The battle lines wavered back and forth, but on the whole the Republican candidate lost votes. He might be all right, but after all we know what Harrison will do, while this man might be influenced by his friends to undertake some radical change. Back of the personal liberty idea lay that of the wide-open town, which was something different from personal liberty as many interpreted it. The gambling trust, the vice trust, and in fact the entire underworld used the personal liberty argument when they had in mind the continuation of their own personal profit in various forms of commercialized vice. They went for Harrison, but disillusionment was ahead, for after the report of the Vice Commission came out Harrison broke up the redlight district in response to the pressure of public opinion.

The truth was that the opposition succeeded in convincing many that I was a "reformer," and I was unable to escape from the implications of that pregnant term. In vain to protest against being classed as a Puritan and to profess liberal views. In vain did the eloquent Clarence Darrow in one of the most powerful speeches of his career come to my rescue; in vain the support of liberal foreign papers. Was I not from a silk-stocking district? Was I not in the University? Had I not pursued the grafters, and beaten the machine? Was I not supported by many idealists and enthusiasts? So, much against my will, I was hustled away into the camp of the narrow-minded and the illiberal, and what was still more embarrassing, into the camp of the rich and the well-born. If in reality I had been rich and in reality a puritanical reformer of the type described, perhaps I might have enjoyed the situation, or at least I would have been endeared to the hearts of the well-to-do and the "unco guid." But even this satisfaction was denied me, as I knew the halo had no other significance than that of a campaign decoration, designed to warn away from me the publicans and sinners and regular fellows with whose ideas I had much more in common than those of the group to which consigned.

I thought of the time Horace Greeley tried to enter Girard College and was stopped at the gate by the guard, who explained to him that under the terms of the deed no clergyman could be allowed to enter. "The hell you say," retorted Greeley. "Come right in," said the guard. But I could find no equivalent formula. If my managers had been thoughtful enough to produce some woman at the psychological moment, demanding that I take care of some bastard son, I should probably have been elected.

In my inner headquarters hung one of those dreadful lithographs that usually deface the landscape during electoral struggles. It was impressive in its dimensions, but seemed to me a terrible distortion of my features. My managers flaunted it before me, and labeled it "Nitro Charley, the Yeggman's Friend," assuring me it would win many votes in the tougher districts of the city. Perhaps it did, but not enough.

The vote was:

Harrison	177,000
Merriam	160,000
Rodriguez (Socialist)	25,000

And Harrison was a better mayor than he had ever been before, interpreter of the sentiment of the City.

One of the most interesting municipal campaigns was that of 1927, sometimes called the America First episode.[1] In this the Democratic candidate was Mayor Dever, who was nominated in the primaries without opposition, and Thompson, who won against Litsinger by a very large majority. The real contest lasted only about three weeks, but was fast and furious while it was on.

As usual the organizations changed places. The anti-Brennan forces supported the Republican candidate, and the anti-Thompson factions, while publicly paraded in support of the party candidate, were quietly in opposition. All this

[1] The Chicago primary of 1926 is described by C. H. Woody in a volume by that name.

was done decently and in order and with many professions of regularity, but few were deceived inside the group of experts who understood what was happening.

The religious issue was discreetly in the background, but a powerful factor in determining many votes. Dever as a Catholic was hard for many Independent Republican voters to swallow, and gave them the necessary pretext for remaining regular. The Eucharistic Congress of the preceding summer had intensified religious feeling, and Dever kissing the Cardinal's ring was a picture freely circulated, with a view to emphasizing it. The robes of a Defender of the Faith may have hung a little awkwardly upon Thompson, but when religious prejudice is aroused almost any scarecrow will serve the purpose.

The Ku Klux vote proved to be more solid and coherent than the Catholic, many of whom broke away from Dever upon other grounds, finding thirst more powerful than religious emotion for the moment.

Business interests were in large measure with the Democratic candidate, although an influential public utility element followed the lead of Insull in supporting the Republican. The labor group was divided with many of the strongest leaders upon both sides, although Dever was the only man who had ever been mayor with a union card in his pocket. A certain group in labor supported the candidacy of Thompson with great energy. To this the influence of Governor Small, to whom the labor group was under obligations for aid in legislative battles, was in some measure responsible, in so far as it was a bona fide case of genuine support on principle.

The issue would normally have been a comparison between the records of two men, each of whom had been mayor; and from the Democratic side this was the argument made. The disgraceful nature of Thompson's eight years was indicated, and the brighter four years of Dever, with specific instances and illustrations to clinch the case. With this as a matter of course went the incidental comparison between the personalities of the respective candidates.

An interesting contrast appears in this campaign between a nominal issue and an actual issue. The nominal issue presented by the Thompson candidacy was that of "America First." This was a survival of the campaign of the previous year in which this slogan had been employed in the contest against Senator McKinley and in behalf of Frank Smith, the challenger. It was now resurrected for the purposes of a municipal campaign.

The actual issue was the enforcement of the liquor law. Dever, elected as a wet, a dripping wet, he called himself, had been angered by the complicity of the police in bootlegging and crime, and determined to put an end to the whole system by rigid enforcement of the liquor law. To this end he had revoked some 5000 licenses, and what was more serious had refused to restore them. Consternation had fallen upon the faithful who had supported him, especially among the nationalities such as the Poles and the Italians and many Jewish groups, to say nothing of his own Irish.

Thompson declared himself wetter than the Atlantic Ocean, promised to open up 10,000 new places, and to take the police away from the task of frisking hip pockets and inspecting refrigerators. But this was not enough, he thought.

America First must be made the forefront of the battle. As one of the opposition speakers explained it, after all other proposed issues had been abandoned as hopeless:—

Thompson himself spoke up and said, "I have figured it

out. The issue will be America First." The others were puzzled and said, "Well, what does America First have to do with it?" But Thompson said: "That's just it—it hasn't anything to do with it, and that is why it will make a good issue. If anyone opposes us we will say he is not for America First; he is for America second or third or he is perhaps not a good American at all. Everybody is for America First, and if anyone is against us we will say he is disloyal."

To make a connection with local matters, the Superintendent of Schools, McAndrew, was denounced as a tool of King George, and as an instrument for introducing pro-British propaganda in the school system. King George must keep his snoot out of Chicago, and in long harangues the charge was made that the textbooks were being modified to please the British, that Washington had been called a traitor, that the names of Polish and German Revolutionary heroes were being omitted or reduced to subordinate positions.

The only specific value of the America First slogan was that it gave a basis of appeal to the teachers against McAndrew, who was highly unpopular for reasons having nothing to do with British propaganda, while its general value lay in the appeal to anti-British elements who at the same time were wet, as in the case of the Germans and the Irish; and further that it avoided the necessity of discussing and defending the Thompson administrations of eight years' duration or of comparing them with the years under Dever. It is plain that neither Poles, nor Italians, nor Czechs would be moved by an appeal against England, their traditional friend, but that Germans and Irish might be affected by the gesture, especially if they were faltering and inclining to the support of a wet.

This was the spectacular feature of the campaign, but it may be doubted whether it did not cost more votes than it gained, because it opened the candidate to the most deadly of all political weapons, that of ridicule. Had the campaign been extended longer than the short three weeks it was waged, it is probable that the later collapse in the primaries of 1928 would have come at that time. One objective proof of this is that polls taken three weeks before the election showed 65% and as high as 67% of the voters for Thompson, while at the end the actual figure was 51%, and this was slipping fast. If America First had progressed as rapidly in the same direction for two weeks more, the tumble would have come a year earlier than it did.

Two other factors are of importance. One is the colored vote, and the other the personality of the candidates. Early in the campaign a great colored meeting was held, which was attended by Thompson, and the opposition press featured him as kissing a negro baby. In reality this was of course a symbol for an attitude toward the colored group and of alliance with colored leaders of not too reputable a character. The cry of "Africa First" was raised by some, and in the course of the campaign feeling ran high upon this topic. The colored vote was solidified and brought out and doubtless many white voters were influenced by the situation. But again many a voter was more thirsty than afraid of the black man.

Democrats used this issue, although not Dever himself, hoping to offset the influence of the wet problem, but in turn it served to divert attention from the consideration of the real question of the campaign, the relative fitness of the candidates and their probable behavior in office. It tended to substitute emotional reactions for reason, a game at which the Deverites were from the outset outplayed.

Dever came from humble origins, fighting his way up, a tanner by trade, a battling lawyer of the West Side, an alderman from one of the most crowded wards in the city, a friend of municipal ownership of traction lines, once something of a radical, and finally a judge for twelve years. Thompson was a rich man's son, with a fortune in his hand, without serious purpose, drifting with the tide. But Dever's dignity was mistaken by some for "high-hatting," and Thompson's bravado for courage and his rough words for a sign that he belonged in sympathy with the many. A little more righteous indignation on the part of Dever, a little more willingness to link Thompson with Insull, and the battle might have been won in spite of all the initial handicaps and the blunders on the field. Above all, had Dever remained wet as when he was elected and avoided a policy wholly unexpected by his friends and followers, the election would have been a foregone conclusion.

A million voters came to the polls and the count was:

Thompson	515,716
Dever	432,678
Robertson	51,347

THE PINEAPPLE PRIMARY

The Pinapple Primary of 1928 was a revolt against the demagoguery and corruption behind the America First campaign, and is in many ways one of the most notable of primary battles. It was remarkable in the strength of the allied forces entrenched, in the violence of their tactics, and in the overwhelming rout of those apparently invincible. The primary involved the control of a delegation to the National Convention, the governorship, a United States Senatorship, congressmen, legislators, state's attorney, sheriff and other important county offices, and a variety of other positions, some important and some not. And capping all an $80,000,000 bond issue for municipal improvements, full of fat pickings for the faithful, a clever mixture of the City Plan and Gang Plan. To the City Hall strength was added the support of Governor Small and the state administration and that of Frank Smith in his campaign for vindication. The fact that Smith had twice been turned back from the Senate, that Small had just been ordered to return $600,000 in interest on public funds and that Thompson's antics were a national disgrace, that organized crime was running wild and citizens alarmed, did not appear to cause the confederates to pause. The stakes were high and the outcome did not seem dubious. Viewed some few weeks away, it seemed certain that Small would be reëlected governor, Smith once more sent to the Senate, Crowe returned as chief prosecutor, and much rich booty brought to the city hall camp.

The first cloud came when the foes of Small united unexpectedly upon Emmerson, when a young lawyer named Glenn obtained a clear field for opposition to Smith, and when a complete ticket appeared against the America First combination. But even then the prospects of a local overthrow of the confederacy seemed a far cry to the experienced eye. The mayor at the first of his term was apparently in the height of his power and Crowe's support was powerful and dominant. The Democrats had no serious primary battle and a deal with the organization ensured some votes for the City Hall.

The attack seems weak; Deneen is busy in Washington with important affairs and not likely to be on the field for long. Prominent men seem reluctant to step to the front in opposition to the forces of the City Hall and the state's Attorney, well intrenched, ruthless and vindictive. Business has little to say; labor is friendly, in part.

The campaign opens auspiciously with an impressive "convention" where the clans are rallied. America First is made the slogan, and Thompson is its prophet. The workers swarm through every ward and precinct, more numerous than ever in the history of the town. Meetings are well organized and well attended. The speakers are trained in the corporation counsel's office, and the singers of "Big Bill the Builder" are especially instructed in the same high office. The bugles and the flags are busy and the wagging jaws. Joe Haas, the right-hand man of Deneen, dies, and his office and prestige are gone. "Nothing to it," say the wise ones.

The state's attorney is especially well supported. He has the endorsement of a dozen well-known judges of the higher court, testifying to his efficiency; he has the endorsement of the Committee of Fifteen (anti-vice) ; he has (in his pocket) the endorsement of four thousand members of the Chicago Bar, and apparently he has the endorsement of the Chicago Crime Commission.

The activity and the pressure of the workers increases, and in instances becomes intimidation, where a joint in the harness may be found, as a defective boiler or a building that might be rigidly inspected. The confederated forces decide to Draft Coolidge in addition to America First already emblazoned on many billboards; and headquarters are opened for that purpose. No protest from the White House.

And now intimidation passes over into violence, not authorized by the larger leaders, but growing out of a campaign where all seems possible. "Diamond Joe" Esposito, anti-candidate for ward committeemen, is found with fifty-eight bullets in his body. Deneen attends his funeral. But that very night the home of the Senator is bombed, and an hour later the home of Judge Swanson, candidate for state's attorney. Real pineapples, these, and not firecrackers or inoffensive alarms. The state's attorney promptly says they must have bombed themselves to get publicity and sympathy. And nobody is arrested.

But now begins a revolution. A citizen's committee plucks up courage to make a fight against Crowe. Dire threats are made against its chairman, and bomb insurance is demanded where meetings are to be held. Deneen's followers demand his return and the Senator takes the field in person. Other heavy guns begin to thunder. The big Swede, Swanson, tells a simple story of the escape of his sleeping wife and two little grandchildren and wonders what man would bomb these little ones for the sake of office, and what manner of man could charge another with that crime. Dead silence now in audiences, and a few brushing away a tear. The gray-haired Loesch with his seventy-six years takes the field and declares against Crowe. The Bar Association, after much trembling, takes courage and polls its members on state's attorney, to find the vote five to one against him, offsetting Crowe's list of lawyers. The Crime Commission breaks its hypnotic trance and demands the nomination of Swanson.

But more. The newspapers and the orators now link Governor Small and Thompson and "Squire" Insull in an agreement for the control of Chicago traction. What are the articles of the agreement, and what is the consideration? Hot shot these, and reaching into all ranks, and all classes; the kind that Dever would not fire against Thompson in 1927. And now the newspaper polls indicate a landslide against the City Hall. Incredible this and the voters are polled again before the result is printed, and the slide goes on.

The Cave of Adullam is alarmed but not despairing yet.

"America First." "Draft Coolidge." "Deneen made terms with vice when he was state's attorney." "The campaign manager is an imported Dry." A Federal dry agent shoots a citizen and a desperate attempt is made to stage a struggle between the City Hall and the Nation over this incident, and to show incidentally that the opponents of Crowe are the drys; and that the fundamental issue is the old question of the wets against the drys. A shrewd move, but it only starts a feeble flame that quickly dies out.

The City remains cold to the old ballyhoo. Even more it begins to cackle at "America First" as a slogan of gangsters. An interesting incident this, the opening of a barrage well worth describing. Litsinger is a hardboiled and clever candidate for Board of Review (of taxes) but not much disturbed emotionally about political idealism. But Thompson stirs him. "And what kind of a fellow is this Ed Litsinger who was born back of the Yards, raised by his old mother, but when he made a lot of money moved over to the North Side and lives in a fine apartment while his old mother is dying in a shack?" Unexpectedly he discovered what kind of a fellow Ed was, for Ed was angry and turned loose his guns, without careful weighing of facts or grooming of adjectives. He relates the story of his old German mother, who passed away many years ago and denounces the lying attacks upon him. Then he turns upon Thompson and discovers that is what the crowds are waiting for, and the thicker the mixture the better they like it. He rains the blows. King George? What about King Bill, King Len (Small), King Graft and some of the other kings. The knock-out is "hide of rhinoceros and brain of a baboon." And the crowds cry for more.

Panic falls on the confederates. Crowe sinks in a collapse. Thompson will resign if Crowe is defeated. "Your mayor does not have to be abused and perhaps indicted. He will not spend half his time defending himself against the state's attorney. He ate regular before he was mayor and he will eat regular again."

But the battle is not lost yet. The forces of the opposition organization are weak and cannot man the polls in the 2600 precincts of the city. "America First" will swarm them, and will invoke the spirits of violence and fraud to help the count. What they cannot buy they will steal. With the police, the state's attorney, the sheriff, why not? So in darker corners of the city, votes are cast, but counted as orders are given. Workers are kidnapped, and in the 20th ward a car of gunmen slip up to fill the opposition committeeman with bullets. Murder, Assault, Fraud, stand by the ballot box, and indeed might turn the tide if the contest of the votes were close. Not this time, for the tide runs high. 700,000 come to the polls in this primary contest, more than voted for Coolidge in 1924. The deal with the Democratic organization had made it possible for organization Democrats to cross the lines and lend a helping hand, but other Democrats unexpectedly came along in greater numbers and for other purposes. When the votes are counted Crowe is buried by 200,000. Small is overthrown by 250,000 in Chicago and 500,000 in the whole state. Thompson is beaten for committeeman in his own ward, although elected a delegate to the national convention, and the bulk of the City Hall slate is smashed, although not all.

And this is not a class movement, or a nationalistic movement, or a regional movement, for it sweeps all sides and angles of the city and the country districts as well. Only here and there does a point stand out. Even the Black Belt falters and fails to help much. The most powerful political machine in the history of the city at the height of its power with a picturesque figure at its head, and a slogan of "America First" on its banners, has been defeated and routed. Other machines will be contrived, but none with greater strength will fall harder.

It sometimes happens that the triumph of the primary is undone in the election following, but in this case the enthusiasm of the Spring was carried over until the Fall. In the November election the voters with pitiless accuracy sifted the wheat from the chaff, and chose their standard-bearers on whatever national party ticket they might be found.

CHAPTER IX

CHICAGO EMERGING

AND finally arises the question, Is there a Chicago emerging from this confusion of novel, complex and shifting elements; a new interest and a new loyalty to a new center?

Every city must struggle hard to find its own life, its own individuality, its own soul. Time-stained urban centers like London and Paris achieved their personality long ago, and trace their experience back through winding centuries. This is our city, men say, and women and children. Its name and fame are ours. It is ourselves written large, thrown upon the screen; and its heights and depths, its grandeur and its meanness are ours. We begin to assume a proprietary and responsible interest in its conduct. In the old days this interest was a landowners' interest in large part, even in urban centers where the emphasis was less and less on land and more and more upon trade; but now as the number of property owners diminishes year by year enthusiasm and loyalty are transferred and taken up by the citizens who have no land and never will have in most cases. But they too become enthusiasts and bearers of the torch.

In various ways this spirit finds expression. In some song or poem or piece of art; some majestic building; some stately street; some humbler but familiar section of the town, perhaps, entwined with rich experiences; some brilliant personality, illuminating the lives of men; in some great trial or some great triumph that has been inwrought in the experience of the community; some series of preeminences in which the city has a part and of which the citizen becomes a part. These events and experiences may be other than political in nature, some great achievement, some spectacle, demonstration, discovery, the cumulation of which, or the poignancy of which stirs the citizen's interest and allegiance, invests a group situation with an emotional quality and blends it with the deeper aspirations of his nature, with the subtle patterns of his temperament.

The city must struggle hard for life and being. Closely pressed, it is, by competing and conflicting rivalries of other groups;—of the economic classes, of the religious associations, of the social aggregations both within and without, by the rival claims of state and nation and common humanity. In modern times the city cannot be the only divinity, and the altar on which civic enthusiasm burns is only one in a great pantheon. Slowly the city must develop those common understandings about common affairs that lie at the basis of government, the sense of individual and group advantage in the city setting, standards of achievement, inventions of common advantage, and some of the great idealisms that sweep men's souls.

The satisfaction of substantial interests lies at the center of these urban groups, for they must have some functional value in the lives of men, unless they survive merely as traditions and artistic reminders of experiences now dead. To see and know these interests makes the community of advantage which is the basis of solidarity. As time goes on experience, woven of the stuff of common life, covers these interests with a golden glow of civic feeling that may at times be mightier than gold or steel, for it may direct their course and conduct.

Is there such a Chicago? Or is it lost in the selfish and narrow struggles of gangs and groups who snatch their own momentary advantage and look upon the city merely as the mother of opportunity? One may paint a picture or catch a mood in which Chicago is crooked politicians, grafting labor lords, predatory rich, slothful middle class, selfish nationalities, jealous worshipers of God, gangsters, killers, thieves:—mocking justice, indifferent to law, regardless of order, reckless of the common weal. And the picture and the mood would be real.

Perhaps a citizen of Chicago is not a competent witness, or cannot be accepted as an impartial observer. If it be so, then so be it. But it is also possible to look at what the observer indicates and form an independent judgment. At any rate there is another picture and another mood which is also Chicago.

There is a Chicago in which there is a central mass of material advantages in a strategic economic location with labor and capital and hinterland, and the hum of profitable industry rising from within its walls. There are more smoke-stacks than spires, it is true; more smoke than incense; its greatest monuments are those to business and trade. But this may also be found true of America and of modern industrial civilization.

There is a Chicago in which the politicians function by serving the public, rather than by robbing them; in which business assumes responsibility for the commonwealth as well as the class weal; in which labor takes its part in shouldering the common responsibility; in which nationalities compete in presenting vigorous and public-spirited leaders; in which the whole community rises from its indifference and shakes off its sloth; in which law and order and legal and social justice not only exist but grow and develop new forms to meet the new conditions.

The spirit of this new Chicago is transforming a city of

brick into a city of marble; shaping lakes and parks, streets, ways and playgrounds into a beautiful and useful whole, which soon will be one of the physical marvels of the world, adding to the urban beauty spots of historic fame.

On the heels of a physical development comes an unfolding program of housing and recreation, as notable in its own way as the stone and steel of structural plan.

Science, social science, the humanities, education, art and music, are building their temples, and weaving their shapes of beauty and power in many forms, unheralded and unseen even. Schools, health, recreation; these are not minor trails of social progress, but major upward ways.

Common experiences are not wanting. Chicago faced and conquered ruin on a waste of smoking ashes and did not flinch; raised a "model city" by the Lake and invited the world to see and appraise; struggled for its political life with public utility interests in the nineties and with the greed of the gangsters in our own day. It is out of periods of stress like this that a common spirit is welded and common standards of public action are formed.

It rose en masse against the attempt of the constitution makers of 1922 to restrict its representation perpetually, and carries on the battle for home rule and common government of the Chicago Region; struggles with neighboring cities and states to maintain its outlet for waterway development.

If Thompson was three times elected mayor, the Harrisons, father and son, were ten times triumphant. Chicago rose to Roosevelt who carried every ward in 1904, and again swept the city in 1912; to Swanson in 1928; and in numerous referendum votes has shown the existence of a common judgment of discriminating and mature nature. Chicago gave Thompson only 35% of its vote in 1919; drove him from the field in 1923; elected him in 1927 as a wet protest and routed him in less than a year by a majority of 250,000 (two to one) in a Republican primary, and compelled a complete reorganization of his program.

Chicago has never rested lightly whether under the yoke of its gangsters, its public utilities, or its reformers, or its racial or religious extremists, but has from time to time unhorsed them all and fled their control. If it has had no towering civic leaders to adorn its local hall of fame, neither has it fallen into the hands of a Tammany like that of New York or a predatory organization like that which grips Philadelphia for long and dreary periods of time.

As in other American cities, its politicians have been forced to use the language of public service, and to carry through a program of expenditure, with improvement incidental in motive perhaps but not unsubstantial in fact. "Bill the Builder" was from one point of view a pathetic spectacle as was his "Eight Years of Progress" with its elaborate charts and diagrams, but unintentionally this was a recognition of the triumph of the planning spirit in the city. And the attacks upon the schools were always in the name of the schools and in the alleged protection of their genuine interests.

If Chicago's traditions are few, the binding and often galling limitations of tradition are also weak, and the obstacles to inventiveness are relatively small. The artificialities of tradition are not in the way of progress, for neither ancient prestige nor ancient evil and suffering have become habitual. There are no moss-grown survivals to reckon with in the government; no social heritage from which the life has passed; no feudal castles fixing their hold on the Lake Front; no slums that have become a landmark and have lost their power to challenge sympathy; no class whose forefathers also dwelt here in misery and without hope; no mass of timid souls accustomed to being herded by their betters, deferring to their masters.

The value of traditions is great when it is based upon some sound principle of organization adapted to the time, but otherwise they become shackles instead of supports; obstacles to progress instead of aids or incentives. In a changing age and in a swiftly moving period like that into which we swing they will be less useful and more obstructive. For the urban industrial era into which we come demands many adaptations and adjustments of uncomfortable survivals, and the rôle of invention, experiment, accommodation will be larger than ever before. We will progressively inherit less and invent more, as we go on in swifter periods of social change.

Aspirations have their value as well as traditions, and hopes are useful as well as history, if they have a solid basis of economic life and biological advantage. In this sense Chicago is a free city, free to move forward when the word comes, and the way is clear.

Nor does Chicago bear the burdens of a national capital as do most of the world's great centers, except New York. It does not have the custody of the nation's governing equipment and personnel, nor the responsibilities that go with them, as do London and Paris and Berlin and Rome and Vienna.

In a way this lessens the prestige of the city, but it also opens the road for a development of a more strictly urban nature than is otherwise the case. It tends to produce a more definitely city character and less of a national, and permits the urban qualities, whatever they may be, to appear more clearly. In this sense, Chicago is destined to be one of the world's great urban centers and one of the urban leaders in the evolution of the strictly civic characteristics. It will be freer for the local experiment, less bound by the traditions and present needs of the national group.

The strength of Chicago lies in its broad economic basis, in its new blend of racial types, in its dynamic energy and drive, in its free spirit and its free position, in its open way to leadership of urban progress. These are not destiny itself, but the materials out of which the garment may be woven on the loom of time. What they will be, *chi lo sa,* who knows that?